TREASON

The Biden Administration's Strategic and Malicious Destruction of America's Sovereignty

BY

J.J. CARRELL

TREASON

The Biden Administration's Strategic and Malicious Destruction of America's Sovereignty

Book Cover Design: Constance Ramos Carrell

Edited: Dr. Lily Bruckner, Owner-Be Iron Consulting

ISBN 979-8-218-60248-2 PAPERBACK
ISBN 979-8-218-61134-7 eBook

Published in the United States of America
1 2 3 4 5 6 7 8 9 10

ISBN 979-8-218-60248-2

I dedicate this book to podcasters and investigative journalists.

We are the new media!

CONTENTS

FOREWORD

A Warrior in The Battle of All Times

J.J. Carrell, a retired Border Patrol Agent, epitomizes heroism, and *TREASON* is a heroic book. It examines some of the worst and most threatening aspects of human civilization as manifested by the open U.S. border under the Biden Administration and related outrageous acts aimed at the destruction of the nation.

There are several kinds of heroism and J.J. embodies them. There is the courage of border patrol agent, policeman, and soldier on the front lines. We consider them heroes when they knowingly risk their own lives to save the lives of other people as part of their official duties. They may also be motivated to save their comrades, or to defend their homeland or to protect human freedom. J. J. is a former U.S. Border Agent who risked his life for all those motivations, but who retired from the service when the Biden Administration would not let the guardians of our borders do their work.

There is another kind of heroism that is much less common, the valor of standing up against your own government, or your own agency, or even your own comrades when they become corrupt. This is a much more difficult form of heroism because it threatens one's very identity. As a physician in the health freedom movement, I find very few of my medical colleagues, really a miniscule number, will do anything that risks their hard-earned credentials, their esteem in the medical community, or their income. J.J., in his life and in this book, displays that kind of courage.

There is yet another kind of heroism that has more intellectual roots—the heroism of the truth seeker who will not be stopped from searching for and expressing the truth. This, too, is a rare form of courage because when a truth seeker keeps on looking deeper and deeper into any area of life, he or she soon runs into trouble with one or another group bent on covering up corruption and on destroying truth seekers. In his first book, *INVADED*, and now in his second book, *TREASON*, J.J. has kept on examining the world around him on the broadest political scale, leading him to face globalism or what my wife, Ginger, and I call the global predators who are seeking increased domination over the world.

There is an additional form of heroism that relates to or underpins all the others—spiritual courage through a belief in God or higher values and ideals. This kind of courage is especially strengthened when we believe that God expects us to bring our gifts to improving the quality of life on Earth. J.J. embodies how a man conducts himself when he has received instructions from God.

There is still another kind of courage or heroism displayed by individuals acting on their own, without any official role such as first responder or military, yet they risk their lives to save others. Most parents, for example, will risk their lives to save their children. Some people will even take grave risks to save strangers, for example, by pulling them from a burning car or a freezing lake. These more private expressions of heroism are rare because they are not done as part of one's professional identity or official role as a first responder or soldier. I don't know if J.J. has ever risked his life to save another's life outside of his official duties, but if I were a drowning stranger, I'd feel blessed to have someone like him come upon me.

Right now we desperately need heroes. Not to be worshipped or to be found flawless. Not to be seen as saviors. We need them to inspire us! Because in the end, we who believe in human freedom surely need a massive dose of inspiration to bolster our courage and determination.

As J.J. describes, the world is locked in a great battle between good and evil. On the one side are the villains who come in many disguises. Some call themselves Democrats or Republicans, some call themselves Progressives or Communists, some even call themselves Globalists, although usually they hide or muddle their identity. But they are basically collectivists who are driven to victimize, exploit, enslave, or murder millions of human beings to build their empires.

Understanding Empires

Predatory kingdoms and empires had their early beginnings about ten thousand years ago. At that time, humans began to give up living independently as small groups of nomadic hunters and gatherers and started living in a more sedentary fashion by cultivating the land and keeping livestock. Soon they found themselves building walls, such as the famous ancient city of Jerico, to defend themselves from marauders or nearby towns and cities. By a few thousand years ago, much of the world was dominated by violent, evil individuals who ran kingdoms and empires. The tendency for the worst, most violent humans of all to seek to rule everyone in sight eventually led to predatory globalism and the desire of these worst humans of all to rule the world. That is the world today, a world on the verge of succumbing to conflicting global empires, two of the largest seeking to reduce humanity to slavery.

The thrust toward global domination has been never-ending since the dawn of civilization and it continues to this day in a global, highly technological, bureaucratic manner, involving what we call the Western and the Eastern Global Empires. The Western Global Empire is a loose coalition of progressives (Communists), corrupt capitalists, billionaires, the World Economic Forum, the EU, the international banking system, most global corporations, and agencies like the UN and WHO. Except for President Donald Trump, all recent U.S. Presidents of both parties have openly supported globalism. This reflects the moral and political decline of Western Civilization.

The Eastern Global Empire is centered in the Chinese Communist Party and its worldwide influence through the UN and WHO and by its massive infiltration of Western institutions. These two empires, the Eastern and the Western, collaborate and compete as it suits them, often through the UN and WHO. And their main opposition consists of freedom-loving people around the world, many of them motivated by Judeo-Christian values. Today this opposition is centered in the United States in the constitution-oriented, patriotic, freedom-oriented movement called America First; but it is growing in other sovereign nations as well.

Ultimately, this wonderful book is about the struggle between good and evil, manifested in the conflict between individual freedom and collectivism, between genuine free enterprise and corrupt monopolistic global capitalism, between Judeo-Christian principles and hateful versions of atheism, between freedom-loving republics and a totalitarian global governance, and between all of us and the wealthiest and most powerful forces in the world. This is The Battle of All Times in which J.J. Carrell is a powerful warrior. His new book, *TREASON*, gives powerful descriptions and explanations of what is going on in the United States and prepares us to further engage in our fight for human freedom. The book is well-written in the first-person, which makes it very engaging and lends it a sense of personal conviction and reality.

Peter R. Breggin MD and Ginger Ross Breggin
Authors of COVID-19 and the Global Predators: We Are the Prey

TREASON

The crime of betraying one's country, especially by attempting to kill the sovereign or overthrow the government.

PROLOGUE

As of this writing, Donald Trump has won the presidential election and will be sworn in as the 47th President of the United States of America.

The severity of damage to the United States of America intentionally caused by Joe Biden has not yet been fully experienced or understood.

My last book, *INVADED: The Intentional Destruction of the American Immigration System*, covered the Biden Administration's first two years in office. The first of those two years, I was still serving in the United States Border Patrol as a Deputy Patrol Agent in Charge in San Diego Sector. I witnessed the genesis of the treasonous directives that poured down to the border from Washington, D.C.

The first year of Joe Biden's presidency was surreal. I watched in horror as the most secure border in the history of the United States of America was instantly destroyed. The Border Patrol was turned upside down and we began to follow unconstitutional orders laying the foundation of chaos and uncertainty. At that time, the United States Border Patrol was approaching our 100-year anniversary. In 96 years, the Border Patrol never functioned in this capacity. If an Agent was ever caught committing the acts that Agents were forced to follow under this administration, that Agent would have been immediately arrested for crimes against the United States of America while under the color of duty.

I watched the border literally be dismantled. The construction of the border wall was halted. I saw my 24 years of hard work evaporate in an instant. My body, beaten up by the rigors of being a Border Patrol Agent, ached as my life's work was in shambles. I witnessed the invasion of millions of illegal aliens from across the world gather at the border, cross the border, and then be transported into America through a web of government corruption and lucrative partnerships with non-governmental organizations (NGOs). I decided that I could no longer work under a traitorous President and Department of Homeland Security (DHS) Secretary, so I retired.

Even though I witnessed the strategic and purposeful destruction of the immigration system up close and personal, I could never have imagined what would happen to America in the last two years of Joe Biden's term in office.

As *INVADED* went to print, the predictions I made from 24 years' experience and research were materializing rapidly in real time. However, even with all my experience and understanding of how the system was being manipulated and coerced, I could never have imagined the level of treason this presidential administration achieved. A great example of not fully comprehending the plans Joe Biden and his DHS Secretary Alejandro Mayorkas had in place to destroy America's sovereignty was my prediction that within six months of his time in office the daily arrests of illegal aliens would grow to 10,000. I was shocked when I witnessed my prediction was off by DOUBLE! In December 2023, there were numerous days when the daily arrests of illegal aliens rose to over 20,000!

For the remainder of Joe Biden's term in office, I dedicated myself to challenging the mainstream media through hundreds of interviews on big and small podcasts, major cable news shows, and on national syndicated radio. I wrote an Amazon Best Selling book, and I traveled across America filming two documentaries *WHAT IS TREASON? #TRAFFICKED* and *WHAT IS TREASON? #INVADED*. I then found myself testifying in front of Congress on child sex trafficking and the unbelievable fact that the federal government had lost over 320,000 Unaccompanied Alien Children, called UACs.

After my time in the Border Patrol, writing and researching a bestselling book, filming two documentaries, and then doing hundreds of interviews and speeches; I have come to the realization that the federal government of the United States of America is evil.

I state with complete certainty that the federal government of the United States of America is the enemy.

The individuals running our government hate America and they have weaponized the invasion of tens of millions of illegal aliens into America as a tool to fundamentally transform America. They are traitors and need to be arrested and brought to justice.

The intentional act of opening the borders of the United States of America is treason. In this book, I am going to lay out the evidence of this treason as I would present a criminal case to an Assistant United States Attorney (AUSA). I am going to clearly articulate who, how and why this criminal act was carried out against our nation. I will provide detailed evidence of what the manifestation of this crime has wrought American cities and towns. You will recoil from much of this evidence as it will make you uncomfortable. You will be uncomfortable because the evidence of treason is ugly, and the horrors of child sex trafficking are evil in its most pure form. I will lay out a case of treason against Joe Biden, Kamala Harris, Alejandro Mayorkas, and the administrative state that controls our government.

Do not look away because ignorance is no longer an alibi. Instead, ignorance is now synonymous with being complicit. Everyone must choose a side in this war for the soul of America. Do not fool yourself into thinking you can sit this one out because you can't. The weak and the undecided will be devoured first.

The idea that our own government, the government of the United States of America, is run by traitors that want to destroy our country is difficult to hear and even more difficult to digest. When you finish this book, all the evidence will be presented, and the verdict will be obvious.

The pieces of evidence will form dots on a blank sheet of paper. All these dots will be connected, and a picture will emerge. The picture will simply be a picture of a crime. Do not look away. Instead, look directly at that picture because there is nothing stronger or more powerful than the truth no matter how difficult it is to accept.

What picture will you see?
TREASON!

CHAPTER 1

Four Years of Treason

Prior to January 20, 2021, meetings at the highest levels of government were held before Joe Biden being sworn in as the 46th President of the United States of America. In these meetings it was agreed upon that the weaponization of illegal immigration was going to be the tool used to fundamentally transform America. Was I at those meeting? No. Do I know anyone who attended those meetings? No. How do I know that these meetings occurred? I know because I sat in a position of authority in the Border Patrol that allowed me to see the ninety-four Executive Orders cascade down from the White House to Border Patrol stations across the nation on day one of Biden's presidency. These Executive Orders were calculated and planned to obliterate every immigration policy President Trump had in place that provided America with the most secure border in her history. Illegal immigration was the vehicle chosen to fundamentally transform America. This vehicle was designed, built, and test driven prior to day one of this traitorous administration.

I witnessed the daily arrest numbers of illegal aliens skyrocket the moment Joe Biden was announced the winner of the most corrupt presidential election ever. Why? Because Joe Biden declared the border was open and then Biden, with his feeble mind and body, signed one Executive Order after another, totaling 296 in his first year in office all on immigration. These 296 Executive Orders destroyed the most secure border in American history allowing the largest invasion ever seen in modern history. These Executive Orders laid the foundation to the greatest betrayal of the American people of all time.

The endless Executive Orders, malicious anti-American policies, and the refusal to enforce immigration laws was done intentionally, strategically, and purposely. The doors of the border were kicked wide open and Biden and his administration smugly smiled as their plan to fundamentally transform America had begun.

By the end of Biden's term in office, his Customs and Border Protection (CBP) will have arrested approximately 12 million illegal aliens from over 180 nations.[1] After arresting this staggering number of illegal aliens, CBP will have released over 95% of them onto the streets of America. In my 24-year career as a Journeyman Agent, Task Force Supervisor, and Deputy Patrol Agent in Charge, I arrested both directly and indirectly at least 100,000 illegal aliens. Do you know how many of those 100,000 illegal aliens I released onto the streets of America? ZERO! Why? Because it is against the Immigration and Nationality Act (INA).[2] The INA is the bible of immigration law. How did the Border Patrol go from strictly adhering to the INA to ignoring law and following unconstitutional orders to the detriment of the country?

The change happened all at once!

Department of Homeland Security (DHS) Secretary Alejandro Mayorkas took the INA, ignored its laws, and then bastardized every single policy, turning the INA into a welcoming manifesto to the world. Mayorkas, under the Biden Administration, did what the anti-America Left does best and that is redefine the language. When you can change the meanings of words and phrases to soften the lie, the narrative changes and becomes an afront to reality. Mayorkas sent out internal memos demanding the use of the legal term "illegal alien" be replaced with "undocumented migrant." Mayorkas changed the category of "arrests" to "encounters." The phrase "illegal entry" was now "legal pathway." Mayorkas radically manipulated immigration policy by creating new policy out of whole cloth. Border Patrol Agents and ICE Officers were confused and did not know what was happening to their respective agencies and to the rule of law they swore an oath to defend and protect.

Mayorkas redefined the roles and responsibilities of the United States Border Patrol. Border Patrol Agents were reassigned to transport and processing duties. These duties included taking illegal aliens to the hospital, feeding babies, providing meals, processing people, and lastly, driving deportable illegal aliens to the nearest city and "street releasing" them onto the streets of America. Border Patrol morale hit rock bottom, and a national Border Patrol suicide epidemic consumed the agency.

Border Patrol Agents that worked for me on my ATV Unit on the violent Tijuana border and on my anti-human and narcotic smuggling unit called the Coastal Border Enforcement Team (CBET) were contacting me in despair because they were releasing terrorists and criminals into America. In the spring of 2023, Border Patrol Agents from my old station, Imperial Beach Border Patrol Station, notified me that there were approximately 2,000 men from the middle east and the continent of Africa camping out on the American side of the border. All of these illegal aliens were single adult military aged men. Each day on this hilltop overlooking a vista covering the Pacific Ocean to the San Ysidro Port of Entry, Border Patrol Agents would arrest and transport 500 of the approximately 2,000 middle eastern and African men to the station to be processed. At the same time, they were transporting 500 illegal aliens to the station, the cartels on the Mexican side would send over another 500 illegal aliens from the middle east and the continent of Africa.

It would take the Border Patrol Agents 24 hours to process the five hundred illegal aliens and then they would start the insidious process all over again the next day. Border Patrol Agents called and texted me in fear because the number of Special Interest Aliens (SIAs) that were being identified reached fifty in every 24-hour cycle. SIAs are individuals that are nationals of terrorist nations or have traveled through terrorist sponsored nations. When you hear or read the term Special Interest Alien, think terrorist. Whenever an SIA is identified, a special unit called the Joint Terrorism Task Force (JTTF) would immediately respond to the Border Patrol station. JTTF is an FBI run taskforce populated with Border Patrol Agents, ICE Officers, Homeland Security Investigators (HSI), and other alphabet agencies. This task force is specially trained to interrogate SIAs and they all have access to special criminal databases. The average Border Patrol Agent does not have either the required clearance or training to access these needed databases. I will cover SIAs in detail in a later chapter, but SIAs are an enormous issue with severe consequences. "In Fiscal Year (FY) 2022, which ended as of last October, there was also a 600% spike in potential "national security risk" migrants, a total of 25,627 individuals. But that crisis of potential terrorists coming across the southern border has seemingly gotten exponentially worse this fiscal year."[3]

The Border Patrol arrests so many SIAs now that JTTF cannot respond to all the requests. So, Border Patrol Agents that have not had the proper training and do not have the necessary criminal database access to determine who is standing in front of them, just quickly process the SIAs and then the Border Patrol promptly releases them. As numerous Border Patrol Agents have told me directly and with fear in their voices, "I know that I am releasing terrorists into America! There is nothing I can do about it!"

Former Commissioner of the U.S. Customs and Border Protection, Mark Morgan, asks the most important question:

> *How many more bodies have to pile up before we wake up and we understand that border security is synonymous with national security. We've...encountered hundreds of thousands of what we call 'spe-*

cial interest aliens' that we know come from countries that sponsor, harbor and facilitate terrorism; yet we're releasing them every day without properly vetting them...This is why I say that our borders are more vulnerable today than they were on 9/11.[4]

During this same four-year time frame in which 12 million illegal aliens were arrested and released, another 15 to 18 million illegal aliens have crossed the open border and absconded. These illegal aliens are labeled "got-a-ways." Eighty percent of the approximately 2,000 miles of the southern border is left unprotected. Meaning for the first time in the Border Patrol's 100 years of existence, 1,600 miles of the southern border does not have a single Agent standing guard. DHS/CBP openly admits to losing three million got-a-ways in four years. When I state that number to current and retired Border Patrol Agents, they all laugh at the absurdity of the low number.

The northern border is no better. The northern border spans 5,525 miles of shared land with Canada. To fully understand the severity of the criminality and vulnerability of the Canadian border, look no further than Border Patrol's Swanton Sector. Swanton Sector's area of operation (AOR) covers Vermont, New York, and New Hampshire. In fiscal year 2024, Border Patrol Agents in Swanton Sector arrested 19,385 illegal aliens from 97 different countries.[5] These arrests set a new record. What was the last record? Well, you would have to add the arrest totals from the last 17 years in the Swanton Sector together! Now, understand that approximately 2,000 Border Patrol Agents are assigned to cover 5,525 miles of the northern border. Out of the 2,000 Agents assigned to the northern border, maybe 500 Border Patrol Agents work a given shift to cover the ENTIRE northern border with Canada.

The Biden Administration's attack on America's sovereignty wasn't just focused on the border. DHS Secretary Mayorkas is an empire builder, and the Republicans are the equivalent of preschool children learning how to stack blocks. Mayorkas brilliantly had the nation focused on the southern border as he attacked the homeland on multiple fronts.

Mayorkas created an actual app for mobile devices called the CBP One Mobile Application (CBP One App) which allowed illegal aliens to apply for a humanitarian parole authority via their phone.[6] This humanitarian parole is being used as a precursor to the asylum process. These humanitarian parole cases awaiting asylum hearings are taking years to materialize as the backlog of asylum cases are now over four million. How many foreign nationals have applied to this app? 64.3 million![7] Every single day, CBP issues 1,450 new CBP appointments. As of September 2024, CBP issued over 815,000 appointments and then released them all into America. I want the reader to think about this app similar to the app called Open Table where you make reservations to your favorite restaurant. Open Table has more security features than the boondoggle CBP One App. DHS and CBP make the unbelievable claim that the CBP One App has security features and is safe from bad foreign actors. Really?

The CBP One App has geofencing that blocks all requests for an appointment to enter America for any user south of Mexico City. The insanely sophomoric belief by DHS is that an individual applying for an appointment must be in or north of Mexico City in order to present oneself to an Immigration Inspector at the designated U.S. ports of entry. In typical government stupidity and arrogance, these safety features blew up in the collective faces of the traitors. Human smuggling cartels, with their endless resources and who are now under the total control of the ruthless narco cartels, found a workaround for the geofencing. The smuggling cartels were savvy enough to see how lucrative it is to have the United States government do the actual smuggling providing the cartels with a new stream of revenue without any risk. After hacking the geofencing, the cartels were able to control who and from where all CBP One appointments were assigned to. How bad has this vulnerability been exploited? Let's read a statement in August of 2023 from House Committee on Homeland Security Chairman Mark E. Green, MD (R-TN):

> *The Biden administration has continuously shown violent cartels that they may operate as they please at our Southwest border. As I warned earlier this year, the cause of this humanitarian crisis is simple: migrants tested the system, called home, and millions came once they received confirmation of Secretary Mayorkas' catch-and-release practices. According to this week's bombshell report, drug cartels have seized on the newest iteration. This is further proof that the Biden administration's use of the CBP One app is reckless and made a mockery of our homeland security—plain and simple.*
>
> *These reports come on the heels of Secretary Mayorkas' testimony before the House Judiciary Committee last week during which he assured that the 'CBP One app cuts out the smuggling organizations that impose such tragedy and trauma on vulnerable individuals purely for the sake of profit.' The dichotomy of these two events would be comical if not so terrifying that the person tasked with securing our homeland is so out of touch. President Biden and Secretary Mayorkas have provided cartel organizations more innovative ways to evade our laws, rake in money from human and drug trafficking, and wreak havoc in our country.* [8]

To further drive home the point on how fraudulent and vulnerable this purposefully bad CBP One App has made America, look no further than from the data itself from the period of January 2023 to September 2023:

- *Overall, **95.8 percent** of all inadmissible aliens who scheduled appointments through the app during this time were ultimately issued a "Notice to Appear" (NTA) and released into the United States on parole.*

- *The documents show **278,431 appointments scheduled**, with **266,846 of these individuals released** into the interior.*
- *Individuals from a number of countries of concern made appointments through the app and were overwhelmingly released into the country.*
    - *Out of **57,381 appointments made by Venezuelan nationals, 55,690 were released** on parole, a rate of **97 percent**.*
    - *Out of **20,948 appointments made by Russian nationals, 19,780 were released** on parole, a rate of **94 percent**.*
    - *Out of **2,279 appointments made by Uzbek nationals, 1,866 were released** on parole, a rate of **82 percent**.*
    - *Out of **801 appointments made by Belarusian nationals, 787 were released** on parole, a rate of **98 percent**.*
    - *Out of **246 appointments made by Afghan nationals, 229 were released** on parole, a rate of **93 percent**.*
    - *Out of **36 appointments made by Chinese nationals, 32 were released** on parole, a rate of **88 percent**.*
    - *Out of **18 appointments made by Iranian nationals, 16 were released** on parole, a rate of **88 percent**.*
- *The app has consistently been used to release otherwise inadmissible aliens from Mexico and Northern Triangle countries.*
    - *Out of **58,772 appointments made by Mexican nationals, 55,099 were released** on parole, a rate of **93 percent.***
    - *Out of **20,776 appointments made by Hondurans, 20,060 were released on parole**, a rate of **96 percent.***
    - *Out of **3,939 appointments made by Guatemalans, 3,717 were released on parole**, a rate of **94 percent.***
- *Other nations represented in the release statistics include Egypt, Iraq, Lebanon, Kyrgyzstan, Pakistan, and Yemen.*[9]

Since that statement from Congressman Green and House Committee on Homeland Security, nothing has changed. No new security features have been added and the Mexican cartels still run America's immigration system from Mexico. This is not hyperbole but a simple statement of truth. You may think, "Well Congressman Green is a Republican and he surely holds a negative bias against Democrats." Ok, then let us review the August 2024 conclusion from the Department of Homeland Security Office of Inspector General titled, "CBP Did Not Thoroughly Plan for CBP One™ Risks, and Opportunities to Implement Improvements Exist":

> *The CBP One™ Appointment feature was not fully ready to fulfill its purpose—to streamline the POE experience and facilitate a safe and orderly arrival for noncitizens—when CBP implemented it in January 2023. Although CBP promptly applied controls to mitigate CBP One™ weaknesses after its implementation, it did not conduct a formalized risk assessment prior to the application's expansion. As a result, noncitizens using the application when it was first introduced experienced application crashes, received frequent error messages, faced language barriers, and may not have always had an equal opportunity to secure an appointment. Additionally, CBP may be missing an important opportunity to leverage CBP One™ information to identify suspicious trends across the eight Southwest Border POEs. Historically, CBP has not received advance information about noncitizens prior to their arrival at POEs. The introduction of CBP One™ changes that and could allow CBP to conduct and supply POE officers with trend analyses to enhance their ability to identify and disrupt national security threats, such as human trafficking. Finally, security vulnerabilities within the CBP One™ application and its supporting infrastructure operating systems could compromise the security of CBP One™ information. Without*

> *a process to ensure all corrective patches are timely implemented and assets properly configured, CBP One™ data could be at risk of exploitation.*[8]

The list of issues, concerns, and outright disbelief of the CBP One App could demand an entire book to itself. My biggest point that I want to drive home throughout this book is the level of calculated deceit, deliberate maliciousness, and planned treason the Biden Administration has undertaken to destroy America using illegal immigration to create chaos, fear, and uncertainty. Nothing Biden and Mayorkas have implemented was bad policy or incompetence, but instead the implementation of these "legal pathways" have been strategically brilliant. This coupled with the feebleness of the Republican Patry, the plan to fundamentally transform America is materializing in real time.

Not to be outdone by the CBP One App, the height of arrogance and complete lack of concern or fear of being held accountable for blatant criminal actions, CBP has flown illegal aliens into America on commercial and chartered airlines. What is even more brazen is CBP did not even report these "entries" into any CBP data category. Todd Bensman, Senior National Security Fellow for the Center for Immigration Studies, and the Center for Immigration Studies (CIS.org) issued a Freedom of Information Act (FOIA) request asking for data on the little-known part of the CBP One parole program.[10] What is this little-known part of the CBP One App? This part allowed inadmissible aliens, aka illegal aliens, to take commercial flights into America circumventing all immigration protocols. The four nations allowed to abuse this program are Cuba, Haiti, Nicaragua, and Venezuela (later to become known as the CHNV Program). This FOIA information was damning and shocking. The United States government flew 221,456 illegal aliens into America in less than nine months from January 2023 to September 2023. True to the complete arrogance of this administration and after admitting this treason, CBP continued these flights as of this writing. The House Committee on Homeland Security in May of 2024 announced that the number of these illegal alien entries through the CHNV Program has surpassed 400,000.

What could be even worse than our government flying illegal aliens into America on commercial flights? How about the United States of America government contracting chartered airlines to fly illegal aliens from across the globe into America in the dark of night. A podcast called *Monkey Werx US* hosted by an expert on flight patterns, airplane types, cargo capacity, and everything in between exposed flights from one airline contracted by the federal government to fly illegal aliens into America. This airline is Swift Air. Swift Air has been sold multiple times and has suffered bankruptcy, but somehow Swift Air has obtained multimillion dollar federal contracts. In 2023, this single airline made over 7,280 flights into America from foreign nations carrying over 1.4 million illegal alien passengers into airports across America. [11] This is just one airline. How many other federally funded contracted airlines are flying illegal aliens into America off the books? To truly understand the magnitude of this one "pathway," you must watch the full podcast episode. The visual of over 7,280 flights coming into America in one year is stunning to witness. Swift Air made over 7,280 international flights into America using a 737 aircraft holding approximately 200 passengers each and every day in 2023.[11] Understand, this has not stopped to the present day! Who is on these flights? No one knows!

President Joe Biden, Border Czar Kamala Harris, DHS Secretary Mayorkas, and the deep state operatives are traitors, and they have repeatedly committed treason against the body of America for four years. If you isolate each immigration policy, you dissect the genesis of that policy, and who created it, on its own it is a form of treason. Now take every single immigration policy as a complete body of work and intently watch their actions, it is undeniable that what these people have done to America is the embodiment of treason.

I like to use the Carter Administration as a contrast to the Biden Administration. Many current historians and political pundits are already arguing which is the worst presidential administration in American history.

Let's look at the Carter Administration, but more specifically at Jimmy Carter the man. It is difficult to find a point of success in the Carter Presidency. Carter is considered by most to be the worst President in modern American history sans Biden. What no one can argue was that President Carter was a patriot, and he loved America. Carter was horrible at his job, but he was not malicious in his actions. Meaning no one is alleging that President Carter intentionally made decisions to harm America and Americans. We might despise Carter's presidential decisions, but we must acknowledge Carter made those decisions in good faith. Also, President Carter lived an exceptional life of service as evidenced by his devotion to Habit for Humanity.

Now contrast Carter and his presidency to President Joe Biden. Like Carter, Biden has had a tumultuous presidency engulfed in one disastrous decision after another marring his presidency as the worst ever. Unlike Carter, Biden's patriotism and love for his country are heavily questioned. Biden is considered an arrogant grifter, lacking in intellect with an abundance of narcissism. Unlike Carter, Biden is wealthy well beyond the means of a career with a modest annual salary. It has become accepted that Biden and his family has enriched themselves by selling their influence to foreign nations at a great cost to America. Most importantly and, unlike Carter, Biden has made horrible decisions costing Americans their economic status and their very lives. Biden's decisions have been based on what is best for Biden and for the fundamental transformation of America. As unintentionally bad Carter was as a President, Biden is even worse because of his intentional decisions to destroy America.

Joe Biden is worse than a grifting sellout.

Joe Biden is worse than a criminal.

Joe Biden is a traitor!

CHAPTER 2

The Journey of Two Documentaries

My first day working the border was in October 1997 at the Imperial Beach Station in San Diego Sector. I had just graduated from the United States Border Patrol Academy in South Carolina. I remember driving out to the "field" with my other "trainee" buddies and seeing that gigantic Mexican flag waving in the wind in the center of Tijuana. I knew instantly that my life would never be the same and that I would love my new career.

I was so excited and eager to prove my worth to all the Senior Border Patrol Agents. Through hard work and demonstrating that I belonged on the frontlines of the border, I built a reputation for being tough, aggressive, and violent. Those are not the three leading characteristics you put on a resume when you are looking for a private sector job. However, those were the three characteristics that were needed to be a great Border Patrol Agent. If you were not those three things, the border and all the savages roaming on that forgotten piece of land would devour you. As I have written before, and I will state once again – I will never apologize for the things I did in the dark of night to keep America safe. I know with complete certainty that the first people to criticize me, and men like me for the actions we have taken to protect America and Americans could never do what we have done. In fact, if I told any of them to walk into the Tijuana River Valley at 1:00 in the morning and arrest ten prior deported felons, every one of them would be curled up in the fetal position crying for their mommy.

After three years on the job, I was able to stop for a second and take a good long look at the big picture of the border, immigration, and the policies forced on the Journeymen Agents protecting the border. Nothing added up. Why were we over staffing Agents on the border when illegal crossings began to decline? Why was there no Border Patrol staffing in the suburbs where all the Agents lived and saw illegal aliens everywhere in the suburban towns and in the city of San Diego? Why did internal policy trump immigration law? I was required to learn the Immigration and Nationality Act (INA) that governed all immigration laws. I had to memorize that convoluted INA and then have the ability to lawfully apply those laws onto foreign invaders or determine when an individual was lawfully present in the United States. So why were unconstitutional policies created by weak men allowed to stymie and at times shut down the enforcement of the INA?

The questions were always met with indifference, apathy, or outright resentment towards me for even asking the question and they remained unanswered. So, I did what every true law enforcement officer does, I followed the law! This cost me some early promotions and advancement but even in my late 20's, I refused to bend a knee. I am stubborn and to my own detriment, I fight back. However, I have no regrets because I have the respect and trust of the men and women I worked alongside and also the respect from the Agents that worked for me. That respect and trust has infinitely more value than another level of promotion.

I can remember how frustrating those days were. Even in the late 1990s, nothing in the world of immigration made sense. I worked through five presidential administrations from President Clinton to President Biden. It was always a smoke and mirror game of lies and a system entrenched in securing the border with imminent failure built in. Every policy that came down from Washington, D.C., or policy created out of whole cloth from some administrative geek sitting in a cubicle in Sector

Headquarters, was antithetical to the INA. That all ended in President Trump's third year in office. President Trump wrestled the control of the Republican Party from the Paul Ryan and Mitch McConnell Republicans.

A new era of border security and American sovereignty rose from the pile of ashes created from a history of lies and deceit. Morale in the United States Border Patrol and in the ranks of ICE soared as the chains of traitorous policies and constraints from years of heavy internal policies were thrown off the Agents and Officers. The Border Patrol and ICE were finally working for the greatest border president in the history of America – Donald Trump. Then in an instant, we worked for the worst border president, the worse leader, and the biggest traitor America had ever seen – Joe Biden.

Border Patrol Agents mark their time in their careers as "before" and "after" President Trump. My last year in the United States Border Patrol was Joe Biden's first year in office. I witnessed the treason firsthand. I watched the most secure border in our nation's history disappear overnight. I watched the 94 Executive Orders on day one and the first-year total of 296 Executive Orders be forced onto patriotic Border Patrol Agents. Biden's Executive Orders on immigration obliterated every successful Trump border policy and created the foundation of treason that would cause untold misery for America.

My times marked in my career of before and after President Trump were hard to stomach. I made my way into special high-speed units, and I created a large maritime narcotic and human smuggling taskforce. Because of the importance of these units, an Assistant United States Attorney was specifically assigned to prosecute the criminals we arrested. I threw myself into these units so that my law enforcement focus was narrow. I was able to shield myself from the lies, distortion, and criminal negligence of the United States government. Despite the continuous negligence of our nation's leaders, I was also able to protect America the best way I knew how within the strict confines of federal immigration law enforcement. I am proud of the dangerous work my units performed. We were extremely successful as a unit and one of our main opponents in the drug war, El Chapo Guzman, rots in maximum security because my unit ripped all his maritime loads for years. One of my best guys testified against El Chapo in court helping to secure his life sentence.

Even with these long stretches of time in special units and task forces, I always wanted to have a strong and loud voice on the border. I wanted to articulate what the border was really like, identify the players on both sides, and express how vulnerable to violence and suffering Americans were because of politicians that believed in a global society and scoffed at the idea of America's sovereignty. One way that I found my voice was when I retired; I wrote my first book. Books are an incredible vehicle to articulate one's beliefs and a thorough way of communicating one's ideas. However, in today's culture and the power of visual communication, I always knew that I wanted to film a documentary about the border. I have come to realize that if I want to grow my platform and enhance my voice, I must utilize all avenues of communication. I must write books and articles, give speeches, testify in front of Congress, host a podcast show, conduct long form interviews and create documentaries.

I remember sitting on my ATV in the Tijuana Slews on a Swing Shift, thinking that one day I would film a documentary telling the horrid story of the border. Never could I have visualized what would happen to me decades later once I retired.

After writing my first book, I gave hundreds of interviews on national cable talk shows, nationally syndicated radio shows, podcasts, and I gave speeches to big and small audiences. I was on a podcast with several retired law enforcement officers, and they were interviewing me about the border and what I thought was the real explanation of the invasion. I speak like I write, and I write like I speak. I am direct and I am unapologetic about my experienced and researched beliefs. I told the podcast hosts that I believed that the invasion of tens of millions of illegal aliens into America was intentional and strategic. That the federal government was purposely destroying the demographics of America to fundamentally change America. One of the hosts of the podcast sent the interview to another podcast host and documentary filmmaker, Ryan Matta. After watching the interview, Ryan Matta invited me to be a guest on his podcast and I agreed. What Ryan was doing was interviewing me to determine what I really thought about the border and if I would speak in those same bold and direct terms. I only know how to be me, and I have no intention to try and be something or someone that I am not. So, I spoke the same and delivered my message with the same vigor and determination.

After the interview, Ryan asked me if he could set up a Zoom call the next day. On this Zoom call, Ryan pitched me a documentary he wanted to film on the border. For several years, I had different parties interested in filming documentaries with me, but the story line was always soft and carefully crafted not to offend. Having been through this before, I told Ryan that any documentary that I would be involved with had to be raw and it had to tell the real story of the border no matter what we exposed. I had no idea who Ryan was, but I believed in him and immediately trusted him, which is rare for me. After discussing our ideas on planning and filming the documentary, we realized that we were aligned. I had one more issue that needed to be answered and that was whether Ryan and his company would cover all the costs. Ryan agreed that his company would cover all costs, and we made an agreement to begin filming. It wasn't until much later that I realized that Ryan Matta's "company" was just him and an editing team. I am still taken aback that Ryan believed so strongly in this project that he rolled the dice on a six-figure production with a guy he had just met. I am still shocked that as thorough as I am, I agreed to film this documentary with Ryan without any real vetting. My decision to partner with Ryan Matta would turn out to be one of the best decisions I made in my life.

Why did we both just jump into this project? Honestly, we both trusted each other. I can't really explain it. Ryan is a heavily tattooed Christian father that is a whirlwind of energy with a fearless attitude. I have no tattoos, but I am also a Christian father, and I can go for days on end without much sleep, and I am also fearless. However, as much as we were the same, we were equally different. But we were a great match because we shared the same vision and strong work ethic and we both brought unique and specialized talents to our newly formed production team.

Less than two months later at midnight on a Friday night, we landed in San Diego and headed straight to the Tijuana border. We began a journey that was going to change everything in our lives and take us both on a path that we didn't even know existed. We were about to learn that our best laid plans were worthless.

Ryan and I planned out the states, cities, and small towns we were going to travel to and film in. I chose San Diego to be our first stop because I knew the layout like the back of my hand, and I knew Agents that would help me get back into the inside. We loaded up our rental car with all Ryan's cameras, sound equipment, and every gadget you could imagine, and headed south from San Diego. We passed by National City and continued down I-5 until we came to Hollister Road. We turned off the interstate and began to drive the side roads to the Imperial Beach Station. About two miles directly south, we could see the border lights on the hill tops. We drove up to the station gates just as the gates magically opened as my guy was waiting for us. I don't think Ryan understood until that moment the kind of access we were going to get. We were on the inside of the Imperial Beach Station compound. We loaded everything up into a Border Patrol vehicle and we were off.

I had not been back to the border since the middle of 2023 when I came back to take pictures and do some final research for my book, *INVADED*. I left the border in 2023 thinking that the machine the federal government needed to destroy America was still not complete. The Agents were still bogged down in long processing times, the movement of illegal aliens was clunky, and the partnership with the NGOs was not efficient or fully funded. In two years, Biden and Mayorkas were making incredible headway on their treasonous plan, but they were behind the curve as the backend of Biden's four-year term had begun. As I drove out to the border, I had a plan of what I was going to film, who I was going to interview, and the story line I was going to follow. Minutes into my first day of filming our documentary, I felt uneasy and unprepared. I didn't recognize the place I had patrolled for a decade.

Ryan could not believe we were between the fences and that we had access to film the invasion on the most fortified section of the border in America. I was in disbelief as I saw hundreds of illegal aliens wandering up and down the border between the primary border fence and the newly constructed "Trump Wall." These illegal aliens did not try and run as they did in my time or even when I was there a year prior. They did the unthinkable, they waved us down so that they could give up and be taken to the Border Patrol station. I looked at my former colleague in amazement. He looked back at me and shrugged and said, "Welcome to the new Patrol!"

I had flashbacks to when me and my boys fought the savages staining the border with our blood and the blood of the invaders. We were hit with large rocks and pieces of broken concrete with rebar protruding out. We were blindsided by boulders lining the border road so that we would drive into them on our ATVs. The savages pulled bailing wire taut between the primary and secondary fences trying to decapitate us as we responded to illegal alien crossings. All that came rushing back as we slowly drove right by the new asylum seekers. I witnessed 24 years of my life's work vanishing.

I remember driving from the Pacific Coast, which marks the southwestern most point of the United States, inland to a location called Whiskey 8 and my anger rapidly rising as a horde of humanity living on our side of the border came into focus.

We stopped our Border Patrol vehicle right on Whiskey 8 and a hundred single adult military aged men were sleeping, milling around, or huddled around burning fires of scrap wood and old tires. I simply could not believe what I was seeing. Whiskey 8 was a section of the border that Border Patrol Agents fought for years to capture back from the Mexican human smugglers. Whiskey 8 sits on top of a large drainage tube that runs approximately a quarter mile underground and is used by smugglers. To the west of Whiskey 8 is the "Gravel Pit" where smugglers trafficked large groups trying to make it to the Tijuana River. To the north of Whiskey 8 was a landmark called, "J.J.'s Dip." That is my landmark. I paid a steep price for the naming rights to that piece of land. I wrecked my ATV in a construction site that wasn't there several hours prior to my shift beginning. A new sewage treatment plant was being built with American taxpayer money to clean Mexican sewage and industrial waste, so a freshly cut trench was created. Not knowing of this deep trench, which did not exist three hours prior to when my shift started, I slammed into it crushing my body. I own that piece of land and now my property is being violated. Endless other Agents have had severe injuries fighting to secure that filthy piece of border including an Agent who was shot in his eye sitting guard on Whiskey 8.

I was now standing among the enemy on American soil that was soaked in Border Patrol blood. Worse than that was an instant feeling of danger. These hundred Middle Eastern, African, and Indian men leered at me as if I were trespassing on their land. They acted indignant that I would interrupt their time and their activities. I was enraged that my Border Patrol would allow this to happen. I was angry that everything I gave to this important and vital mission was now a waste of 24 years of my life. I stood among these men as a stranger, a trespasser on their land. How did this happen? How did we get to this point in our history? Who allowed this to happen? And how did they accomplish it?

Ryan put a camera in my face and began to record a man filled with rage and anger. By the end of the night, that same man would be sad and shaken. In just a few hours, I understood what was happening in real time and I could see what the future held. America was vulnerable. America was in danger. America was suffering under a treasonous government, and the American people had no idea what was taking place on this long miserable stretch of land.

The next two days in San Diego were filled with numerous interviews with current and retired Border Patrol Agents, ICE Officers, and DHS employees. We traveled to several areas of the border within San Diego Sector, and I was left stunned at the number of illegal aliens just allowed to cross over onto American soil and then set up camp there for days if not weeks until they were transported by the Border Patrol to the stations to be processed. A desolate section of the border called Jacumba, California is in the middle of nowhere, but the cartels have designated this to be the location to push illegal aliens through the porous border fence. As I walked among the hundreds of illegal aliens just living on the American side of the border with no shelter, food, or understanding of what to do, I felt like I was in a bad dream. Just a couple of years earlier, every last one of those illegal aliens would have been running through the rocky hillsides trying to escape arrest. Now in a literal twilight zone, these same illegal aliens wander aimlessly in a dusty area the size of two football fields. I watched in complete disbelief as a Border Patrol unit sat about 100 yards away monitoring the situation as a taxi pulled up, picked up several illegals and drove off. The Border Patrol unit didn't move. I just witnessed a smuggling event take place and no one seemed to blink an eye!

What the hell is going on!

I walked up to the Border Patrol unit, introduced myself and spoke to an Agent who seemed despondent and miserable. During our brief conversation, this Agent was completely defeated and resigned to the fact that his career was now a sad pathetic joke. I could not believe what had happened to my Border Patrol in such a short time. We were destroyed. We were a shell of the once proud and strong Patrol. Biden and Mayorkas had killed the Border Patrol!

After filming for 72 hours with almost no sleep, Ryan and I boarded our respective planes and flew back to Detroit and Kansas City. I sat in the dark airplane traveling back to Kansas City confused, angry, and frustrated. Everything I had planned with Ryan was meaningless. The government and their NGO partners were no longer ineffective, clunky, and underfunded. Instead, I saw a well-oiled machine that was extremely efficient and fully funded. Sitting in the back of the airplane, I tried to wrap my head around how deep and entrenched this treason was. I wondered if the rest of the border was functioning at this pace and tempo. I was exhausted, but what kept me awake the entire flight was the thought of what the hell did I just experience and how in the hell am I going to articulate what I know now.

Ryan and I spent the next five months traveling across the southern border, the east and west coastlines, and into middle America. We documented things that shocked me and made me shake my head. Even after spending 24 years in law enforcement, I could not believe what I was seeing. I struggled to understand how the federal government had constructed a machine this large and this efficient. Each trip of this journey brought a different aspect to the totality of the treason. However, one despicable evil showed its head every trip we took. This evil was everywhere we went and in every interview we conducted. Driving across Texas, Ryan and I looked at each other and we had an honest discussion of what we both realized was the issue dominating the story of the open border – child sex trafficking.

When Ryan and I were planning our filming schedule and what aspects of the open border we were going to cover, we knew we were going to discuss the intentionality of the open borders, narcotics, crime, and human suffering caused by human trafficking, to include child trafficking. In my career, I saw child trafficking and I witnessed the suffering and hopelessness of the entire illegal immigration world. But child trafficking was not that widespread. Yes, we had to deal with it, and we watched children being drugged and presented as a "family unit" under President Obama's ridiculous no family separation policies. We witnessed parents throwing their young children into the bushes or leaving the children on the smuggling trails to slow us down as we pursued them. However, under Biden this evil of child trafficking exploded to heights never seen before. Ryan and I could be in Washington, D.C., Colorado, Texas, or California; it didn't matter where we were or who we were talking to, child trafficking, and more specifically, child sex trafficking dominated every aspect of our filming.

There is a country song "Help Somebody" written by Jeffrey Steele and Kip Raines and recorded by Van Zant that has a great line that makes me laugh every time I think about it, "If you want to hear God laugh, tell Him your plans!" If I was more spiritually aware when Ryan and I were discussing this issue as we drove from Denver International Airport to Estes Park, Colorado, I would have heard God laugh. Somewhere between the airport and the beautiful mountains of Estes Park, Ryan and I made an agreement that if God will allow us to sell enough copies of *WHAT IS TREASON? #INVADED* we would take those profits and travel back out to film a documentary on the horrors of child sex trafficking.

After God finished laughing at His two foolish followers; He changed our plans.

After five months of filming, early one Saturday morning in late August I got a text from Ryan saying we had a problem. This was alarming to me because we had had zero issues throughout the entire filming of

WHAT IS TREASON? #INVADED. In fact, throughout my entire life, everything that I have achieved has been difficult. I admit that when I look back on my life, I realize that many, if not all, of my difficulties and struggles were my fault. I was so determined and sure that I was walking down the right path that I would continue to run into that brick wall knowing I was meant to knock it down. I tried repeatedly, throughout my life, to knock the walls down all the while God had a door wide open for me and all I had to do was open my eyes and walk through it.

There have only been two situations in my life that were uncharacteristically easy, and both situations should have been the most difficult. The first one was the greatest gift God ever gave me, my son! My wife and I adopted our son, and we knew the birth parents two months into their decision to give us the responsibility to raise and love their son. Seven months is a long time for things to be difficult and to go sideways. Strangely and more accurately, God made the adoption flawless and as easy as it could have been. Throughout the entire process, I never had anxiety, fear, or worry. I just knew this was what God wanted and months later my wife and I were parents. In an instant, we both felt love we did not know existed. It was both powerful and beautiful.

The second situation was filming this documentary. We didn't have enough money. We didn't have enough experience. We didn't have enough of the right people to interview. We didn't have a full understanding of what to do or what to expect. Honestly, looking back we didn't have anything that was needed to be successful. However, we had two dudes with strong work ethics and the desire to speak the truth. And we knew God would guide us. We just didn't know God had a completely different plan for us.

Ryan and I never missed a flight. We never ran out of money. We miraculously met all the right people to interview. We were introduced to and met people we didn't even know existed until we were on this journey. We never lost any film. We never felt overwhelmed when we should have felt overwhelmed the entire time. We received endless interview requests to promote our documentary when we had no budget for marketing. Everything we didn't have and needed was provided. If I am completely honest, Ryan and I felt as if we were along for the ride, that we were being guided. Unbeknownst to us, this whole journey was directed, and we were not in charge, we just did our part the best we knew how.

I got up from my bed that Saturday morning and as I walked downstairs to my office, I anxiously called Ryan, "What is wrong?" I asked. "Well, I can't put any of the child sex trafficking into *#INVADED* because there is too much footage. The child sex trafficking is a documentary on its own!" Ryan replied. Stunned, I listened to Ryan continue, "We have enough footage to create three documentaries on child sex trafficking!" I let that statement hang in the air for a moment and then I asked, "What do you want to do?" He replied, "I want to create two documentaries." We had already agreed to premiere our documentary in the 2A Film Festival in Greenville, Texas outside of Dallas on September 13th and I asked the most important question, "Ryan, can you edit that much footage in 25 days?" In typical Ryan Matta fashion he declared, "Well, I don't have a choice!"

Twenty-five days later, in a beautiful, restored theater in the heart of Texas, a sold-out crowd was standing, wiping tears from their eyes, and applauding our work. God had laughed at our plans, but I believe He was pleased by our obedience and proud of what we created.

We had two documentaries. One that proved that our government intentionally and strategically opened the borders to fundamentally transform America. And the other documentary proved that our federal government is the world's largest child sex trafficking organization in modern history.

Treason is difficult to digest.

CHAPTER 3

Non-Governmental Organizations

I thought I understood the significance of Non-Governmental Organizations (NGOs), their partnership with the federal government, and the vital role they play in the destruction of America's sovereignty. I thought after 24 years in the United States Border Patrol, witnessing up close and personal the uneasiness of dealing with these organizations, that I had a solid understanding of who they are and what they do. Flying home after the first 72 hours of filming my documentary in San Diego, I realized I had no knowledge of the depth and complexity of criminal activity these NGOs were engaged in. I also had no gauge to measure the importance every NGO played in the ultimate success of fundamentally transforming the United States of America. However, I would soon discover the NGOs were the missing link in the machine needed to transport 30 million illegal aliens into and across America.

When the decision was made to flood America with tens of millions of illegal aliens through an intentional invasion, I truly believe the traitors in the incoming White House did not expect the level of success they would have with opening the borders. I believe Biden and Mayorkas struggled to get a handle on the massive hordes of humanity that crossed day after day. The issue of how to move tens of thousands of illegal aliens from the border to the interior of America every day became a huge public relations nightmare. The Biden Administration banked on the continued ignorance of the American public so that they could continue the treason unabated. However, when thousands of illegal aliens could not be transported from the border to the Border Patrol stations to be processed and then released onto the streets of America, Biden had a major issue. The investigative journalists in the new social media world forced the main street media to show video footage of 10,000 people living under a bridge in Eagle Pass, Texas and that began to slowly awaken Americans from their long slumber.[12]

Mayorkas and CBP had been working with the NGOs since they took power in January 2021. The funds and the personnel needed to complete such an incredible feat took time to create and to get running effectively. I saw the beginning of the local and state NGO's involvement in 2021 prior to my retirement. I saw the emergence of powerful national and international NGOs when I returned to the border to conduct research for my book in 2023. Even in the early part of 2023, the Border Patrol, ICE, and the NGOs were not totally coordinated yet. The components of this massive machine were not working properly but that would seemingly change overnight in late 2023, heading into 2024.

The powerful NGOs cloaked in the protective cover of God and religion, were now extremely well-funded as the engine to the machine was humming. Where was all the funding coming from? From you and me! America was funding the international NGOs through the United Nations (UN) and the International Organization for Migration (IOM) which operates inside the UN. The United States of America is funding her own death. America is committing suicide and the NGOs, and our corrupt politicians have all become incredibly wealthy to the tune of billions of dollars. Todd Bensman from the Center for Immigration Studies (CIS.org) detailed this scam to perfection in an article he wrote in January 2024 titled, *Biden Admin. Sends Millions to Religious Nonprofits Facilitating Mass Illegal Migration.* This is how the money is laundered. Just in 2024, the Regional Refugee and Migrant Response Plan (RMRP), an arm of the UN, had $1.6 billion to dole out to over 200 nonprofit groups (NGOs). These 200 plus organizations would then hand migrants cash, debit cards, food, shelter, clothing, medical treatment and with total hubris, they also offered "humanitarian transportation" to the Mexico/U.S. border.[13] IOM also received over $1.4 billion in one year from the United States State Department and United States Agency for International Development (USAID).

The UN and IOM facilitated the entire world to travel to the United States border and then break our laws of sovereignty. Where did the UN get $1.6 billion and IOM get $1.4 billion from in 2024? Better yet, where did the UN and IOM get billions of dollars from in the last four years? You know the answer! Biden and his administration laundered billions of dollars through the UN and IOM to the religious NGOs who then took American taxpayer's money and handed it right over to the tens of millions of future illegal aliens. Who were the main religious NGOs – Jewish Family Services, Hebrew Immigrant Aid Society (HIAS), Lutheran Family Services, Catholic Charities, Seventh Day Adventists, and other evangelical religious organizations.

Bensman takes one of these NGOs, HIAS, as an example of how insidious these government and NGO partnerships have become:

> *A prime example is the self-described "Jewish American" nonprofit organization HIAS of Silver Spring, Md. (incorporated in 1903 as the Hebrew Immigrant Aid Society), which has pledged $17.1 million in aid to immigrants in at least seven Latin American nations during 2024, the UN's RMRP planning documents show. It turns out that in FY 2022, 47 percent of revenue reported by HIAS came as grants from government agencies, the majority from the State Department, but some also from the Department of Homeland Security, according to the group's tax filings and other sources, with*

the balance coming from a mix of major corporate sponsors and other sources.

But there can be little question about the origins and purpose of at least some of HIAS's $17 million pledge to the UN's Latin America migrant trails project. Last year, the State Department's PRM gave HIAS a $6 million grant for, according to USAspending.gov, a database that tracks federal spending.[13]

What prominent member of the Biden Administration was previously on the Board of HIAS? Well, that would be DHS Secretary Alejandro Mayorkas! The CEO of HIAS, Mark Hetfield, was thrilled when "Ali" was appointed to DHS:

We at HIAS have been so blessed to have Ali Mayorkas on our board of directors and are thrilled to have him nominated to be the next Secretary of Homeland Security. Ali has consistently demonstrated that he is not only a strong and highly respected leader, but an empathetic one who knows the heart of the stranger, as the child of a Holocaust survivor, as a Latino, and as a refugee and immigrant himself. Ali is uniquely suited to rebuild public trust in the Department of Homeland Security as he knows that America is at its greatest when we build bridges, not walls.[14]

I am so tired of the phrase "build bridges not walls." Especially when all the money to build bridges goes directly to fund NGOs like HIAS. There was a slight conflict of interest in play here when the leader of DHS served on the board of directors of an NGO and then grants tens of millions of dollars to said NGO.

The partnerships with these NGOs are all connected to each other and to the individuals inside the government machine. Board members are former government officials and government officials are former board members and the incestuous funding merry go round endlessly spins around and around. There is no better example of these incestuous relationships than Mayorkas and HIAS, "When I was very young, the United States provided my family and me a place of refuge. Now, I have been nominated to be the DHS Secretary and oversee the protection of all Americans and those who flee persecution in search of a better life for themselves and their loved ones."[15] Mayorkas, or as HIAS insiders call him "Ali," was not named a board member twenty years ago, but in the year prior to Biden taking the office of President in 2020 and then appointing "Ali" as the new DHS Secretary in 2021.[15] Do you think the position of being a HIAS board member could have had any influence on what NGO received tens of millions of dollars of American taxpayer money?

These international NGOs have no loyalty to the United States of America. They have no allegiance to any nation's sovereignty. However, they have complete loyalty to the one-world government and the extremely insane desire to reset the power structure in the world. The UN does not even try to disguise their involvement in the unprecedented movement of the world into the western nations. Just go to the IOM's webpage where they openly declare their desire to "collaborate" with NGOs to fulfill the IOM's mission:

> *IOM's collaboration with NGOs is defined in Article 1(2) of its constitution, according to which the Organization "shall cooperate closely with international organizations, governmental and non-governmental, concerned with migration, refugees and human resources in order, inter alia, to facilitate the co-ordination of international activities in these fields. Such cooperation shall be carried out in the mutual respect of the competencies of the organizations concerned."*

> *Over 60 NGOs currently hold Observer status with the Organization. IOM is actively encouraging NGO participation at its Council and the International Dialogue on Migration and hopes that the trend towards increased NGO participation in migration policy dialogue will continue. Also at Headquarters level, IOM convenes regular annual consultations and briefings for a wider NGO audience. Most of the programmatic cooperation between NGOs and IOM, however, takes place at field level.*
>
> *Cooperation between IOM and NGOs occurs in various contexts and reflects the diverse relationships between the two actors.*[16]

It is important to visit the website link listing the 60 NGOs that currently hold Observer status with IOM.[17] The same names we see working inside the United States are the same international NGOs working outside and against the United States. The major NGOs working inside of our borders are controlled by international organizations. Our government is paying foreign entities to destroy America in the tune of tens of billions of dollars annually.

The best location to witness the treason playing out in all its glory is in the Darien Gap in Panama. The Darien Gap is the brutal and dangerous crossing location migrants use to travel through to get to the United States. This 60-mile roadless stretch of jungle connecting Columbia and Panama is ground zero for migrant murders, deaths, rapes, and assaults. Over a million migrants have used this path to enter Central America on their journey to the promised land. Who is there in the jungle ready to help the migrants on their journey? Every American funded NGO you can imagine.

HIAS is properly funded, and they are eager to assist every nationality on the globe, especially anyone that fits into the sexually perverse world:

> *As political, social, and economic crises become more acute around the world, more refugees and migrants are making the risky journey through the Darién Gap, a dangerous stretch of jungle that connects Colombia to Panama. In 2022, almost 250,000 people crossed the jungle, which is set to rise in 2023 to 500,000. Among them are growing numbers of gender-based violence (GBV) survivors, women at risk of experiencing sexual violence, and LGBTQ people.*[18]

I believe most Americans can confidently state that we have our fill of LGBTQXYZ people in America! Thanks, HIAS, but we are good!

Secretary Mayorkas visited the Darien Gap as the surge of migrants began to overwhelm the bottleneck in Panama. Mayorkas didn't go down to the jungle to strategize how to stop this invasion and force the Panamanian government to help mitigate this disaster. Instead, Mayorkas was there in the jungle to ensure the proper facilities were constructed to help every migrant make their way to America's border. Mayorkas created a place for migrants to be fed, sheltered, clothed, and medicated all for the efficiency of millions of migrants to get to America as safely and quickly as possible. Investigative journalist Michael Yon saw Mayorkas land in the Darien Gap in April 2022. You don't trust Michael Yon like I do? You don't think Mayorkas has built facilities in foreign nations to increase the flow of illegal aliens into America? Well, how about hearing the treason committed by Mayorkas from Mayorkas himself as he arrogantly stated on ABC's *This Week*, "We have built safe mobility offices in Colombia, Ecuador, Guatemala, Costa Rica to reach people where they are so they don't have to take the perilous journey."[19]

Who built these "Safe Mobility Offices" (SMOs) littering Central America at American taxpayer expense? Mayorkas did! Your tax dollars funded brick and mortar buildings in foreign nations to undermine America's safety and security. Who staffed these SMOs that not only provided life's necessities, but helped with American immigration documentation? Foreign governments and NGOS! Let me be as clear as I can here: foreign nations and international NGOs hostile to the United States of America are and have been running our immigration system. These foreign entities control the number of migrants, type of foreign nationals, and where these migrants cross into America. Numerous individuals inside DHS, CBP and Border Patrol have made it completely clear to me that the NGOs run our immigration system.

What do billions of dollars given to these NGOs look like in real time? As America suffers from homelessness, unemployment, economic hardships, and economic upheaval here in America, NGOs like Medical Teams International (MIT) spend our monies on future foreign invaders. MIT is positioned in the Darien Gap to provide all the necessary medical aid needed. Where did the funds come from to keep this organization running? The same funding structure many of the NGOs are paid through, the United States Department of State and their section titled, U.S. Bureau of Population, Refugees, and Migration (PRM). What is the mission statement of the PRM? Let's take a look:

> *The mission of the Bureau of Population, Refugees, and Migration (PRM) is to provide protection, ease suffering, and resolve the plight of persecuted and uprooted people around the world on behalf of the American people by working with other governments and international partners, sharing the burden of providing life-sustaining assistance and seeking durable solutions by working through multilateral systems to build global partnerships, ensure compliance with international norms and standards and promote best practices in humanitarian response.*[20]

I believe several valid questions need to be asked:

- Why has the United States of America government created a global migration crisis by exclaiming to the world that our borders are open?
- Why has the U.S. government funded all the international NGOs to facilitate this migration crisis?
- Why has the U.S. government spent taxpayer monies on infrastructure in foreign nations to ensure safe passage to America's southern border?

Every religious NGO cloaked in the blanket of God, every NGO funded by the U.S. government directly or through the money laundering structure of the UN, and every nefarious NGO are actively helping the invasion of America, and they deliver the enemy to the doorstep of America. This is where the international NGOs seamlessly blend into the homegrown NGOs. This is where the blurring of the lines happens. This is where international funding ends and internal funding begins. This imaginary line is hidden so that the powers outside of America and the traitors running our nation can combine forces and begin to implement the most devastating demographic shift in the history of our nation. This is where the partnership between DHS and NGOs takes over the movement of 30 million illegal aliens into America and disburses them across 50 states.

DHS does not have the manpower to move tens of millions of illegal aliens from the border and place them in states across America. DHS has created a situation where the government is completely dependent on NGOs as the mechanism needed to move people. In my documentary, WHAT IS TREASON? #TRAFFICKED, I interviewed a DHS employee who sent Electronic Fund Transfers (EFTs) to the NGOs. I asked this employee which NGO she had oversight of, and she replied that she paid

Jewish Family Services. I asked her what the biggest EFT was that she sent Jewish Family Services, and her response shocked me, "$600 million."[21] Stunned, I asked if that was for several years, and the DHS employee laughed at me because this was just for several months of service. Then she made the most profound statement, "The government does not run the NGOs, the NGOs run the government." [21] I had several follow up questions, one question being was this compensation equally paid to the other numerous NGOs working with the federal government and the answer was yes!

The DHS employee said the atmosphere in this department within DHS that is housed in Washington, D.C., is one of fear and chaos because this entire treasonous operation is now outside of the control of the federal government. DHS is held hostage by the NGOs because without the NGOs, the operation would come to a shrieking halt. The DHS employee stated that money is not an issue and whatever an NGO demanded, they were given. There is absolutely no oversight or accountability. She laughed at me when I asked her if she was the individual responsible for tracking the money sent to Jewish Family Services. She laughed because when that $600 million left her office, she was on to the next emergency.

In fact, she described a money laundering scheme that was incredible. This is how it goes. Jewish Family Services receives the $600 million contract for three months of very undefined services. Smaller NGOs with broad ranging names that are subcontractors for Jewish Family Services begin to make funding demands for clothing, food, medical, shelter and other pressing needs. These services would range from a million dollars to tens of millions of dollars and the government paid them without question and without any accountability. What was shocking to this DHS employee was that when she sent the EFTs, the EFTs didn't go to their respective subcontractor's bank accounts. The EFTs were delivered to the same Jewish Family Services account that received the $600 million! [21] This is theft! Catholic Charities, Lutheran Family Services, and on and on, are all receiving the same insane payments. Our government is spending tens of billions of dollars to fundamentally change America. Our government knows what is happening and they don't care because the ends justify the means. Do you think that Mayorkas and the individuals running our government care about the cost needed to destroy America?

In conjunction with funding the major NGOs on the border. The government created another money laundering machine called the Shelter and Services Program (SSP) that is funded by DHS and administrated by the Federal Emergency Management Agency (FEMA). SSP is the instrument that funnels money to local and state governments and NGOs to provide shelter, food, medical care, and transportation for illegal aliens. As large metropolitan cities' budgets began to collapse under the enormous weight of caring for hundreds of thousands to millions of illegal aliens, the federal government tried in vain to backstop these cities with SSP money. The Federation for American Immigration Reform (FAIR) cited the cost to the American taxpayer in 2023 exceeded $300 million and in 2024 it would surpass $340 million.[22] The idea that the federal government only spent $640 million in two fiscal years is absurd. There is not one governmental website or governmental watchdog organization that knows the real number of actual dollars spent on illegal aliens. The government does that on purpose. Let me give you an example of what I am talking about in this same article published by FAIR.

In this article FAIR writes about lawmakers being split on the amount needed to fund the SSP program. They weren't arguing about the funding in terms of millions, but in the billions:

> *Lawmakers remain split on the program. Earlier this year, a group of House Democrats called for increased funding of the program, asking for $3 billion to fund it and citing a "resounding need from*

> *cities and towns across the country for increased federal support to provide migrants with short term humanitarian services." Meanwhile, Rep. Chip Roy (R-Texas) says of the program that, absent H.R. 2 being enacted into law, taxpayers "will continue to bail out NGOs and sanctuary jurisdictions that enable illegal immigration." In its FY25 proposed budget, the Biden administration requested $4.7 billion for a Southwest Border Contingency Fund to replace the SSP Program, while continuing to offer similar services to illegal aliens.*[22]

To further prove my point that we have no rational idea of the true cost of the NGO partnership let's look at the first Continuing Resolution (CR) passed by Speaker Johnson and the Republican House in 2024. A CR is not an annual budget, but a stop gap measure to just keep the government funded. In this first CR passed by Democrats and Republicans through a Republican controlled House, Speaker Johnson funded the NGOs with a $7.9 billion package.[23] Not for a year. Not for six months, but for several weeks. This partnership between our federal government and NGOs is a financial windfall for every NGO big and small. We are talking about tens of billions of dollars a year with zero accountability or oversight.

The CR Bill of 2024 was a stark reminder that this treason is a uniparty issue. The Democrat's traitorous policies are created and implemented only because Republicans fund it. There is no way Nancy Pelosi would have brought that grotesque spending bill to the House floor for a vote. She would have been laughed off the stage because no Republican would assign his or her name to such a bill. However, covering this CR with a Republican House Speaker, the bill becomes a Conservative bill. Both sides vote for its passage, and they all stand in unison talking about the "hard work and bipartisanship effort" they demonstrated to help

America. In reality, the uniparty appropriated billions of dollars to illegal aliens and further funded our demise. But our Congress is working hard!

NGOs of all sizes are functioning across America. They are in every state of our nation. The constant movement of these NGOs remarkedly move in incredible coordination. Millions of illegals are processed out of Border Patrol custody and land right in the arms of NGOs swarming the border. Every illegal alien has thousands of dollars attached to them. Millions of get-a-ways also find their way into the security of NGOs. The NGOs do not make the distinction between an arrested and processed illegal alien and an illegal alien that circumvented the open border and absconded. The NGOs do not tell immigration authorities because there is no system or audit done to verify who comes through the NGO system. Billions of dollars are spent on illegal aliens through the NGOs if they are processed or not. The national security of America is a sad joke. America has never been this vulnerable to attack and takeover from within her borders.

The depth of collusion and deceit between the United States government and the endless number of NGOs, both internationally and domestically, is staggering. The number of NGOs that pop up, fade away because of criminal activity, and then spring back up under a different name would make Americans furious. This depth and level of vicious treason attacking America has never been defeated by any nation in the history of civilization. No great historical world power or run of the mill country has ever overcome this intense of an attack from within and survived. Not the Greeks. Not the Ottomans. Not the Romans. Despite America's hubris and arrogance, how could we believe we are immune to treason and the destructive effects of internal warfare?

The Non-Governmental Organizations have been weaponized to hide in plain sight, the strategic and intentional plan to destroy America from within. The purposeful transformation of our demographics from a nation of citizens to a nation of non-citizens has hit an apex. The demographic change is under way as native birth rates rapidly decline, and illegal aliens procreate at an exponentially higher rate. What our leaders have imposed on America is now a bad math problem and America is the negative in this equation.

CHAPTER 4

Demographic Upheaval

There are 195 nations on planet Earth and over 180 nations are represented in the Border Patrol arrest data. The entire world has descended onto our borders and then have illegally entered America. Every first world and every third world population are here. Hundreds of languages and dialects can now be heard in every small town and major metropolitan city in America. The belief that diversity is a strength is a lie! Having 50 million illegal aliens residing in America that do not have the ability or intellect to learn to speak the English language is now considered diversity. Having 50 million illegal aliens who share no cultural, societal, or religious norms is now considered diversity. Having 50 million illegal aliens completely dependent on the government for every necessity of life is now considered diversity.

I don't want or need any more diversity!

This intentional demographic change in America is simply a change from citizens to non-citizens. To fundamentally transform America, the anti-American Left decided that the mass invasion of third world illegal aliens is the most effective and efficient way to change the population of the United States of America. The traitors running our nation also believe that it is not just the immediate invaders that will make the change; it will be their offspring that will cement the complete demographic shift of America. The new world order traitors have learned that there is no changing the beliefs of the current population of Americans because we have a profound understanding of the Constitution and of our God given rights. Now contrast a God fearing patriotic American clinging to his Bible and his guns to an illegal alien from the Middle East, Africa, Central America or even Europe. Almost 100% of these illegal aliens can't speak English, have zero understanding about the United States Constitution, and have no knowledge of what type of government we have in America. And no, our form of government is not a democracy, it's a Republic.

Which population is easier to change? Which population needs and wants the government in every aspect of their lives because that is all they know? What population will heel immediately to governmental pressure or edict? Which population will fight the government to their own death? Which population has loyalty to our founding fathers, our founding documents and to a nation founded on the principles of Divine Providence? Answer those questions and you have your answer to why this illegal demographic shift is happening.

The Left and even the cowardly Republicans will maliciously assert race into this discussion to muddy the waters to create fear of voicing common sense. This has nothing to do with race. Every skin tone, ethnicity, religion, and every other identity group is pouring over the border into America. This is a statement of the total upheaval of our population in America from patriots to foreign invaders. If the white population decreased and the black population increased, no one would care. Americans have been lied to for decades that America is racist. We are not. We don't care about what color of Americans are decreasing or increasing because we are just Americans. What we all care about is the artificial change to our population.

The infamous clip of then Vice President Joe Biden pontificating on the positivity of demographic change in America is still unnerving and infuriating. Biden, in his characteristic arrogance, stated:

> *There is a second thing in that black box: an unrelenting stream of immigration, nonstop, nonstop. Folks like me who are Caucasian, of European descent, for the first time in 2017 we'll be in an absolute minority in the United States of America, absolute minority. Fewer than 50% of the people in America from then and on will be white European stock. That's not a bad thing, that's a source of our strength.*[24]

The arrogance of Biden and people like him is truly unbelievable. What men like Biden always leave out of the conversation is the important distinction that it is legal immigration that should be championed. What Biden did then, and he does now is conflate legal and illegal immigration. We can have a robust discussion on the need to decrease, increase, or stay the same on legal immigration, but what we will never agree on is that illegal immigration is good and needed in America. On a side note, when you watch Biden pontificate his views of "unrelenting stream of immigration" please look to his left and see the smug little face of Ali Mayorkas!

Because of the decreasing belief in God, rampant abortion, the lie that motherhood is bad, and coupled with many other societal changes, American women are reproducing below the replacement level of 2.1 births. Since 2023, American women are below the replacement level at the staggering number of 1.62 births per 1,000 population. Similar birth rates are devastating many western nations across the globe. Let's dive a little deeper into the numbers. From the *World Population Review*, the United States estimated birth rate in 2024 is 11.013 per 1,000 population.[25] Not good. Now let's look at other country's birth rates per 1,000 that are invading our nation with the facilitation of our government – Niger 44.458, Somalia 42.091, Afghanistan 33.834, Sudan 32.012, Palestine 26.835, Iraq 26.339, Tajikistan 24.702, Haiti 22.435, Guatemala 20.439, Venezuela 16.099, and on and on we go! Numbers don't lie. Our bad math problem is obvious. We are looking at a 2:1, a 3:1, and even a 4:1 birth rate higher than American women!

There are 50 million illegal aliens living in America. That means 1:6 to 1:7 residents in America are illegal aliens. Staggering, but true! Take our non-replacement birth rate and compare it to say the 86,000 Afghanis we brought to America when Biden pulled out of Afghanistan like the old fool that he is. Before you do that let's go to the CBP.gov website to see how many more Afghanis we have allowed to enter America. Well, well, there seems to be no nation of Afghanistan category to verify the illegal entries and releases into America.[1] Why? That is rhetorical of course because we all know why. Since Afghanistan is out, let's take Venezuela as the comparative nation versus America. We have allowed in over one million Venezuelans in less than four years. Applying one million Venezuelans to the birth rate equation compared to one million population of Americans we have a nasty population birth problem. The Venezuelans will reproduce (in one birth) cycle 16,099 to America's 1,620.[1] What about Haiti's over 500,000 illegal alien population equaling 11,217 births in one year. Remember this is only the number of Venezuelans and Haitians we know about. You can conservatively double, triple, and even quadruple CBP's arrest totals in terms of Haitian and Venezuelan get-a-ways.

Let's fill out this math equation. Let's put 50 million illegal aliens residing in America on one end of the equation and place the variable of births at an average of three times that of American births. The variable would be America's birth rate of 11.013 times three giving us an illegal alien birth rate of 33.039 per 1,000 population per year. We would then divide 1,000 into 50 million, giving us 50,000. We then take 50,000 and times that number by the birth rate of 33.069 and that gives us 1,651,950 illegal alien births in a single year. In a later chapter I will thoroughly disprove the grotesque abuse of the 14th Amendment destroying the myth of birthright citizenship. Let us go to CBP.gov and locate the FY2023 arrest numbers – 3,201,144.[1] The release rate of illegal aliens into America is between 95% - 97%. For this equation we will use a release rate onto the streets of America at 95% totaling 3,041,086 for FY2023. For the sake of this equation, I will not add the millions of get-a-ways, or the millions of illegal aliens flown into America and not counted in CBP data. Now take the number of 3,041,086 illegal aliens arrested and released and add the illegal alien births of 1,651,950 and we have a total illegal alien population growth in America for FY2023 at 4,693,036.

What was the total number of American citizen births in 2023? 3,596,017

We have a serious problem!

We can play the game that the number of illegal aliens living in the U.S. is lower and the birth rate is not as high as three times, but the outcome of destructive illegal alien population growth is still profoundly evident. Lowering some or all the variables does not change the demographic upheaval that has gripped our nation. This demographic shift from citizens to non-citizens is severe and it is altering our nation. You may not like who I am, how I write, how I speak, or what color my skin is, but it doesn't matter because statistics are simply statistics. You can attack the messenger, but it will not change the message. The message is clear – the United States of America's federal government is the enemy of the citizens of this great nation. PERIOD!

What does this demographic change look like currently in America?

Let's take a look at the destruction.

I love to take the macro problem and bring it down to the streets of America. Look no further than Springfield, Ohio. You remember Springfield because the moderators of the only presidential debate between Trump and Harris mocked Trump as a nut job as Harris cackled. What did the moderators and Harris mock and laugh at Trump about? Trump made the claim that illegal alien Haitians were eating the pets, the dogs and cats, of the American citizens living in Springfield. The laughing and ridiculing ended immediately after the debate as what Trump claimed was in fact, TRUE. The newly placed illegal aliens from Haiti were eating the pets. There are endless articles and videos of Haitian illegal aliens eating pets. My favorite example is the body cam footage of a Haitian woman being arrested for eating a cat on her driveway. The police officer commands the Haitian woman covered in blood to smile into his body camera so the video could show cat fur stuck between her teeth.[26] What makes Springfield, Ohio a great example of the demographic shift argument is not that a Haitian woman was arrested for eating someone's pet cat, but because Springfield has a population of approximately 60,000 residents with over a third being Haitian illegal aliens. In four years, the small town of Springfield went from 40,000 residents to 60,000 when Biden strategically placed over 20,000 illegal Haitians in this community.[27]

The town of Springfield is dead, they just don't know it yet. That population of Haitians will exponentially grow from insane birth rates and because a direct pipeline from Port au Prince to Springfield has been developed. The American population is being displaced because of housing shortages, residents moving out, and more and more Haitians moving in. The culinary appetite of the Haitians is the least of Springfield's problems. Crime, education, an STD outbreak, medical facilities being overrun, and yes, births are skyrocketing in Springfield.

Before we leave the state of Ohio, let's take some time to investigate the population shift in a small town called Lockland, a suburb of the city of Cincinnati.[28] An important fact of this investigation is that Lockland has a population of 3,500. Have you ever heard of a nation called Mauritania? I hadn't either because the real name of this nation nestled on the continent of Africa is The Islamic Republic of Mauritania. Three fun facts about this third world nation are: it is Islamic ruled, it is the poorest nation on the continent of Africa, and the most fun fact, is that girls were just recently allowed to attend school! What does Lockland, Ohio and the nation of Mauritania have in common? Not much. However, the Mauritanians learned about pipeline building from the Haitians. The Mauritania to Lockland pipeline is over 4,400 miles, but it is direct. Biden and his traitors have helped over 3,000 Mauritanians take that pipeline into Lockland. Remember, Lockland has only 3,500 residents. Not anymore! Welcome to what is called population growth. A suburb with the infrastructure to handle 3,500 residents now must accommodate over 6,000 residents and that number grows daily. Crime, fires (yes fires), housing shortages, education, and a severe decline in the quality of life are just some of the fun changes occurring in Lockland.

Americans love to live in the current moment. However, we must look to the future in terms of our demographic transformation. What does the future look like if the trend of allowing millions of illegal aliens to invade our nation continues? Steven A. Camarota and Karen Zeigler from CIS.org did a demographic analysis based on the government's monthly Current Population Survey (CPS). If the current trends continue, Mr. Camarota and Ms. Zeigler, state, "the foreign-born population will reach 62.5 million in 2030 and 82.2 million by 2040 — larger than the current combined populations of 30 states plus the District of Columbia. It would also be larger than the current total populations of the Northeast (57 million), the Midwest (69 million), or the West (79 million)."[29] And they also state a fact that I know to be true as well, "There also is some undercount in this data, so the actual number of foreign residents in the United States is larger."[29] What the authors of this study mean is the real population count of illegal aliens living in America is even worse than what they have uncovered. We only know what we can quantify and what we know. In the last four years of this insanity, 80% of the southern border has been unmanned and unprotected. My best experienced and researched estimation of the number of illegal alien get-a-ways is between 15 - 18 million. Unbelievably, that number could be even higher.

As I conducted research for this chapter, I was shocked at the level of propaganda from the government and left-wing think tanks and websites. Google's AI places the number of illegal aliens living in America at 11.7 million as of July 2023. That is not even close to the factual truth. I guess that is why they call it propaganda. As I wrote in *INVADED*, the agreed upon number of illegal aliens living inside our borders stood at 22 million in 2019. This number was from a Yale/MIT study in 2019.[30] Yale and MIT (not your bastion of conservative thought) pushed every demographic and immigration data point into an algorithm and ran that algorithm one million times. Their study claimed that the height of illegal aliens living in America was 29 million. The solid number of 22 million illegal aliens was the average. Six years and another 30 million invaders later, Google's AI and every left-wing pundit still uses a number from 2016! Members of Congress openly admit that the true number of illegal aliens in America is 50 million. The truth about the cause of the tens of millions of illegal aliens living in our nation is due to the unholy alliance between both political parties. The Democrats create the traitorous policies, and the Republicans fund the treason.

Population increases across America have exploded exclusively from illegal immigration. What I always find interesting is the Left makes accusations about the evil of racism that is embedded into the fabric of the American society. Why would anyone want to travel thousands of miles to come to a nation of racists that will abuse you? The Left are irrational and illogical, all the time. Even the left-wing website, www.migrationpolicy.org, must admit that the world has decided to come to America:

> *Worldwide, the United States is home to more international migrants than any other country, and more than the next four*

> *countries—Germany, Saudi Arabia, Russia, and the United Kingdom—combined, according to the most recent UN Population Division data, from mid-2020. While the U.S. population represents about 5 percent of the total world population, close to 20 percent of all global migrants reside in the United States.*[31]

Could you even begin to calculate what percentage of the world's migrants are here since this study was conducted in 2020! Four years of open borders and the numbers above seem insignificant.

As this invasion continues and another five to ten thousand illegal aliens cross into America daily, our sovereignty continues to be destroyed. The value of our citizenship has become almost worthless. The cries and accusations of racism and xenophobia have become meaningless because they are without merit. The enlightened among us tells the basket of deplorables that unfettered immigration is great for America. It is great for the unwashed masses in middle America, just not for Martha's Vineyard and the elite enclaves with gated residences. The elites lecture us about the importance of diversity when they live in the whitest bubbles on the planet. We have been lied to and abused by the powerful elite in this nation. Their pronouncements are so imbecilic and baseless that it makes it clear they did not obtain their wealth and status because of their brain, but through connections and corruption.

Demographics of a nation are important. Borders protect the sovereignty of a nation. Demographic altering populations of illegal aliens do not produce positive outcomes. If one million illegal aliens are great for America, why not ten million? If ten million illegal aliens are great for America, why not 20 million? If 20 million illegal aliens are great for America, why not 50 million? If 50 million illegal aliens are great for America, why not 100 million? Why stop there? Rationally, if those statements are true then why not replace us all, all 350 million Americans.

America became the most powerful nation in the history of civilization because of us!

Us being Americans!

CHAPTER 5

The Destruction of Big Cities

The financial cost of providing every life necessity to illegal aliens in the major metropolitan cities in America has been crippling. The untold costs of negative societal changes from oppressive crime, complete budgetary collapses erasing essential services, and the destruction of the quality of life where entire neighborhoods have been changed overnight, have caused these same sanctuary cities to cry "uncle." The metropolitan cities of Chicago, D.C., Philadelphia, Los Angeles, San Francisco, San Diego, Boston, Denver, and every other big city across America is realizing the days of pontificating from their superior moral pedestal are over. These same cities that once spoke down to the rest of America in harsh condescending language are now begging for help. Help is coming, but not in the form these crazed Leftists want.

I am going to focus on three major cities that have become the focal point of this invasion. These three cities, New York City, Chicago, and Denver, have several aspects in common: they are led by incompetent mayors, they are sanctuary cities, and they are financially in ruins. The financial costs these cities cite in their budgetary reports exclude federal dollars and thus are fictitious, at best, outright lies, at worst. These sanctuary cities and states do not count billions of federal dollars in their budgets, assuring the cost of illegal alien services appear much lower than the actual financial outlay. Their cities are broken; and their future is destined for chaos, violence, and uncertainty.

The greatest example of the invasion into major cities in America is New York City. Once upon a time, New York City Mayor Adams was welcoming in every illegal immigrant he could locate. Mayor Adams used to chastise people like me as being racist and a xenophobe because deplorables like me didn't appreciate or understand the value of the illegal immigrant:

> *When you think about it, the days I spent with our essential employees, a substantial number of them were undocumented. They were delivering out Uber Eats, they were stocking our stores, they were out in the streets keeping our city running. We have to expand NYC Care to make sure everyone has healthcare. We need to make sure we have proper translation services in our schools.*[32]

Oh, how times have changed! Being unqualified to run a large city let alone a popsicle stand, Mayor Adams does not have the intellectual capacity or the ability to critically think past the immediate present. After welcoming illegal aliens into his city of 8.5 million residents, the mayor knew he had miscalculated everything. By the end of 2024, NYC admits the cost of housing, feeding, medicating, educating, and handing out preloaded cash cards, cost the city over ten billion dollars, $4.75 billion in 2024 alone.[33] I don't believe those numbers are correct as I believe you can at least double that dollar amount. However, I always use their own data because the best-case scenario they provide is devastating on its own.

Mayor Adams has turned 180 degrees. He is now so bullish on illegal aliens that he has sided with incoming Border Czar, Tom Homan. Adams is so pliable and has changed his tune so quickly that if you close your eyes and filter out his heavy New York accent, you may think you are listening to me! Mayor Adams, ever the morally and intellectually weak politician, is trying to cover all his bases stating that he and Homan are on the same page and that, "We're going to protect the rights of immigrants in this city that are hardworking, giving back to the city in a real way. We're not going to be a safe haven for those who commit repeated violent crimes against innocent migrants, immigrants and long-standing New Yorkers."[34] Notice the subtleness of his use of the term "immigrant" and "migrant." No distinction of legal or illegal. This is an important distinction that must be made in any discussion on this topic. Adams knows how he is using this term, and he doesn't really care about the crime, drugs, sex trafficking and changes to New York City's quality of life caused by "immigrants" and "migrants." What Adams and all politicians care about is the next election and he needs votes.

What could have changed the mind of this bluest of blue Mayors? It was that Donald Trump will be President on January 20, 2025, and all federal funds backstopping the financial bleeding in NYC is going to stop immediately. Mayor Adams will be left holding the bag on January 20, 2025. Because of the insane sanctuary city policies once championed by Adams, NYC has well over one million illegal aliens inside the city's boundaries. There is no more money to contract 50% of all hotels in NYC for illegal aliens. It will be January in New York when the federal bribes end and there is no worse place to spend the winter months on the streets homeless than NYC. Mayor Adams knew that this situation was dire back in 2023 in a letter to his constituents:

> *They do not have the authorization to work, so we have to provide shelter. We have supplied food and access to healthcare. We have enrolled children in schools. We have opened almost 200 emergency sites, including more than a dozen large scale humanitarian relief centers. And we have assisted migrants with asylum applications.*

> *But we are past our breaking point. New Yorkers' compassion may be limitless, but our resources are not. And our partners at the state and federal levels know this. We continue to face impossible decisions about allocating our resources, and that means a lose-lose for our most vulnerable New Yorkers as well as those seeking asylum.*[36]

Mayor Adams continued in his letter outlining the costs associated with the total care of foreigners living in his city illegally:

> *Let me put it in perspective for New Yorkers. For each family seeking asylum through the city's care, we spend an average of $383 per night to provide shelter, food, medical care, and social services. With more than 57,300 individuals currently in our care, on an average night, it amounts to $9.8 million a day, almost $300 million a month, and nearly $3.6 billion a year.*
>
> *But this is the floor, not the ceiling. This is only an estimate if the number of migrants in our care stays the same over time. It is clear to us, however, that without policy changes, the number of migrants arriving will continue to grow. This will increase our cost(s). If we continue down this unsustainable track, with an average of almost 34,000 households a night over the course of just this fiscal year, that will increase cost(s) to $4.7 billion.*
>
> *Hear me, if things do not change, our new estimates have us spending nearly $5 billion on this crisis in the current fiscal year. That's up from the $1.4 billion we spent last fiscal year. And it nearly equals the budgets of the Sanitation Department, our Parks Department, and the FDNY combined.*[35]

This letter in 2023 was a far cry from the hubris of Mayor Adams welcoming illegal aliens arriving on buses in 2022, "As the Mayor of New

York, you know, I don't weigh in on immigration issues, border issues. Ah, I have to provide services for families that are here and that is what I am going to do."[36] The city is crumbling. Crime has consumed the city to the point that the state of New York has called in the National Guard to provide protection on the subway platforms. How is that working? Not so good. An illegal alien savage from Guatemala lit a woman on fire as she fell asleep on the subway train.[37] This savage was deported in 2018 under Trump when we had a border and consequences for crossing illegally. Under Biden, this animal just walked across the border, received a free plane ticket to NYC, and he set up shop. New York City paid for this savage to live in New York City for free from April 2023 to the day he set that woman on fire and murdered her. Mayor Adams knows the political fallout is coming because these third world crimes are beginning to accelerate and he needs a fall guy for his arrogance, hubris and for his miscalculation that Kamla Harris was going to win the election thus continuing this treason.

Neighborhoods that were once small little enclaves tucked away in the sprawling big city have been destroyed by illegal aliens. The neighborhood of Clinton is one such neighborhood. While filming our documentary series, *WHAT IS TREASON?*, we drove around this little neighborhood. What we saw was startling. Turning off a main street in New York City, we ran into a sea of single adult military aged men roaming the sidewalk. We drove around an entire city block with several large buildings housing over 3,000 of these illegal aliens. All the men looked like they were from either the Middle East or the continent of Africa. They can't work and they are completely dependent on government assistance. The federal government fraudulently welcomed them into America under the guise of asylum without any work authorization documents. At that moment of filming, 3,000 illegal alien men were living in the one city block. Now the number has grown to over 6,000 with proposals to increase that number to 9,000 in one city block. The city has transformed this idyllic enclave to a crime ridden and dangerous neighborhood.[38] New York City voted for Biden in overwhelming numbers exceeding 90%, so they are getting exactly what they voted for. I have no sympathy for them because the residents of NYC voted for this disaster all the while vilifying the rest of us deplorables. One of the residents named Kristina so perfectly exemplifies the stupidity and the inability to comprehend what has be forced unto them as she asked for compassion for the thousands of men that were terrorizing the Clinton neighborhood, "I hope that everyone here can understand that as frustrating and as disastrous as the situation is, it is important to remember that the people who are in our neighborhood today have suffered enormously."[38] Kristina and her kind are asking for empathy and compassion for the same men that are raping and pillaging their community! You can't make this up!

Rumor has it and I can't confirm, Mayor Adams is going to daily mass at St. Patrick's Cathedral. He has reportedly been seen lighting candles and placing pictures of Tom Homan next to the Virgin Mary. If this is true, smart move because that's all Mayor Adams has now – prayers!

Let's move from one intellectually deficient mayor to another, Chicago Mayor Johnson. To be fair to Mayor Adams, Johnson is significantly dumber, not much, but enough that there is an evident gap between Adams and Johnson.

Chicago was the first city outside the border that we traveled to and began filming because Chicago is the epicenter of the invasion. Crime, societal collapse, and monetary corruption caused by the invasion are in your face in Chicago. Chicago made an intentional decision to strategically place the illegal aliens in a specific geographical area. That geographical area would be the south and west side of Chicago, the poorest neighborhoods in Chicago and some would say in all of America.

The south side of Chicago is a burnt-out shell of a community. There is no industry, no grocery stores, no businesses but there are endless dilapidated and shuttered buildings. We can have a sound discussion on why these communities are burnt out and what, if anything, can be done to improve them. What can't be argued is taking billions of dollars and ignoring these communities to ensure foreign invaders are provided with every necessity needed to survive and prosper.

The dominate nationality of the illegal alien population in Chicago is from Venezuela. There are hundreds of thousands of Venezuelans living in Chicago, displacing black residents, which has now created an explosive situation with sides being drawn by race. I interviewed numerous people living in the notorious south side of Chicago. I interviewed black residents that are street pastors, mega church pastors, businessmen, soup kitchen personnel, and current and former gangbangers and criminals. They all stated to me with complete certainty that there was going to be a war, a war between the Venezuelans and the blacks. Why? Because Chicago's Aldermen (think city council) has diverted billions of dollars to the illegal aliens from the poorest residents in all of America.

Chicago has diverted hundreds of millions to billions of dollars from their poorest constituents to an ever-growing illegal alien population. The stated cost of illegal aliens in the state of Illinois is all over the place because all of the costs associated with illegal immigration are not included in every report. From a commonsense perspective, don't you immediately question why the total costs of illegal aliens to our nation, states and cities are never exact? Illinois State Representative Chris Miller detailed the enormous burden illegal aliens have placed on the state budget since July 2022, "The cost of providing services to illegal immigrants is costing Illinois taxpayers an estimated $2.84 billion since July 1, 2022. This does not include education costs or other various state and local services."[39] Representative Miller goes on to state the obvious, "The billions of taxpayer dollars being spent on illegal immigrants directly takes away funds that could be used to support essential programs for all Illinois citizens, including seniors and those most economically and socially vulnerable. Illinois is one of only five states in the nation that provide Medicare-like benefits, at taxpayer cost, to illegal immigrants."[39] To reiterate, this estimation does not include education costs and excludes the first year and a half of Biden's presidency and this report was written in April 2024. The real costs for the state of Illinois are at least double, maybe even triple, the $2.84 billion costs stated in Representative Miller's report.

Another State Representative Davidsmeyer blasted Illinois Governor Pritzker for the unforgiveable funding of illegal aliens:

> *$638 million in taxpayer funds to address the migrant crisis created by Chicago's sanctuary city, Illinois' sanctuary state, and the Biden Administration's failure to secure the border. Illinois taxpayers are already on the hook for more than $2 billion in costs to provide free healthcare benefits to illegal immigrants. When is enough enough?*[40]

Representative Davidsmeyer is right to place the blame of Governor Pritzker and the city of Chicago. The estimated funds wasted on illegal aliens are unfathomable. Mayor Johnson ignores the cries of his constituents confidently knowing the votes will, as always, land in his favor. Historically, Chicago elections make the presidential election of 2020 look like child's play.

The city of Chicago is in a budget deficit of over one billion dollars. What did the sanctuary city of Chicago spend over a billion dollars on? One Chicago resident named Zoe Leigh declared, "Johnson should be convicted of treason. We are dealing with a mayor who is a democratic socialist, and he's bringing an agenda to Chicago that's just not going to work. And it is an agenda of illegal immigration that has gotten out of hand since last year. We are $1.2 billion in the deficit because of this illegal immigration scam. I call it a Ponzi scheme."[41] In April of 2024, Chicago City Council voted to appropriate another $70 million for illegal aliens and residents exploded with one Alderman, Anthony Beale, asking the most important question, "When are we going to help us? When are we going to help the people here?" Another Alderman Yancy followed Beale's question with a profound and direct statement despite voting for the additional $70 million appropriation for illegal aliens, "But Black Chicago is on life support."[42]

What is Mayor Johnson's view on all this spending and fighting on illegal aliens:

> *We need the president to extend the same economic opportunities long term for our undocumented brothers and sisters, so they can build a better life here in the city of Chicago or wherever else they decide to live." Johnson followed that utterly useless statement with this pronouncement, "I want to make this emphatically clear: Chicago will never turn its back on people who wish to call the city of Chicago their home.*[43]

Mayor Johnson has done what every sanctuary state governor and federal politician has done and that is place the safety and representation of American citizens below that of the illegal alien. Like Mayor Adams of New York City, I find Mayor Johnson lacking in both intelligence and political instincts. These are lightweights in the political jungle. In fact, they are simply puppets who are having their strings pulled by the more powerful and more corrupt "leaders" inside and outside of our nation.

Mayor Johnson has oversight of all of Chicago, including the south and west sides of Chicago that are literally dead zones. Any hope has evaporated. Any belief that there is a way out of the extreme poverty that envelops these communities is gone. Resentment grows each day as this betrayal continues. It is not just the obscene spending on illegal aliens that is so offensive, it is the replacement of black residents in these historical black neighborhoods with illegal aliens. It is showering these illegal aliens with thousands of dollars monthly for rent, food, education, and medical expenses when black residents "fight for the scraps."

American homeless men and women sleep in tents on the side of the highways in Chicago when less than a block away, illegal aliens sleep in hotels and renovated building in downtown Chicago. Homeless individuals are literally freezing to death while two hundred yards away illegal aliens sit in warming buses wearing their new clothes, eating their freshly cooked meals, all the while staying warm and safe. These warming buses sit idling along the curb of the processing centers to ensure every illegal alien remains comfortable as they wait to be transported to an all-expense paid hotel or newly renovated building. Homeless individuals have tried repeatedly to enter these warming buses on frigid nights in Chicago only to be denied as the warming buses are for "immigrants only."[21]

Chicago is sitting on an explosive race war created by Democrat elites that run both the state and every city in Illinois. Crime has exploded as illegal aliens that are predominately single adult military aged males engage in knife fights, prostitution, assaults, drug dealing, and violence. These hotels and shelters are breeding grounds for criminals and criminal activities. The financial cost to the state of Illinois and to the city of Chicago is in the billions. As the needs of hundreds of thousands of illegal aliens do not only need but demand continued services, the date of January 20, 2025, is rapidly approaching. Once the billions of dollars of federal aid instantly dry up and every service screeches to a halt, chaos will erupt and engulf the city of Chicago. Then we will see a city collapse from the stupidity of the elected leaders. One may argue that our founding fathers were correct in that we get the government we elect. Chicago is a living breathing example of our founder's understanding of human behavior.

We go from two of the dumbest mayors in America to one of the most ideologically driven beta males in America, Denver's Mayor Johnston. Just like Mayor Adams, Johnston was all in for illegal aliens. Johnston and the city of Denver are morally upright unlike the racists that fill the red states of America. Johnston and the city of Denver not only speak their beliefs, but they put their money where their mouths are to the tune of over $356 million spent on illegal aliens. Mayor Johnston cares so much about illegal aliens that he cut services to the sanctuary residents of Denver. He cut the recreation center's hours, suspended public event permits, and made more cuts to the Denver Motor Vehicle Division. In fact, the sanctuary city mayor made a reasonable statement after spending hundreds of millions of dollars, "What we know is it's unsustainable for us to permanently serve the number of people we're serving with the types of services we're providing."[44]

Mayor Johnston saw the writing on the wall all the way back in January 2024 when he echoed the fear shared by Mayor Adams as he tried to deflect blame to the feds, "The challenge we have is you have someone who will arrive in Denver who's been admitted on an asylum claim, but their court date is six years away. And they're in Denver for six years without the ability to work and support themselves and that means we have to support them. And that's not what they want to do or what we want them to do."[45] Johnston followed up with a pat on the city's back then added more blame on the feds, "We know what it takes to do this successfully, and we just need that help. Yes, we need federal dollars, but the most important thing is we need work authorization for folks who may arrive, and we need those resources at the border so you can have more security at the border and so you can help process those asylum claims so the folks who do arrive here can work."[45]

Let's put all of Denver's funding issues into context. This is from an article in January 2024 and every funding data point they predicted happened in excess. The city of Denver created a report that stated if this happens then the spending on illegal aliens would equal the spending on XYZ services.

- *$59.8 million by April 2024, the same amount as the Department of Transportation's operations.*
- *$103.2 million by July 2024, the same amount as the funding for Denver County's jail operations managed by the sheriff.*
- *$135 million by September 2024, it would equal all transportation and infrastructure spending.*
- *$152.2 million by October, amount allocated for the Denver Police Patrol Districts Division.*
- *$181 million by December, equal to the funding for the Department of Parks and Recreation and Cultural Facilities, plus the Office of Human Services.*[46]

Then a moment of clarity, even if it was fleeting, came from one of the sanctuary councilmembers Amanda Sawyer, "We are desperate for federal help. I'm concerned about having to come to a financial point where we might have to reduce services that we're providing to our tax-paying residents."[46]

What happens when you are a sanctuary city? Denver knows firsthand. Homelessness and services begin to stretch, then snap. Crime spikes and "hot spots" becomes a commonly used phrase. Two of Denver's city councilmembers have begun to ring the alarm bell of "hot spots" of crime in Denver, but they soften the spike in crime and who is committing the crimes saying, "The vast, vast majority of people who are entering our program are fantastic humans who want a better life. Not all of them. And we know that's the case because it's happening in District 5."[47]

Our representatives are a direct reflection of the society that appointed them to positions of authority. Denver, like New York City and Chicago, are run by mentally deficient individuals; people with a low IQ, an inability to think critically, and individuals that are tied to their ideology. All three of these cities share a common bond - they are led by bad representatives and the residents have voted for the chaos they live in. The representatives and the residents make over the top excuses for the third world criminal behavior of illegal aliens, and they try in vain to justify their actions as noble. They vigorously try to persuade the deplorables that being raped, murdered, and assaulted is a good thing, as long as you care.

Here is a great example of the hubris that the noble cause of exhausting all resources on foreigners is a good thing. Example A: Denver's health care services. Denver's largest healthcare provider and hospital, Denver Health, has seen over 8,000 illegal alien patients resulting in over 20,000 appointments in 2023.[48] What was the financial number associated with the 20,000 appointments for illegal aliens? How does $136,000,000 make you feel? Before that number sinks in remember that this is for one year, for one healthcare provider, and it is all free for the illegal aliens! Denver Health CEO Lynne cried the blues of this situation, "I suspect that no other hospital in the state of Colorado can say that and there has been no reimbursement for that and quite frankly it is an ongoing conversation with the city, with the state and with the federal government."[48] What happens when your largest healthcare provider and hospital is servicing thousands of illegal aliens with no reimbursement: you cut services! What services did Lynne cut? Well, let CEO Lynne tell us, "We have 78 inpatient beds that we devote to all substance abuse disorders as well as mental health, we've closed between 15 and 20 of them because we simply can't do it financially."[48]

Google Colorado rural hospitals and sit back and watch article after article populate discussing the closures of rural hospitals around the state. One of the main reasons for the closures is potential failure of reimbursement. With Colorado being an ultra-liberal state, every article refuses to connect illegal aliens to the lack of reimbursements. These articles portray a story as if American citizens are walking into these rural hospitals, getting treatments, and then throwing their hands up and yelling, "Sorry! I'm not paying!" Hospitals will bleed you dry for your money so the thought that these hospitals are closing due to everything under the sun except the fact that thousands of illegal aliens have crippled the healthcare system is a joke. These hospitals are crumbling under the crushing weight of illegal aliens and their refusal to pay. Period!

Johnston takes the cake when it comes to stupidity and arrogance. He has openly declared that Denver cannot sustain this growing situation of illegal aliens. The mayor is so stressed about this problem that he had one of Denver's Spanish-speaking city officials, Andres Carrera, beg the illegal aliens to leave Denver. Here are the words of a sanctimonious bastard, "...the opportunities are over..."[49] Carrera reportedly tells the group in Spanish. "New York gives you more. Chicago gives you more. So, I suggest you go there where there is longer-term shelter. There are also more job opportunities there."[49] Then Carrera offers a depressing look into life in Denver if they stay, "We are not going to block you if you want to say here. If you stay here, you are going to suffer even more and I don't want to see this."[49] You can't make this stuff up!

Johnston takes his arrogance one step further. Even after bemoaning the collapse of Denver without federal help, Johnston lays out what type of help he will allow. Unfortunately, the help is coming from another political party and the new Border Czar, Tom Homan. Johnston, all of 150 pounds and a soft, slender build, puffed his little bird chest out and stated, "More than us having DPD stationed at the county line to keep them out, you would have 50,000 Denverites there. It's like the Tiananmen Square moment with the rose and the gun, right? You'd have every one of those Highland moms who came out for the migrants. And you do not want to mess with them."[50] Not the Highland moms! Homan went right at this beta male as only Homan can:

> *But look, me and the Denver mayor, we agree on one thing—he's willing to go to jail, I'm willing to put him in jail because there there's a statute. It's Title 8 United States Code 1324 (iii). And what it says is it's a felony if you knowingly harbor and conceal an illegal alien from immigration authorities. It's also a felony to impede a federal law enforcement officer.*[51]

What do gutless blowhards like Denver Mayor Johnston do when directly challenged from an alpha male, they cower in fear. Johnston is the quintessential beta when he responded to Homan's direct blow, "Would I have taken it back if I could? Yes, I probably wouldn't have used that image. That's the image I hope we can avoid. What I was trying to say is this is an outcome I hope we can avoid in this country. I think none of us want that."[52] When asked if he would be willing to go to jail, Johnston meekly stated, "Yeah, I'm not afraid of that, and I'm also not seeking that. I think the goal is we want to be able to negotiate with reasonable people how to solve hard problems."[52]

I would fork over a thousand dollars to watch Johnston versus Homan on a pay per view. It would be over in a second, but it is always worth witnessing God's natural order takeover as a weak, pathetic, and cowardly man kneels before a powerful alpha.

The nation's big metropolitan cities are in crisis. The sophomoric leaders of those cities know that they are heading into dangerous times. Even as they hold onto their liberal ideologies, they are actively seeking help from their enemies, the Trump deplorables. As much as I want to sit back and watch those cities burn to the ground, I know the horde of illegal aliens will not and have not stayed in those blue sanctuaries. Instead, they have seeped into every small town and mid-size city across America.

Just like cancer, if you do not treat it, it spreads.

The cancer has spread.

CHAPTER 6

Hollowing Out of Small Town America

Where do 50 million illegal aliens go? They don't all go to the major metropolitan cities; they scatter to small towns and cities. Small towns you've never heard of. Small towns that always felt protected from the insanity of big city politics. Not anymore. The treason of the federal government to flood our nation with 30 million illegal aliens in four years has a profound negative impact on our nation. Small towns are waking up to discover that their small rural community's population has doubled literally overnight. Their population is unrecognizable in terms of language, customs, appearances, and cultural norms.

People are frightened. People are terrified. People are angry and resentful because their lives have been killed. The total takeovers of towns have been swift; and these takeovers can't be undone without pain and suffering for all involved. When your population increases by 100% and the total population increase is from a third world nation, nothing good will happen. Conversely, everything bad will happen and it will happen all at once. The native residents will move out for fear of being the last one holding the door thus losing everything. Businesses close. Schools and services close or become shells of their former selves because there is no one left paying taxes. What is left is a community of illegal aliens from the third world. This community will be a haven for crime, hopelessness, and despair. This community will become a "no go zone" and it will become a major suck on a state's resources. In effect this community will just become an extension of the third world it came from, but now it just resides in America.

What does this look like in reality? Ask the residents of Logansport, Indiana. Logansport is a small town with a population of 38,000 with a 30% population increase of illegal alien Haitians. Logansport sits just 80 miles north of Indianapolis and Indiana's Attorney General Todd Rokita believes this Haitian dump was coordinated by Biden and Harris, "Illegal immigration caused by 'border czar' Kamala Harris' perversion and misapplication of federal law has made every state a border state and imposed unsustainable costs on Logansport and other cities across the nation."[53] AG Rokita continued his allegation of the intentional destruction of Indiana, "It has also created serious sex and labor trafficking risks in all communities. I'm creatively trying to use every tool in the law to stop the Left's intentional destruction of Indiana."[53]

Logansport's school system is being overwhelmed by non-English students causing many residents to condemn this invasion. Housing has become a major issue as a Logansport resident Candice Espinoza bluntly stated, "It's just overrun. We don't have space for everybody, so the housing has been taken over and our schools have been taken over; pretty much the whole town has been taken over."[54] Do cultural norms and women feeling protected have any value? It seems to have value to multiple residents in Logansport as Haitian men act just a little differently, as one resident stated "...[They] stop in front of our porch and just stop and stare. They don't say a word. They just stare. It's unnerving."[54] I am sure these white women are just racist xenophobes clinging to their Bibles and their guns! I sure hope these racist residents aren't told about the sharp increase in tuberculosis and HIV that is now commonplace in Logansport.

The new residents of Logansport are from 28 different countries and speak a total of 27 different languages. The Mayor of Logansport, Mayor

Martin, has said that assimilation has become a big issue because of cultural differences. Really? Are there any benefits for Logansport outside of the obvious diversity? Interestingly, there seems to be a huge benefit not for Logansport, but for a certain company in the area called Tyson which has a large poultry plant just outside of Logansport.[55] The demographic movement of thousands of individuals into specific communities is coordinated and strategic. There are influential powers at play and politicians are becoming wealthy and more powerful because of this treason.

Staying in Indiana, we look at the small town of Seymour. Seymour is about one hour south of Indianapolis with a population of approximately 21,000. Just like Logansport, the illegal alien situation is bad. Indiana's Attorney General Rokita makes the argument against open borders and the chilling effect it has on his Indiana small towns, "The influx of these illegal aliens, which are coming from over 150 different countries, have strained our schools and the children of taxpayers are suffering as a result. It has caused unneeded stress on law enforcement, local hospitals and healthcare facilities, and our housing and labor markets."[56] The Brookings Institute did an analysis for the Indiana Economic Development Corp. In this report, Brookings detailed a 174% growth in the Latino and Hispanic population, AKA illegal aliens, and that was BEFORE Biden took office. Even then, Brookings stated the quiet part out loud, "While this growth has provided many workforce and economic development opportunities for the small city, it has also led to increasing challenges in meeting the needs of the growing population."[56] Again, reports like this always revolve around economics with a complete refusal to account for the devastating costs connected to large illegal alien populations. The Brookings Institute and other think tanks are great to quote but if you want the truth go to the residents like Seymour's City Council Representative Lucas, "I've had teachers reach out to me, elementary teachers, who will have 28 kids in a class and 20 of them are English learners. And then seven of them were level ones who speak zero English...and you can just see the challenges that our teachers are facing day to day."[56] Lucas also lamented about the crime associated with illegal aliens as he made a statement the citizens of the United States of America all agree with:

> *I love this town, and I see what it's turning into and there are a lot of very, very nice immigrants. And I've said this publicly...'If people want to come here legally and live here and raise their family and assimilate into our culture—one family in one house, pay taxes, keep your money here locally, and start a business—we welcome those people with open arms. But, for the people who are just coming here to plunder our resources for a job only to move on? We'd just as soon you'd go somewhere else.*[56]

Amen!

Let's drive east to Charleroi, Pennsylvania to see what the effect of increasing your population by 60% with Haitians and Liberians looks like. Charleroi had a population of approximately 4,000 until the Biden Administration brought in 2,500 Haitians and Liberians. One resident concisely described what Charleroi is like now, "This is beyond immigration at this point, it feels like an invasion."[57] Charleroi is just south of Pittsburgh. The movement of large groups of illegal aliens out of the city to rural America has become the norm. The use of NGOs to facilitate this movement is critical to the success of demographic change. The NGO servicing the complete demographic upheaval of Charleroi is the Pittsburgh charter of Jewish Family and Community Services (JFCS). Business has been extremely profitable for JFCS. How good? Well, in 2023 this NGO reported a profit of $12.5 million with over $6 million coming from government grants and the other profit came from other NGOs like, wait for it, HIAS.[58] I love how JWCS reports their funding as profit as if they are a business. This is all a giant Ponzi scheme of government grants being awarded to NGOs and then those NGOs spread that money around to other NGOs. In criminal legal terms this is called money laundering. This is the icing on the cake – JFCS's executives enjoy generous salaries: The CEO earned $215,590, the CFO $148,601, and the COO $125,218 — all subsidized by taxpayers.[58]

The demographic destruction of small towns like Charleroi is something that does not just happen. There is a malicious and strategic intent on the part of our government. "If you showed people in Haiti a map of the United States, the likelihood that they'd put their finger on Charleroi, PA and decide to come here is close to zero."[60] That is as factually true of a statement that you will ever find. So, if that statement is true, then how did thousands of illegal Haitians find their way to this specific small town and small towns like it? The answer is these specific groups of illegal aliens are strategically guided to these areas through the web of NGOs. By using NGOs, the federal government has plausible deniability. I wrote about Springfield, Ohio in a previous chapter and the same forces that brought mass destruction to Springfield are bringing Haitians into Charleroi. Want an example? Ohio Governor Mike DeWine stated, "Springfield is having a resurgence in manufacturing and job creation. Some of that is thanks to the dramatic influx of Haitian migrants who have arrived in the city over the past three years to fill jobs."[60] Why does the movement of illegal aliens always find locations in need of workers? More specifically, when these illegal aliens arrive in these geographic areas needing workers, why do the companies pay these illegal aliens well below the living wage? Why is an invasion of illegal aliens always good for business and economic growth while at the same time a complete societal decline occurs? Why are third world foreigners that can't read or write in their native language, can't speak English, have no job skills, and share no cultural norms with Americans always categorized as a net positive for America? While according to

Governor DeWine all the terrible criminal actions committed by illegal aliens in Springfield are lies! The only lies being told come from the political elite like DeWine.

Businesses get cheap labor and what else is positive? Nothing! Now let's quickly list the negatives – Americans are replaced by cheaper labor, schools are overcrowded and need specialized language teachers, crime skyrockets, housing shortages and property values decline, less taxes are collected, medical costs soar, long-lost medical conditions arise, and lastly the community gets hallowed out. What is left is a community that took decades, or hundreds of years, to build is now decaying. Residents that called their community home for generations move out and leave a community that now resembles the third world nation from which the illegal aliens escaped from. The irony of all ironies is that the businesses that needed workers initially benefitted from the influx of cheap labor, now sit vacant because they drove out all their customers.

Instead of listening to all the eggheads in the media, academia, and lying politicians; let's listen to the residents of these small towns. In an interview for American Compass, Charleroi resident, Tom Altmiller, is having none of the lies, "I don't believe that argument of, they had to bring that population here to save Charleroi, has any validity. We aren't prepared for it. We don't have the tax base for it. This is a town of 4,000 people hanging on the best they can. So, whoever is responsible for putting them here? That is an act of negligence."[59] Another resident, Andy Armbruster, tackles the lie of needed workers in Charleroi, "They say 'we can't find people to work.' Well, that's a half truth. There are people who would work if you paid them the going wage for the work. But they want to pay less and so they ended up getting involved with these agencies that bring in these workers."[59] Charleroi Fire Chief Robert Whiten Jr. stated with complete frustration about the culture and lack of understanding of how to drive a car, "I have never seen a town respond to so many of these calls.

Our response area has more vehicles [driven] into buildings than anywhere else. I just can't figure it out. Most departments have structure fires, fire alarms, medical calls, you know, but we have a lot of cars into buildings."[59] Read that again, "A lot of cars into buildings." Finally, the massive influx of illegal aliens leads to the destruction of the school system. The Charleroi school system had to place 45 Haitian children in a 60-person kindergarten class. Charleroi spent $400,000 on two English Language Learners (ELL) educators, an ELL coach, a registrar, and an interpreter. They expect to see the cost grow to another $300,000 next year.[59] When you lay out the facts, the imbecilic arguments of the Left are worthless.

On to another small town that has been decimated, Whitewater, Wisconsin. Whitewater is a town with approximately 15,000 residents. The Biden Administration artificially added a 10% population increase of Venezuelans and Nicaraguans. What could go wrong? I spoke with the Chief of Police Dan Meyer, and he was exasperated.[21] Chief Meyer told me that he has never seen this level or type of criminality. Crimes never experienced in this small town have been normalized. Kidnapping, child abuse, domestic abuse, narcotics, prostitution, and the list goes on and on. When I spoke with Chief Meyer, he seemed like a genuinely nice guy. He was smart and articulated the town's pressing issues with the influx of foreign nationals. What I do not respect is the constant need to backpedal or to clarify why he and other leaders are not racist and how diversity is a strength. Instead, I want leaders to speak the truth.

The Police Chief wrote a letter to President Biden in 2022 enumerating the issues and the needs of town of Whitewater. Chief Meyer didn't want the letter to become as political as it did because as he stated, "The intent behind it [the letter] really is to make sure that we as a community, or we as city leadership, are doing everything within our power to obtain the resources that we sorely need, prior to going to referendum and asking our community members to pay for something like this through taxation." Why did Chief Meyer feel a need to further articulate the meaning of his letter to the White House? Well, it could be that the Chief inadvertently spoke the truth about diversity when his letter asked for more police resources. And why would the small town need more police staffing if everything was rainbows and unicorns? Because that is the fairy tale told to America. The truth lies in the statistical increase in crime in Whitewater that tried in vain to hide. One example of these statistics is between 2010 to 2021, the Whitewater Police Department had in total approximately 2,400 traffic stops. In 2022, the number of vehicle stops was 1,719 and in 2023, they saw just over 1,200 traffic stops.[61] Just to make sure you read those last two sentences correctly, in less than two years the police officers in Whitewater surpassed the total number of traffic stops from the past twelve years combined! Whitewater authorities have no idea who is in their community as Chief Meyer explained, "I can't tell you how many times we've [Whitewater police] had contacts with somebody and unbeknownst to that officer, it's the second, third, maybe fourth time that we've had contact with that person. And every single time, we've gotten a different name and date of birth for that person."[61]

On a side note, why do Americans have to follow the law or face consequences but individuals that break our laws from foreign nations are instantly forgiven or worse, their criminal activity is ignored. Let's play a quick game of, "What Would Happen If..." What would happen to you if you were stopped by law enforcement while driving around town with no license, no insurance, and you gave the police officer a fraudulent name and date of birth? You are in big trouble. You will pay significant fines, and you might be taken to the police station to sort things out. Now what if the same scenario happens and you are an illegal alien from Honduras? Nothing!

In a nation founded on law and order, these situations are unjust, unsafe and they undercut the foundation on what has allowed America to prosper. Law and order are the bedrocks of our nation's foundation that allow for opportunity and freedom. If you remove the foundational bedrocks of law and order, you get chaos. Chaos destroys freedom and opportunity.

The small towns across America suffer from the same stupidity and fear that manifests from Leftist doctrine. Crime is soaring in Whitewater and their small town is rapidly changing but thank God, diversity is a strength, and Whitewater is drowning in it. There is nothing more impactful than listening to a "Karen" that runs a nonprofit about the beauty of people that share nothing in common with you and your neighbors. Marjorie Stoneman runs the local community group Whitewater Unites Lives. I love the titles of their organizations; they are always filled with words to deceive and contradict the truth. Why not just come out being bold and screaming the truth? Call your organization The Death of Whitewater. I would, at least, have to respect that for its honesty. What is it about Venezuelans and Nicaraguans that make Whitewater so much better than before the invasion, "The community is more diverse than it was when I was growing up and I love it. I'm so glad my son had a chance to meet more people that don't look like him or speak the same language."[61] I am so glad her son gets to learn new languages and see different faces even if that means the city's finite resources are stretched beyond the breaking point and the entire town becomes unrecognizable.

Has anyone else hit their breaking point on diversity and the losers that pedal this insanity? I could literally go from one small town to another for several more pages and I would be just touching the tip of the iceberg. There are endless border towns that have been decimated. There are untold rural towns scattered across America where the news media just hasn't gotten to yet. The idea that 50 million illegal aliens moved into the big cities in America and then the rural towns are walled off from the rest of the nation is absurd on its face. Instead, all of America is being adversely affected.

I want to focus on one more town in America, Aurora, Colorado. Aurora is a suburb of Denver that has been completely overrun by tens of thousands of Venezuelan illegal aliens. Aurora has a population of approximately 400,000. You might say that it isn't a small town, but you would be incorrect. Aurora is a sleepy little suburb of the large city of Denver, and it functions as a small town. Let me explain in terms of the police force. If I took the ratio of the number of police per 1,000 residents as in the state of California or Nevada, your police to 1,000 residents' ratio would be 3 to 1,000. Using that ratio, Aurora would need over 1,200 officers. In reality, Auora has 748 police officers for the entire population. That tells me crime is not a big issue in Aurora. But that has completely changed now that Tren de Aragua (TDA), a violent gang from Venezuela has descended into this suburb.

First, let's dive into who and what makes up TDA. TDA has spread across 20 different states in America. Just in the summer of 2024, TDA occupied six states. Under the lawlessness of sanctuary cities and states, the complicity of the Biden Administration, and the strategic placement of certain illegal alien populations, TDA has franchised out of Chicago and New York City. TDA is a prison gang from Venezuela. Remember when everyone in the media mocked Trump as he stated the Venezuelan government had released all the prisoners from jails and patients from mental institutions? I don't hear the mocking anymore! TDA focuses on human trafficking, drugs, kidnapping, extortion, and every other third world crime. They are vicious and many believe they rival the ruthlessness of El Salvador's MS13.

The Biden Administration placed tens of thousands of illegal aliens from Venezuela into the suburb of Aurora. I remember driving through Aurora in August as we were filming our documentary. We came to a stop light on a busy city street. I watched ten young men in their late teens and early twenties descend onto the stopped traffic and begin to wash the windows of the trapped cars waiting for the light to change. They all wore hoodies and heavy jackets even as the temperatures reached the high 90's.

I turned to my documentary filmmaker partner, Ryan Matta, and I calmly told him that this is just the beginning of Aurora's problems. He asked me what I meant, and I said that these guys are illegal aliens from Central America/Venezuela, and they are all criminals. I explained to Ryan that this is always how it begins. Once a certain group of illegal aliens gain a foothold in a town, they call all their friends and relatives to come. This is what has happened to Aurora.

If you follow the migration of Venezuelans into America and follow the migration from the big cities to rural America, you can predict the next stronghold of TDA. Gangs are parasites and they need a host to feed off. TDA feeds off their own people as they set up their criminal enterprise. It is a perfect business model. TDA can hide inside the large Venezuelan illegal population and build their business in plain sight.

TDA has taken over entire apartment complexes all the while the sanctuary mayor, city council, and even the governor lied about the existence of TDA. They lied until they had to admit the truth, their community in Aurora had been taken over by a violent prison gang from a foreign nation. So much for diversity! Why did Venezuelans think it was ok to come to America? Well Texas Governor Abbott explained, "The fact of the matter is, this is something that has exploded in the aftermath of the president saying that if you're from Venezuela, you'll be allowed in the United States."[62]

What was the initial response of the Aurora Mayor, City Council, City Manager, and the Police Department in September of 2024 after TDA had taken over the city. Well, exactly what you would expect from a blue sanctuary city led by the morally elite:

> *We would like to clear the record about the widely reported presence of Tren de Aragua (TdA) in Aurora and across the metro area. We want to provide an update about the facts of the situation and the*

Aurora Police Department's collaborative, ongoing efforts to investigate and aggressively pursue criminal activity linked to TdA members and associates.

The city's duty is to make sure it gathers and presents factual, accurate, and comprehensive information about any issue affecting the community. We reiterate that the safety, security, and well-being of community members and visitors is of paramount concern to us and the city.

As for the perception and reality of public safety in Aurora, please understand that issues experienced at a select few properties do not apply to the city as a whole or large portions of it. TdA has not "taken over" the city. The overstated claims fueled by social media and through select news organizations are simply not true. Again, TdA's presence in Aurora is limited to specific properties, all of which the city has been addressing in various ways for months.[63]

Not to be outdone, Colorado Governor Jarod Polis, a gutless beta male, had his spokesperson, Shelby Wieman, mock the only brave city councilwoman, Danielle Jurinsky, with a statement about the TDA situation. Wieman proudly mocked the entire TDA criminal activity, "The Governor has already let the Mayor know that the State is ready to support the local police department with assistance from state troopers and the Colorado Bureau of Investigation if needed. But, according to police intelligence this purported invasion is largely a feature of Danielle Jurinsky's imagination."[63] The Aurora Mayor Coffman piled on to the mocking led by the Governor's office by stating:

I'm trying to be realistic on how I portray this, but I am worried that there is a tendency, inherently, to exaggerate and to say this incident

> *that's isolated to three buildings under the same ownership with the same people — concentration of Venezuelan migrants — is the city of Aurora, that the entire city is unsafe. And that narrative isn't true, and that's a destructive narrative to the economic health of this city.*[63]

Fast forward to December 2024 and the discussion that this is a conspiracy theory has quickly faded to a discussion of "Dear God! What do we do?" Kidnappings were on the rise as one of two kidnapped victims sadly told a reporter, "I thought I was going to die. I started praying silently, telling God if I had to go, to take me to him."[64] The Chief of Police Todd Chamberlain seems to have changed his tune about TDA criminals in his suburb. Chief Chamberlain was questioned about a home invasion, "But when you look at the circumstances of this, when you look at the events of this, when you look at the individuals involved in this, when you look at the veracity and the violence involved in this, again, it is not a big step for me to say that they are TdA gang members."[65] That seems to be a far cry of "Nothing to see here!"[66] in September to less than three months later exclaiming, "We have a real problem with TDA!"[67] Even the Chief of Police has had enough, "Yeah, I'm fired up. Something is seriously wrong and we are going to try to fix it as best we can. And we have been."[68]

What about the Governor and the Mayor's new tune:

> *Governor Polis congratulates the city of Aurora and the Aurora Police Department for these arrests. The state added staff and resources to the task force in July and convened federal officials over the summer. The state stands ready to assist Aurora PD. Governor Polis is calling for additional public safety investments during the upcoming legislative session to crack down on crime and urges the legislature to approve those requests to make Colorado safer.*[68]

Wow that is totally different than "it's a wild imagination!" Aurora Mayor Mike Coffman said, "Today's swift and decisive action to apprehend the 14 probable gang suspects, and maybe more, demonstrates precisely why we brought the chief here and why he has my full support."[68] Pretty strong language regarding a prison gang from Venezuela that was mocked as "imaginary" just a few months prior.

I want to frame this invasion like it is cancer. All cancers have a beginning point, then it spreads and attacks the body. The invasion of 30 million illegal aliens in four years also has beginning points. The four open borders of America are the genesis of Stage 4 cancer; and it is spreading across the body of America. The cancer is aggressive, and it is attacking everything inside of our body. The doctors, who are our elected representatives, have simply walked away, allowing the cancer to wildly spread. The cancer spreads like the hordes of illegal aliens that devour our cities and small towns. Our representatives are welcoming thousands of illegal aliens to America daily. The equivalence of what our representatives are doing to the body of America is the same as if our cancer doctor injected more cancer cells into our body every day.

After we find a brave doctor to stop this disease from consuming our body, the two most important questions must be answered:

Who allowed this cancer to enter America?

Why would those culpable do this to our nation?

Once those questions are answered, swift justice must be doled out.

CHAPTER 7

Special Interest Aliens – Terrorists

How vulnerable is the United States of America to terrorist attacks? Very!

Biden's open borders have allowed approximately 12 million illegal aliens to cross the border, surrender to the Border Patrol, and then be released into America with zero vetting. When DHS Secretary Mayorkas makes the false statement that all individuals that cross the border are thoroughly vetted, he is lying. Yes, every illegal alien that "presents" himself/herself to the Port of Entry or is arrested crossing the border is inputted into the DHS and FBI database. If a person has been in America before and he has committed a crime or been deported, he will have a criminal history. However, if he has never been to the United States of America then he could have never committed a crime in America. Outside of a nation reciprocating criminal databases with the U.S. (which is rare) if the person is a criminal from another nation but has never set foot inside the United States, he will be vetted clean. Do you now see the absurdity of Mayorkas' claim that everyone has been vetted?

Unbelievably, even if a person committed horrible crimes inside or outside of America, he will still be released from Border Patrol custody into America. A person could have committed murder, or had a prior deportation, and guess what, he is still released. I understand a new reader to this treason instantly screams that this can't be true. Sorry, it is! In

September 2024, Immigration and Customs Enforcement (ICE) released a report late on a Friday afternoon, hoping to have the contents of this report buried in the weekend news cycle, detailing releasing hundreds of thousands of criminals into America. In this report, ICE was forced to admit that out of the seven million illegal aliens on the Non-Detained Docket (NDD), ICE released 662,566 criminal illegal aliens onto the streets of America. Let me explain the NDD so you better understand the open abuse of immigration law under Biden and Mayorkas. Better yet, let's have the senior fellow at the American Immigration Council, Aaron Reichlin-Melnick, explain this insanity:

> *ICE's non-detained docket is a list of every person the United States believes is a removable non-citizen who is physically present in the United States and who is not currently held in ICE detention. So non-detained does not mean not in detention. It means specifically not in ICE detention. So there are people who are on ICE's non-detained list, who are in federal prison, for example.*[69]

Before we continue, let me reiterate what our government has created. The federal government has released over seven million illegal aliens into America that they knew were deportable aliens. To make matters worse, as of July 2024, DHS knowingly released 662,566 criminal aliens from that seven million NDD group. ICE had the nerve to try and soften the blow by placing the total 662,566 criminals into two categories: Convicted Criminals 435,719 and Criminal Pending Charges 226,847. Doesn't that make you feel better? But wait, it's beyond comprehension when you dive into what type of criminals ICE released into our communities. ICE admitted to these numbers below of individuals NOT in ICE detention:

> *Among those not in ICE detention, there are 425,431 convicted criminals and 222,141 with pending criminal charges.*

These are, in many cases, violent criminals. Some 62,231 were convicted of assault, 14,301 were convicted of burglary, and 13,099 were convicted of homicide. An additional 2,521 have kidnapping convictions and 15,811 have sexual-assault convictions.

There are an additional 1,845 with pending homicide charges, 42,915 with assault charges, 3,266 with burglary charges, and 4,250 with assault charges. ICE records showed 792 illegal immigrants on their docket convicted of arson, 2,200 convicted of "commercialized sex offenses," 9,461 convicted of sex offenses not involving assault or commercialized sex, and 13,413 convicted of "weapon charges."[70]

I want to pause here for a second so we can all digest what ICE has admitted. ICE has admitted to releasing almost 15,000 murderers and almost 16,000 sexual predators to include over 11,000 rapists. ICE knew that these people were murderers and sexual predators and still decided to release them into America!

Let me walk you through how this works in real time under this administration and let me make this as clear as I can – the Border Patrol never did this prior to the Mayorkas tyranny. After the Biden administration took office, a Border Patrol Agent finds an individual squatting on the north side of the border and that individual is arrested and taken to the Border Patrol station. Once in the station, the Border Patrol Agent takes the illegal alien's biographical data and inputs that data into the DHS and FBI criminal database. A literal red bar appears on the illegal alien's name indicating that the illegal alien has a criminal history. The Agent clicks on the red bar and the illegal alien's criminal data populates. The Border Patrol Agent sees that the individual standing in front of him has a murder conviction in America and a prior deportation or multiple deportations prior to Biden's presidency. What this Agent does next is criminal, this Border Patrol Agent releases the murderer into America. At the same time, he is releasing this arrested murderer, his coworker next to him is releasing a convicted rapist onto the streets of our nation. No oversight. No follow up. Nothing, absolutely nothing is done to protect Americans from foreign savages.

Understand, that those 662,566 criminals out of the seven million on the NDD are just what the Border Patrol was able to identify. You need to take that number of criminals and multiply it by ten! The number of illegal aliens arrested in the last four years is not seven million, but 12 million. The number of get-a-ways in Biden's four years in office are between 15 – 18 million. The number of criminals released by ICE on the NDD are staggering but that number is as true as unicorns and rainbow candy filling the sky. Our own government has opened the borders of America to the most vile and vicious criminals on planet Earth.

As hard as that data is to digest, I have even worse news to report. As discussed in an earlier chapter, there is a class of illegal aliens that pose an even darker challenge to the safety of America – Special Interest Aliens (SIAs). Who are SIAs? Well, they are terrorists! DHS will try and spilt hairs and label these individuals as people from terrorist nations or people that have traveled through terrorist nations. People working in the dirty immigration business know that all SIAs are potential terrorists.

Americans today have a unique way of seeing the world through the lens that what is happening now has always been that way. Of course, that is an unsophisticated way of thinking. In terms of SIAs, this purposeful debacle has never happened prior to Biden. SIAs have always been a huge concern for our nation because of the maximum destruction one SIA can cause alone. However, prior to Biden taking office, SIA entries and arrests were under control. When you look at the statistics of SIA arrests each fiscal year (FY), the numbers are shocking. In FY21 the number of SIAs arrested by Border Patrol was 3,675. Then Biden entered the picture and opened the border causing the FY22 numbers to spike to 25,627. FY23 was even worse as the number of SIAs arrested by Border Patrol catapulted to over 80,000![71] Internal CBP leaked data state that FY24 surpassed FY2023. Some reports state the number of SIAs arrested will be over 100,000! In the four-year term of President Biden, over 200,000 Special Interest Aliens have been arrested out of the 12 million total illegal aliens apprehended by the Border Patrol. We have another 15 – 18 million illegal alien got-a-ways that are unaccounted, and we have no idea who those individuals are. I tell everyone that will listen – there are over one million SIAs inside America today.

Let's put the over 200,000 arrest total of SIAs from FY2022 to FY24 into context. From 2007 to 2017, the United States Border Patrol arrested 45,006 SIAs.[72] Let that sink in for a second as you truly try to understand the danger America finds herself in. To further prove how rare the occurrence of arresting an SIA is, consider my career in the Border Patrol. In my 24-year career, from being a Journeyman Agent to a senior leader in the Patrol, I arrested at least 100,000 illegal aliens directly and indirectly. Of those 100,000 illegal aliens, I cannot remember five being SIAs. FIVE! Of those five SIAs I arrested, how many do you think were released? ZERO! How many of the over 200,000 SIAs arrested by the Border Patrol in the last three fiscal years were released? ALL OF THEM!

I want to take you back to the "old days" (all four years ago) and tell you what the procedure was when we arrested an SIA compared to the current criminal activity being conducted by Border Patrol Agents and ICE Officers. When that rare occurrence of an SIA arrest happened, everything in my Border Patrol station stopped. As the Deputy Patrol Agent in Charge, I would have to email and call DHS Headquarters in Washington D.C. and provide exact details of the arrest. Agents from the Joint Terrorism Task Force (JTTF) would respond to the station and conduct extensive interviews and interrogations on the subject. The JTTF was made up of every three-letter alphabet law enforcement agency in our government led by the FBI. JTTF have special criminal and terrorist database access that the average Border Patrol Agent does not possess. JTTF Agents also have specialized interrogation training so that they can extract as much information as they can from a suspected terrorist. Each Border Patrol Sector has a JTTF unit. If JTTF determined that the subject was a terrorist, that individual would disappear like in the movie *Men in Black*. If it was determined that the individual could not be connected to a terrorist organization, that individual would be turned back to us, and we would then process that subject for deportation. What we would never do would be release the SIA onto the street. If I had taken an SIA from JTTF and released that subject, I would have had my gun and badge taken from me and I would have been placed on administrative leave. I would then be interrogated as to why I would have made the decision to release a high value SIA. My choices would have been either I was corrupt, or I was incompetent. Either way, my career would have been over.

What does this same scenario look like in the corrupt world of Biden and Mayorkas? There are so many SIAs being arrested, there are not enough JTTF Agents to respond. So, the interviewing and interrogation is left to the average Border Patrol Agent that lacks the criminal and terrorist database access and has not been trained in specialized interrogation techniques. On top of that, Border Patrol Agents are processing hundreds of illegal aliens a day in stations built to hold 100 illegal aliens. Those holding cells now have 500, 600, 1,000 illegal aliens crammed into holding areas that are well beyond capacity. To say the average Border Patrol station is chaotic would be the understatement of the year. Agents are pressed to process faster and faster as the buildup of illegal aliens in the field grows every minute. Agents are processing so quickly and are forced to cut corners, so mistakes are being made and SIAs are being mistakenly released, or they are knowingly released. I receive videos, photos, phone calls, and text messages from Border Patrol Agents showing and describing thousands of single adult military aged men on the border. They are all processed and released into America. My former colleagues tell me that they are scared to death because they know they are releasing terrorists into America. They are seasoned law enforcement agents that know who the hell is standing in front of them, but if the individual can't be determined to be a terrorist and is not on the terror watchlist, he is released.

And what is the "terror watchlist" anyway? Do you believe that every terrorist in the world is on the big bad watchlist? The terror watchlist is simply just a list. It is not an all-consuming document that has every terrorist identified and listed. For that to be the case, the United States would have had to thoroughly vet the over 8 billion people on planet Earth. Do you think that happened? Of course not. So, that terror watchlist is a sample of what or who we know. We all agree that our government has no idea the number of terrorists in the world. In fact, the United States government is so grossly incompetent and corrupt as they have proven over and over again throughout recent history.

Agents are moving so many people through each Border Patrol station that the record checks from DHS and FBI criminal databases are lagging. So much so that Border Patrol Agents are releasing individuals and once they are released, record checks come back revealing that the released individual was in fact on the terrorist watchlist. How often does this happen? Well, more than you want to know.

In 2023, Border Patrol released 15 nationals from Uzbekistan. The FBI went into high gear when it was discovered that these 15 Uzbekistan nationals were smuggled by an individual with ties to ISIS.[73] National Security Council spokesman, Adrienne Watson, assured the nation to not worry because, "There was no indication—and remains no indication—that any of the individuals facilitated by this network have a connection to a foreign terrorist organization or are engaged in plotting a terrorist attack in the United States."[73] After everything we know about the FBI and the national intelligence agencies, do you believe her? Needing to convince us more, Ms. Watson vomited out a bunch of words that meant nothing.

> *We continually assess our security architecture to ensure that we are best poised to respond to threats to the homeland. Moreover, we will continue to constantly recalibrate our screening, vetting, and processing of those encountered entering the United States to ensure that we are taking into account the most up-to-date information at our disposal and with an unyielding commitment to protecting Americans and the homeland from the full range of potential threats.*[73]

Words should have meaning, but because of the endless lies and the lack of trust, words are just words especially when you have experienced the truth. Ms. Watson can spew words like "recalibrate," "screening," "vetting," and "processing" until the cows come home but until the border is closed and our trained personnel can thoroughly screen, vet, and process these individuals; her words are still just words without meaning.

Here is one of my favorite arrests and then release of SIA terrorists by the Border Patrol. In 2024, eight nationals from the Tajikistan that crossed the southern border were arrested by the Border Patrol and taken to the station for processing. As I described above, in the chaotic environment of the processing area, all eight Tajikistanis were not properly vetted and then they were released. Now here is where this situation gets interesting. These eight individuals from a terrorist nation traveled over 7,500 miles together to get to America. After 7,500 miles of togetherness, they dispersed to three different cities – Los Angeles, New York City and Philadelphia. Why would eight dudes travel across the globe and then separate once they get to America? Because they had to get to their respective terror cells. A coordinated multi-agency effort found all eight of these terrorists and deported them.

Great work to find these terrorists but stop and ask, "Was there anymore nationals from Tajikistan in the group that crossed?" Why do I ask that question? I did this job for 24 years. When a group is arrested, Border Patrol Agents fill out a Border Patrol tracking form that we call a "Ready Wet." This form captures the simple biographical information of everyone in the group. So, if I arrested this group of eight Tajikistanis, I would have created a form and on the top right corner I would have written "1of 8". This notation would allow me to keep track of the group and the processing Agent at the station would know that these eight people were in the same arrest group. Reports have been circulating that these eight ISIS terrorists separated prior to entering the border. That opens several more questions, but the main question remains, "Were there other individuals in the group or was it just a group of eight?" Since most of the media have no idea of this system used by the Border Patrol in the field, no follow up questions were asked. Everyone assumes because of the current border situation where group numbers can climb as high as 1 of 1,000, that there were only eight of these terrorists in the group. I do not have the proof but listening to interviews with ICE and Border Patrol managers, I believe there were others in that group. Meaning other ISIS terrorist escaped from being identified.

Is this a one off with this ISIS group or is this a badly hidden secret? The FBI Director whispered about the border threats in a Congressional Hearing:

> *I want to be a little bit careful about how far I can go in an open session. But there is a particular network where some of the overseas facilitators of the smuggling network have ISIS ties that we're very concerned about and that we've been spending an enormous amount of effort with our partners to investigate. Exactly what that network is up to is something that is, again, the subject of our current investigation.*[74]

That is a word salad that reads between the lines of, "We have a serious problem with terrorist organizations." The former ICE Chief of Staff Jon Feere made an excellent point about the vulnerability of our open borders, "When a random person shows up at our border with no paperwork, no known background, our first instinct can't be to simply allow them to enter the United States. And we're going to have to make the tough decision to say no in many instances."[74] Then he hits the million-dollar target, "Now, the odds of a bad person coming through are low when we're talking small numbers. But when we're dealing with mass illegal immigration, as we're experiencing now, the odds of a bad actor coming through increase, and the threats that this administration has created will be felt for years to come."[74]

What are the politicians in charge of the oversight of the DHS and Homeland Security doing? Writing strongly worded letters. Here are some strong words from Congressmen Green from Tennessee of the House Homeland Subcommittee:

> *Unfortunately, the unacceptable security failures that have allowed individuals with terrorist ties to enter the United States through the Southwest Border have become an alarming pattern under the administration... The Department's prioritization of catch, process, and release, presents a grave danger to national security. The Committee has repeatedly and forcefully highlighted the security vulnerabilities inherent in the massive influx of illegal aliens at our border. The Biden Administration and the Department, however, continue to hide their heads in the sand, ignoring the 'blinking red lights' everywhere.*[75]

Everyone knows the danger America is in and nothing gets done. As I write this book, at the end of Biden's term in office, thousands of illegal aliens are arrested and released each and every day. Terrorists are pouring across our borders. The numbers of nationals from Tajikistan that have flooded into America since 2020 is over 1,500. On its face that doesn't seem to be that big of a number compared to 30 million illegal aliens in four years. On the contrary, that number is enormous when you realize that only 26 Tajikistan nationals crossed into America in the previous 14 years![76]

As I write, I have stopped multiple times in amazement at what we have allowed to happen to our nation and what the anti-America Left has accomplished. If I am being truthful, which I always try to be, I must applaud Biden, Harris, Mayorkas, and the other transformational people behind the scenes because they are winning. They have successfully accomplished more in four years than I thought was humanly possible.

Todd Bensman wrote a great article in 2023 for CIS.org titled, *Thousands of 'Special Interest Aliens' Posing Potential National Security Risks Entering via CBP One App.*[77] In this article, Bensman discovered that the unlawful application called the CBP One App (that I wrote about in a previous chapter) is being used to bring in foreign nationals from SIA nations. This is one of those times that I stop and stare in amazement at not only the Left's success but at their arrogance to even try this. Bensman stated that the DHS, using the CBP One App, has brought into America over 7,300 SIAs from 24 terrorist designated countries. I am going to list some of these nations as I believe reading these terrorist nations is important to drive home the depth of this treason - Iran, Lebanon, Syria, Iraq, Afghanistan, Kyrgyz Republic (Kyrgyzstan), and Uzbekistan.[77] This abuse of the immigration system has continued since this article was written in 2023 to the present day.

Bensman quotes a retired FBI counterterrorism agent James G. Conway, who worked for years after 9/11in Mexico trying to vet SIAs and detect terrorists. Conway articulates perfectly the absurdity of this program, and the vulnerable position America is in:

> *That's a really hard target to analyze, and to just shoot from the hip and let them in is absolute insanity in my book. How would you knowingly and wittingly bring people from terrorist countries into the United States with that level of vetting? Some of these terrorism countries don't even have an electric grid let alone a computer system, and you can't scrub them on databases that don't exist. The whole thing is insane to me.*[77]

Agent Conway asks the most poignant question, "Why?" Why would your government open her country to the abuse, pain, suffering, and death caused from terrorism? The answer remains the same – to fundamentally transform the United States of America. To be fair, I want to quote another expert on this topic that is from the other side of American politics as FBI Director Wray echoes Agent Conway, "The only thing we can query is information that we have. So, if we have no information on someone, they've never crossed our radar screen, they've never been a ripple in the pond, there will be no record of them there and so it will be challenging."[77]

The truth about the coming terror attacks have come out of the shadows and out from quiet hushed conversations to live in the exposed daylight. Sarah Adams, a former CIA Targeting Officer and author of the book, *Benghazi: Know Thy Enemy*, was on the Shawn Ryan Show for a second time and made a huge statement that shook the nation. What was the statement Sarah Adams made after Shawn Ryan asked, "You are one hundred percent certain that there are 1,000-plus Al-Qaeda-trained fighters within the United States borders?"[78] Ms. Adams responded, "Well, Al-Qaeda says they trained and deployed 1,000 for this attack. First off I think that there is more than 1,000 Al-Qaeda members in the United States."[78] Ms. Adams continued about other terror organizations inside America's non-existent walls, "Within the thousand terrorists some of them are ISIS."[78]

Wow, Ms. Adams was spot on as an ISIS terror attack occurred on New Year's Day 2025 in New Orleans. This attack was from a U.S. citizen with allegiance to ISIS and as of this writing, 14 people have been killed and another 40 people severely injured. The ISIS terrorist drove his truck through a crowd of people in the French Quarter, jumped out of his truck firing his gun at random people, and then was shot and killed. The investigation is ongoing but immediately the FBI made contradictory statements about it being a terror attack and it not being a terror attack. Diversity, Equity, and Inclusion (DEI) was front and center as representatives from both the local police department and the FBI fumbled their way through press conferences showing the true ineptitude of our law enforcement organizations.

Shawn Ryan posted the perfect retort to the traitorous and felonious government that rule over us:

> *I told you this was coming, @TPASarah told you this was coming, @RooftopLeader told you this was coming, @realLegendAfg told you this was coming, @AhmadMassoud told you this was coming. Congress funded it (you heard this on my show), we warned them, we warned you. Nobody did a damn thing. Now we will continue to see the reality and the consequences of what open borders, and funding terrorism does. Remember, terrorists organizations that Bin Laden's son leads are saying 50-60 Thousand Americans will die, and we are funding it.*[79]

America's sovereignty has been exploited and destroyed. America stands naked and vulnerable because our elected leaders have purposely weakened her. The enemy is living inside of our broken borders waiting on the green light to attack.

The greatest enemy of the American people is our own government!

CHAPTER 8

Criminals

Open borders have dire consequences. Borders open for four years produce catastrophic consequences. The treason committed by the Biden Administration by intentionally opening the borders to vicious criminals has led to third world violence and fear. Sixty to seventy percent of the 30 million illegal aliens allowed into America are single adult military aged men. We have invited the world's criminals into our nation. We have allowed foreign nations to dump their worst into America. We have a standing army of millions of thugs, rapists, murderers, drug dealers, pedophiles, and violent gangs that are allowed to roam our country unimpeded. I don't want anyone to read over what I just wrote, so I want to reiterate it again – there are millions of illegal alien criminals in our country.

I could write an entire volume of books just listing the victims of illegal alien criminals. I will discuss several victims in this chapter to highlight the level of depravity these third world savages have inflicted upon our brothers and sisters. I want to make this point as strongly as I can, every story of illegal aliens raping, murdering, and assaulting Americans that you read or hear about is just a tiny fraction of the truth. The truth is that every single day Americans are being butchered, raped, human trafficked, kidnapped, and assaulted by illegal aliens. The situation is so abysmal that the Left does not even try to deflect the truth or throw vile racist names at people like me that point this out. Instead, the Left knows the volume of these crimes against American citizens cannot be defended or talked away. So, the Left ignores the blatant truth, and they try to normalize the pain and suffering as if this has always been life in America.

I am not the biggest fan of the tough letters from any politician or powerful committee like the House Homeland Security Committee. However, the Chairman of this committee, Congressman Green, put out a report that squarely communicates the dire situation America faces because of the open borders and the criminals pouring in. Chairman Green enumerated the challenges our nation currently faces:

- *Since the start of FY21, the Border Patrol has recorded 43,674 arrests of illegal aliens with criminal backgrounds, a 99% increase from FY17-FY20 combined.*
- *According to one New York county executive, "We have seen an increase in crime, basically because you have these organized gangs that are part of the drug cartels from Mexico and other countries who have come to the metropolitan area... Some of the patterns that we've found on the burglaries of residential and commercial properties have been done by migrants who came here through the current migrant policy."*
- *Sheriff Mark Dannels of Cochise County, Arizona, testified in February 2023 that "border related crime" was "at an all-time high" in his county.*
- *According to figures from the Chicago Police Department, arrests of Venezuelan-born individuals in 2023 were up more than 11,000% compared to 2021.*
- *According to Bradley Schoenleben of the Orange County, California, District Attorney's Office, "We know transnational criminals, including Colombian nationals, are intentionally being arrested at the California border to gain entry into the United States, knowing*

they will be released quickly. Upon release, they commit residential burglaries and other thefts..."

- *The deputy chief patrol agent for the Yuma Sector told the Committee in 2023, "[A]ny crime that can be committed, we do encounter people who have committed them."*[80]

What is so frustrating when trying to communicate the level of crime and criminality caused by illegal aliens is the data is extremely flawed and grossly inaccurate. There are several reasons why the local and national data doesn't come close to reflecting the actual damage caused by illegal alien criminals and violent gang members. The first reason is that local law enforcement does not accurately capture the correct biological data. If I had a dollar for every illegal alien criminal that I processed where the FBI rap sheet showed the suspect as a white United States citizen, I would be rich! Men that were as black as night or Guatemalan nationals staring blankly at me as I asked them questions in English, were inputted by some local police or sheriff as white and a U.S. citizen. Secondly, illegal aliens go to cities and states that are favorable and welcoming to illegal aliens. These are mainly the blue democrat localities. These sanctuary municipalities will not interact with federal immigration law enforcement, and they help conceal the actual nationality of the illegal alien criminal. Lastly, the federal government, on purpose and because of incompetence, does not have any mechanism in place to capture the data of illegal aliens that commit crimes.

Because of the above listed issues, many in the media will use the talking point that illegal aliens commit a lower percentage of crimes than native born Americans. That is a flat out lie, but for the sake of this discussion, let's accept this falsehood as truth. So, when I can provide citated data proving that there are millions of criminal aliens in America and that these millions of criminal aliens commit tens of millions of crimes annually, how does that belief from the Left hold up? How do you tell a mother whose daughter was raped for two solid hours, strangled to death, and then dumped into a creek, that illegal aliens commit less crimes? That horrible scenario I just described happened in 2024. A young 12-year-old girl named Jocelyn Nungaray was walking through a neighborhood in Houston when two savage illegal aliens from Venezuela took her and raped her for two hours. Stop and let that settle in, two hours! After these animals were done with Jocelyn, they murdered her and tossed her little preteen dead body into a shallow creek under a bridge.[81] Jocelyn's mom, Alexis Nungaray's, pain, and sadness will be attached to her forever, "Some days are better than others. Some days I don't cry, some days I just cry for five minutes, some days I'm on and off crying." Asked if she has any political affiliation, Ms. Nungaray flatly stated, "This has turned really political, and I know it seems that I'm going for one side more than the other, but I'm going for the side that's wanting to make change. I'm going for the people that are gonna make a difference and protect these kids, we've lost too many kids."[82]

This rape and murder should have never happened. Think about this logically, if those savages were arrested at the border and deported, those animals would never have been on the same road that young Jocelyn was walking on. To go just one step further, if Biden did not open the borders and then literally welcome these people into America, those two criminals might have never left Venezuela and tried to come to America.

This is happening across America every single day. What is never discussed is the fact that these two Venezuelan illegal aliens did not just end one life, they ended an untold number of lives. Jocelyn's mother's life as she knew it is dead. Ms. Nungaray is still living but the life she had prior to her daughter being raped and murdered is gone forever. Young Jocelyn would have met a young man, fell in love, gotten married, and then had several children. Their children would have met their husbands and wives and had grandchildren for Jocelyn and her husband. When a young person is taken from this life at the hands of savages, the ripple effect is endless. Lives have been completely altered and if you play this ripple effect out to its end, logically the world is also altered. Biden and the transformational anti-Americans own all of this!

I would like to take that same Leftist belief that illegal aliens commit less crimes than Americans and apply it to Rachel Morin who was a mother of five that lived in Maryland. Rachel was taking a run on the Ma & Pa Trail in Maryland when a savage from El Salvador brutally raped and killed her. Now a mother has lost her daughter, and five children have lost their mother. I wonder if it would help the healing process if we just told them that illegal aliens commit less crimes than Americans. Just guessing here, but I don't think that will help. This wasn't the first heinous crime this savage from El Salvador, Victor Martinez-Hernandez, committed. In fact, Martinez had an open Interpol warrant for murder outside the United States. So much for vetting! When he entered the United States, this savage conducted a home invasion in Los Angeles where he assaulted a mother and her nine-year-old daughter. He then traveled across America and landed in Maryland where he destroyed not only Rachel's life but untold lives of family and friends. Rachel's mom, Patty Morin, testified in front of Congress stating, "The open border policy of Joe Biden and Kamala Harris caused my daughter's death. It allowed a dangerous man to flee his home country to avoid capture and bring his reign of terror to American citizens."[83] Patty Morin summed up her frustration with politicians and the media:

> *They're using my daughter like a political flag, and I don't want to underestimate the importance of what's going on at the southern border – we're almost 2,000 miles away from it, and we've had two murders in the county that I live in, and Rachel lived in. So, it has come all the way up, halfway up from the southern border of the*

> *United States. And I really want people to understand that life itself is valuable and precious, and that that is what we need to preserve. And that's what makes this an American crisis, not just a political crisis.*[83]

These vicious acts of violence and death are senseless because they should never have happened. Tarrant County, Texas Sheriff Bill Waybourn testified before the House Oversight Committee describing the state of his jail and the consequences of open borders:

> *Some 264 illegal immigrants sit in jail in Tarrant County, Texas, and among them they face eight counts of murder.*
>
> *The illegal immigrants also face 38 counts of assault with a deadly weapon, five counts of sexual assault, two counts of possession of child pornography, one count of intoxicated homicide and more than 200 other assorted counts.*
>
> *These offenders, [many of which] are gang members and outlaws, have left nothing untouched. While I do not necessarily think these aliens have a higher crime rate, just the fact these people are illegal in our country and committed crimes is the impact.*
>
> *The fact is that illegal aliens should not be in the country in the first place and able to commit these crimes. The solutions aren't hard. Secure the border, stop releasing illegal aliens into the country in droves, and when an illegal alien commits a crime in the community, turn them over to ICE, enforce the law, and remove them from the United States.*[84]

One high profile case this year that set the nation on fire was the murder of Laken Riley. On February 22, 2024, Laken Riley, a 22-year-old Augusta University nursing student, was murdered while she was jogging at the University of Georgia. The coroner stated the cause of death was "combined effects of blunt force head trauma and asphyxia."[85] Laken was hit so many times in her head with a rock that her skull was disfigured. Who did this to a young beautiful woman at the beginning of her life? Another illegal alien. This savage's name is Jose Ibarra. Ibarra is from Venezuela and is reported to have ties to the Venezuelan prison gang, Tren de Aragua. If you want to physically feel the pain of Laken's mother, Allyson Philips, then you must watch the police bodycam video when Mrs. Philips learns the fate of her daughter. In fact, I believe viewing this video should be mandatory for every politician who facilitates open borders. In this police bodycam video, you witness the anguish and pain of a mother losing a daughter. The sound of torment and agony leaving Mrs. Phillips' body is something that I can only describe as a moan from the depth of a mother's soul.[86]

John Philips, Laken Riley's stepfather, read one of Laken's last journal entries at the end of the criminal trail:

> *To my future husband, as silly as I feel writing this, my old small group leader once recommended it. So here I am.*
>
> *To my future husband, I want you to know that I'm thinking about you. I'm working every day to become the best wife I can be by working through my current relationships to best prepare me for ours and our kids one day. I'm focusing on God and what he defines as a faithful Christian life and so that I can best embody those characteristics.*
>
> *I pray that you know that [it] is with my full faith and trust in God, that I know this relationship has been handcrafted by him. I pray that we continue to glorify the Lord, prioritize him in every aspect of our lives, and raise our family, our future family to be God-fearing Christians as*

> *well. I pray God is the center of our relationship as it is a gift from him. I thank him for you before I even know you and can't wait to love you in the best way I know how for the rest of our lives.*
>
> *I pray you know and feel the importance of my love and hopes for our relationship. No matter what challenges we face, I pray that our trust in God and love for one another overrules the obstacle. May our relationship last forever. Your future wife, Laken.*[87]

Allyson Phillips didn't hold back as she continued:

> *This sick, twisted and evil coward showed no regard for Laken or her human life. We are asking that [the] same be done to him. Laken had a beautiful and bright future. She was smart, hardworking, kind, thoughtful, and most importantly, she was a child of God. She had a personal relationship with Jesus, and she loved being the hands and feet of—his hands and feet in this world. She shared her love for our Lord with others through her mission trips, working with elderly at the nursing homes, and through her nursing career.*
>
> *Laken was an amazing friend, sister, niece, daughter and granddaughter. Anyone who knew her knew about her loving heart. Laken's life was not the only life taken on that day that Jose Ibarra attacked her. The life of her family and friends was taken too. None of us will ever be the same. This monster took away our chances to see Laken graduate from nursing school. He took away our ability to meet our future son-in-law. He took—destroyed our chances of meeting our grandchildren, and he took my best friend.*
>
> *He ripped away every beautiful memory we will ever be able to make with her again. This horrific individual robbed us all of our hopes and dreams for Laken. Your Honor, I'm asking you to please give*

Jose Ibarra the same thing he gave us when he made the choice to take Laken's life and destroy ours. He showed no mercy on Laken when she was begging for her life. There's no end to the pain and suffering that he inflicted on our family and our friends.

I am asking you to please give this monster life without any chance of parole, so that he never gets the chance to hurt anyone else ever again.[87]

Can you see the ripples? Can you see the lives that have changed forever? Can you see that the world has changed?

As horrible as the murder of Laken Riley is, brace yourself for the timeline of this monster's journey to Georgia. Ibarra began his journey to America from Venezuela. In September 2022, Ibarra crossed the border illegally in El Paso, Texas. He was arrested by the Border Patrol and then released for further processing. What that means is the Border Patrol simply street released him onto El Paso's streets. Any other time in the 100-year history of the Border Patrol, Ibarra would have been processed and then deported back to Venezuela. Not this time. This time Ibarra found an NGO who then gave Ibarra a taxpayer funded airline ticket to New York City. In September of 2023, Ibarra was arrested by the New York Police Department for "acting in a manner to injure a child less than 17 and a motor vehicle license violation."[90] Ibarra was driving around the busy and dangerous streets of New York City with his five-year-old son in an unregistered and uninsured car. Knowing that Ibarra was an illegal alien and because New York City is a staunch sanctuary city, Ibarra was released before ICE could put an immigration detainer on Ibarra. That did not matter anyway because NYPD does not honor federal immigration law enforcement detainers. Ibarra tires of New York City (who wouldn't) and gets another taxpayer funded flight out of New York City to Georgia. Ibarra's illegal alien brother was already living in Athens, Georgia. Once the two brothers reunited, they were promptly arrested for shoplifting from an Athens Walmart. Once again, law enforcement officials failed by citing the savages from Venezuela with a misdemeanor shoplifting charge and released them with a court date. Of course, Ibarra did not show up for his court hearing for his shoplifting charge and why would he - illegal aliens never face consequences. Also, Athens is a sanctuary city with a large state university. Ibarra's brother Diego had already been arrested for DUI and faced no repercussions. The belief that they were untouchable was repeatedly reenforced all the way back to illegally entering America in 2022.

Three different law enforcement agencies and departments failed Laken Riley. Law enforcement had three opportunities to deport Ibarra, but they held strongly to their illegal orders via open border policies and unconstitutional sanctuary city directives.

Does my statement that our government is the enemy of the people seem more and more plausible?

The statistical data on arrested criminal aliens and their immediate deportation by ICE has sharply decreased under Biden. How much has it decreased?

> *In 2021, illegal immigrants deported because of accusations or convictions of lawbreaking fell to 45,432, from a high of 123,128 in 2019, according to Immigration and Custom Enforcement's annual report on enforcement-removal operations; in 2022, ICE removed just 46,400 aliens. Similarly, ICE prosecutions of illegals for criminal actions have plunged by two-thirds, from 6,739 in 2019 to just 2,208 in 2022.*[89]

Why would arrests and then deportations decrease to these levels? Here's why:

> *Shortly after taking office, in fact, the Biden administration narrowed the criteria for expelling criminal aliens, requiring immigration officials to remove only those deemed an immediate risk to public safety; others, even felony offenders, were permitted to stay. The order also mandated newly extensive investigation of individual cases, which, combined with the border influx, overwhelmed immigration services. The crisis is captured in the numbers: the caseload of immigration-removal operations has soared from about 3 million in 2019 to 6 million under Biden in 2023, while staffing has stayed flat.*[89]

Joe Biden and Mayorkas purposely sabotaged the immigration system in America. They created chaos to jam up the system and allowed the weight of millions of fraudulent parole and asylum cases to break the American immigration system. This is treason! You would be a fool to believe that if you don't live in a southern border state, this illegal alien crime will not touch you. Don't believe me? How about we go as far north as possible from the southern border into Montana. Mexican drug cartels have seized the illegal opioid market in Montana driving the endless overdose deaths on the Indian reservations. The Governor of Montana, Greg Gianforte, explained the situation clearly:

> *I've been to the border a handful of times over the last six years, and the situation has never been more dire for our country. Human traffickers and drug cartels are profiting on catastrophe the Biden administration has made worse, with thousands of illegal crossings each day. We've got a serious problem that's putting the safety of the*

> *American people at risk, and the only person who can fix this mess is the president.*[90]

There is no hiding from this treason. The entire country is feeling the strain from unrelenting crime and the suffering caused by savages from the third world.

The number of crimes and the number of illegal alien criminals living inside of our borders is startling. The website, FAIRus.org, does a great job highlighting the cost of human suffering at the hands of these savages. I want to list just some of the criminal cases FAIR spotlights on their website for the year 2024 that stops in August:

> ***August***
> *On August 4, Mexican national Alberto Martinez-Fidel allegedly shot another man in Montgomery, Alabama, shooting him in the back and buttocks at close range. ICE confirmed that Martinez-Fidel is an illegal alien but stated they do not have additional information regarding his information history, suggesting he entered the U.S. as a "gotaway."*
>
> ***July***
> *On July 8, Honduran national Zelvin Gomez caused a car crash while speeding and driving intoxicated at three times the legal drunk driving limit, killing a 6-year-old girl that was in his vehicle, in Baldwin County, Alabama. The child was not buckled in a car seat. The illegal alien had applied for asylum in the U.S., but his case was rejected.*
>
> ***May***
> *On May 2, Guatemalan national Marvin Perez Lopez allegedly kidnapped and sexually assaulted an 11-year-old girl in his van in*

Palm Beach County, Florida. Although the 20-year-old Perez Lopez tried to keep the girl in his van by force, she managed to escape once her mother banged on the car door and confronted him. When police tracked the illegal alien down at his residence, he attempted to flee. Perez Lopez entered the U.S. illegally in January 2024, surrendered himself to USBP, was given an immigration court date in 2027, and was released into the country by DHS.

April

On April 1, Haitian national Kenol Baptiste fatally stabbed his two roommates in an apartment complex in Middletown, New York. Baptiste illegally entered the U.S. approximately 8 months before the murder – after booking an appointment via the CBP One app and being paroled in – and was awaiting a deportation hearing.

March

On March 11, three Guatemalan nationals – Andres Felipe Morales, Darinel Ordonez Jimenez, and Marcos Felipe Ramirez – kidnapped and sexually assaulted a woman near John Prince Park by Lake Worth Beach, Florida. Palm Beach County Sheriff Ric Bradshaw commented that "[t]he federal government has put the American people in jeopardy" through reckless open-borders policies, and offered the following warning: "Don't think for a minute that what happens at the Mexican border doesn't affect us here." Morales had been pulled over in January for driving without a license, but was not handed over to ICE.

February

On February 14, police arrested Honduran national Junior Manuel Dubon Benitez for allegedly sexually assaulting a 12-year-old girl at a residence in Waterloo, Iowa. The illegal alien entered the U.S. through Hidalgo, Texas, in April 2022 when he was 16.

January

On January 9, ICE arrested Haitian national Pierre Lucard Emile for allegedly raping a developmentally disabled person in Boston, Massachusetts. The illegal alien originally entered the U.S. in Brownsville, Texas, in December 2022, and was simply released into the country with a Notice to Appear (NTA) after being deemed inadmissible. He had previously been arrested for the rape in late September, but local authorities ignored an ICE detainer and instead released him in November with an electronic monitoring tag, forcing ICE to have to track him down.[91]

I could go to one website after another all day long and fill books with pages from cover-to-cover enumerating illegal alien crimes that have destroyed the lives of Americans. Every crime should never have happened because, protected by a secure border, that individual would never have been able to cross the border without being arrested and deported. The part of the sadness, pain, and loss of life that is the hardest to bear is that American citizens are just pawns to be moved in this global cabal to reset the power structure in the world. The rape of a child, the murder of a mother, or the violent assault on an innocent bystander is just part of the process to get to the end. The elites have no compassion, understanding, or empathy for the people most affected by this invasion. Instead, the elites see us, the deplorables, as no better than cattle.

There is an army of millions of illegal alien criminals roaming throughout our country. No state, no city, and no small town will go unaffected by this invasion because this fundamental transformation was strategically planned and implemented. The illegal aliens that will self-deport once Trump comes back to power will not be the criminals. The criminals will fight to stay. A war will erupt across America between the limited law enforcement officers and the millions of illegal alien criminals in our country.

When this war begins and American blood spills onto the streets, remember this treason can be laid at the feet of our government. Our government is the enemy of our nation and the citizens that make America great.

CHAPTER 9

China - People's Liberation Army

"The jungle is filled with Chinese marching to America."

War Correspondent Michael Yon

People's Liberation Army (PLA) of China are pouring over the southern border by the thousands. According to CBP data, in FY22, a grand total of 27,756 Chinese nationals crossed the border illegally and were arrested by the Border Patrol. The doors of the barn were pushed wide open in FY23 to clear a pathway for an explosion of 52,700 Chinese nationals. The flood of Chinese nationals tore the barn down for the massive invasion of 78,701 Chinese nationals illegally crossing into America in FY24. The total number of Chinese nationals that have entered our nation in the last four years is approximately 200,000! All these 200,000 Chinese nationals were released into America.[1]

What do the majority of 200,000 Chinese nationals crossing the border have in common? A lot, according to many experts to include Retired U.S. Colonel Derek Harvey, "We have Chinese nationals of military age coming into Latin America, coming across the southern border. They wear the same clothes, they have the same haircuts, they have the same pocket litter. They have the same, ah, knapsacks. It's like it's a uniform. And they get processed, and they move on."[92] What do you call large groups of men that share all of those similarities? Soldiers! To put this insane annual Chinese arrest number into context, in 2019 Border Patrol arrested a grand total of 2,134 Chinese nationals.[1]

While filming our documentary this summer, I interviewed several active intelligence specialists that would only talk to me off the record. When we got to the subject of Chinese nationals with ties to the PLA, I was left floored by the number that one of the intel specialists gave me, "Over 100,000 PLA soldiers have crossed the border!"[21] After this intel specialist with the alphabet letters behind his name made that statement, I looked at the other two border intel experts for any body language that said their friend had misspoken. Sitting at this table in a country restaurant tucked away in rural Texas, they looked directly at me with their cowboy hats resting low on their foreheads and they simply nodded in agreement. I am an expert on Border Patrol arrest data, and I can read between the lies and propaganda better than the next guy. I knew this PLA situation was bad, but I honestly did not possess the full breadth of this issue. However, when I got back to my Airbnb that night, I combed over the arrest data and cross-checked the other sources I had, and that number made perfect sense.

From January 2021 to the end of Biden's term as president, the United States Border Patrol had arrested approximately 200,000 Chinese nationals. Across all political parties, think tanks, and media, everyone has made the definitive statement that China is our number one adversary. America needs to think like our number one adversary. If you were the President of the People's Republic of China, Xi Jinping, how would you attack America? Would you choose to attack the United States straight on in a modern military battle knowing it would lead to a best-case scenario of mutual destruction? Or would you move your military into America through an open border? Before you answer, let me add several other components to this open border option. Once your military soldiers are inside the enemy's borders, they will be fed, clothed, medicated, and provided housing, at no cost. Better yet, America will fly your soldiers to any part of America that you, China, have ordered your soldiers to report. As President Xi Jinping, which method of warfare would you choose? The answer is obvious, and that border option is being exploited right now! This sounds completely insane and improbable, but this is exactly what is happening right now as you are reading this chapter.

I can only imagine what those internal Chinese military briefings must have been like in 2021 and 2022. At first, the PLA's Generals had to have thought that this was a trap. The Generals had to have been fearful of even briefing President Xi Jinping on what was happening on America's southern border for fear of shaming themselves by falling for such an obvious ensnarement. After tens of thousands of military soldiers had crossed successfully into America and were living in nice hotels with three square meals a day, the Generals were forced to brief Xi Jinping. I am sure this is what happened. Before entering the meeting room, the Generals drew straws to see who would have to present this insane report. As they all sat nervously around a giant wooden table that sat 50 anxious men, President Xi Jinping proudly entered the room commanding respect and fear. There was a deafening silence until Xi Jinping waved his hand impatiently at his Generals to speak. The unfortunate General that drew the shortest straw slowly stood up, cleared his throat, and then proceeded to tell the improbable story of how battalions of Chinese soldiers have crossed the southern border of America with the help of American law enforcement. Pausing to let that incredible statement be consumed, the General took a deep breath and continued explaining that the PLA soldiers were transported by NGOs, paid for by the United States government to strategically placed locations across the United States of America. The room went silent, and the other Generals tilted their heads down as the short strawed General sat down and they waited in fear for the reaction of President Xi Jinping.

President Xi Jinping stood up and pulled the bottom of his suit to straighten it out. Everyone sitting around the table swallowed hard as the President began to speak. For the first time in President Xi Jinping's entire life, he smiled. He reached down to the table and took ahold of a 1,000-year-old crystal glass, and almost laughed as he told his military leaders, "Relax, old man Biden and his administration hate America even more than we do. They have allowed us into their nation with the hope and desire we can destroy America from within!" The entire 50-person delegation of military leaders raised their 1,000-year-old crystal glasses and made a toast to the American government in thanks. Loud cheers filled the room from the communist leaders of the People's Republic of China.

Even the Chinese government knows that the enemy of America is her own government.

With tens of thousands of PLA soldiers inside our walls, what will it look like when they are activated? I had a podcast that ran for a little over a year, *Unrestricted Invasion*, with my cohost Brian O'Shea. Brian is a disabled veteran who was deployed in the Middle East as an intelligence analyst embedded with Special Forces. Brian also worked for the three letter agencies and is considered an expert on China. On one of our shows, we dissected a video of illegal alien Chinese nationals crossing the southern border in San Diego. After Brian identified several soldiers in the video, I asked him to tell me what their activation in America would look like. Brian went on to describe a war inside America. First, Brian made sure that I understood that this war on American soil was not going to have any resemblance of traditional warfare where the enemy places their battalion of soldiers against our battalion of soldiers. Instead, according to Brian, these thousands of PLA soldiers would be broken down into small groups of less than ten soldiers. These smaller groups would have no direct contact or knowledge of the other smaller groups scattered across America. Each group of PLA soldiers would have a specific mission. I asked Brian to describe what a mission would look like. He presented a terrifying situation. Brian first explained that these missions would not be crazed religious fanatics blowing themselves up with IEDs. Instead, they would be well trained soldiers with entry and exist plans. Brian described a horrible situation where a group of ten PLA soldiers would enter the JFK Airport at seven in the morning when the airport was packed with travelers. The soldiers would enter the airport ticketing area and shoot and kill as many Americans as possible then extract out.

Brian O'Shea is not the only China expert that believes that numerous PLA cells are in the United States waiting on their orders to attack. Richard Fisher of the International Assessment and Strategy Center told *The Daily Caller News Foundation*:

> *Ancient Chinese strategists prized the use of subterfuge and surprise to achieve victory, and the two PLA colonels who wrote Unrestricted Warfare in 1999 were full of praise for the tactics of Osama bin Laden. When the Chinese Communist Party starts its war against Taiwan and the United States, Americans should expect that Chinese sleeper agents now in America will hit targets like gas stations and military-age Chinese now crossing our border will be mobilized for assassination attacks and assaults on U.S. military bases.*[93]

Think about that scenario playing out ten, 100, or 1,000 times within a 24-hour or 48-hour time frame. All activities in America would come to a screeching halt. Americans would be terrified to leave their homes. America would come to a standstill. What would the military response to these heavily armed and well-trained soldiers be? What local police department is trained and outfitted to combat this level of threat? Is America ready for a hot war on our soil? Maybe a more important question is - do you trust the government of the United States of America to be able to defend our homeland and her citizens? Take a second and honestly answer that question before you continue to read on.

On another episode of *Unrestricted Invasion,* Brian and I interviewed an investigative journalist named Jennie Taer who at the time worked for *The Daily Caller News Foundation* and now is employed by *The New Post.* Ms. Taer was reporting on the large marijuana grows owned and operated by illegal Chinese nationals. Ms. Taer focused her attention on the state of Maine. She discovered that DHS had located 270 suspected Chinese illegal marijuana grow operations in Maine alone. Republican Maine State Rep. Austin Theriault stated:

> *This is a failure I believe of both the state government and the federal government, and it's time people start taking this more seriously. This is a lack of political will, there's many other areas the government's not afraid to get involved, but for some reason they're not willing to put their foot down and start to crack down on some of these illegal operations and I want to see that happen.*[94]

During our interview, Brian made an incredible observation and connection between the illegal marijuana grows run by Chinese nationals and the infiltration of PLA soldiers. The marijuana grows are a cash industry and these grows can fund the Chinese military here in America. There does not have to be any hidden money transfers from China or from other overseas countries where these transfers could be intercepted and traced. Instead, the Chinese government produces illegal narcotics in America, sells the products for cash then uses the cash to fund the nefarious actions of PLA soldiers.

The Chinese are also working with the Mexican drug cartels to increase the cash flow to do the unthinkable; purchase American land for either more marijuana grows, or worse, land that has military benefit to China. Former head of the DEA's Special Operations Division Derek

Maltz told Taer, "So, not only are they providing this unbelievably important service to the Mexican cartels by picking up the cash and doing the money transfers over the banking apps and stuff like that, but they're using the cash in America to buy land, to buy real estate, to buy property to invest in these grow operations."[94] As these marijuana operations reproduce faster than rabbits in the state of Maine, don't you worry because the government is here to help as the Maine U.S. Attorney's Office declared, "Mainers can be assured that if illegal business activities occur here, the law enforcement community will always do whatever is necessary and appropriate within the law to respond. In order to protect the integrity and capabilities of any investigations, we decline to provide additional comment at this time."[94] I need to reiterate that Maine has at least 270 known illegal marijuana grow operations. Maybe Mainers need a little more reassurance than what was provided!

Maine is a liberal bastion; wherever there are insane liberals, and their crazy policies, crime, chaos, and violence follow. But let me be fair in this situation on illegal Chinese marijuana grows because one conservative red state is as bad off as Maine, maybe worse. That red state would be Oklahoma. How bad is it in Oklahoma? The director of the Oklahoma Bureau of Narcotics and Dangerous Drugs, Donnie Anderson, said that Chinese organized crime "has taken over marijuana in Oklahoma and the United States."[95] Growing marijuana isn't the only crime taking place under Chinese rule on American soil. Chinese illegal aliens are smuggled across the open borders as slaves to work these grows and Chinese women are forced into prostitution to service the marijuana grow bosses.

How lucrative is this marijuana business in the state of Oklahoma?

> *Oklahoma has quickly become a top supplier of illicit weed. Although street prices fluctuate and calculating the value of a black market is complex, officials estimate the value of the illegal mariju-*

> *ana grown in the state at somewhere between $18 billion and $44 billion a year. State investigators have found links between foreign mafias and over 3,000 illegal grows — and they say that more than 80% of the criminal groups are of Chinese origin.*[95]

Now let's reflect on what Brian O'Shea stated about the cash flowing from these grows to the in-house PLA soldiers. I have my share of registered firearms, so I am positive that $18 to $44 billion could purchase enough firearms and any other warfare weaponry needed to engage our citizens in war. After reading about Brian O'Shea, Jennie Taer, billions of dollars in cash profit, and the astounding number of marijuana grows (at least 3,000), we need to ask a very serious question – how is this being allowed to happen and prosper? I always love getting the answer to this question from men like me that did the job and know exactly why the problem exists in the first place. Ray Donovan, former chief of operations of the Drug Enforcement Administration, stated:

> *The challenge we are having is a lack of interest by federal prosecutors to charge illicit marijuana cases. They don't realize all the implications. Marijuana causes so much crime at the local level, gun violence in particular. The same groups selling thousands of pounds of marijuana are also laundering millions of dollars of fentanyl money. It's not just one-dimensional.*[95]

Here is another former Senior DEA Agent, Donald Im, explaining the importance of these Chinese marijuana grows, "The profits from the marijuana trade allow the Chinese organized criminal networks to expand their underground global banking system for cartels and other criminal organizations." [95] Agent Im continued to express his concern about the huge revenue stream that is laundered through an apparatus that is, "the most extensive network of underground banking in the world."[95]

Here is a great follow up question – Why would our federal U.S. Attorneys, selected by the Biden Administration, and District Attorneys, funded by George Soros, an America hating thug, ignore such a large and complex criminal issue run by our greatest enemy, China? Because our government is corrupt. Hard to hear? Hard to digest? Don't want to believe it? Then tell me what the hell is going on!

To further exasperate this situation of PLA soldiers inside America, our own government is allowing Chinese companies and billionaires to purchase land in the United States of America. As every China expert will state, there is no distinction between a Chinese national, a Chinese business, and the Chinese government. China expert Gordon Chang asked a commonsense question:

> *Just for instance, no American may own a square inch of land in China. So why are we allowing Chinese nationals onto our farm and ranch lands where we know they're engaged, many of them, in very dangerous activities? Human trafficking operations on Oklahoma farmland owned by Chinese nationals, illegal marijuana grows all over the place, the spread of the Triads in American rural communities– none of this has to happen. Also, they don't allow our social media platforms in China, so why do we allow theirs in ours?*[96]

When I write a book like this or articles that I write on platforms like Substack or Re:Public, I like to use sources from every media outlet there is because the facts find their way to the light no matter how hard the truth is pushed into the darkness. Let's use a quote from the not so conservative news outlet, NPR, "China owns 380,000 acres of land in the U.S. Concerns over Chinese land ownership grew in 2021 after a Chinese company bought land near an Air Force base in Grand Forks, North Dakota."[96] NPR continued, "[They] reported that an investigation into a cluster of farms called cannabis "grow" operations in New Mexico revealed businesses that 'employ and are managed and funded largely by Chinese people.' The investigation found that marijuana has become 'big business in the U.S., where about half of states have legalized it for adult recreational use and about two-thirds have legalized it for medical use.'"[96]

ProPublica, another news outlet I don't visit daily stated:

> *'Thousands of Chinese immigrant laborers suffer abuse and exploitation in a U.S. marijuana underworld dominated by Chinese mafias.' During raids, inspections, and investigations of over a thousand farms in recent years, Oklahoma state law enforcement found many abuses: 'bosses threaten and beat workers, sexually assault them, steal their wages, confiscate their IDs, restrict their movements and force them to work in dangerous heat with noxious chemicals and pesticides.'*[96]

And then there is the very disturbing topic of America selling large sections of land near our military bases to Chinese businessmen and to Chinese companies. *The New Post* published an article on the number of Chinese owned American land and the disturbing Chinese land purchases near 19 of our military bases:

> *China has been buying up strategically placed farmland next to military installations across the US, raising national security fears over potential espionage or even sabotage.*
>
> *The Post has identified 19 bases across the US from Florida to Hawaii which are in close proximity to land bought up by Chinese entities and could be exploited by spies working for the communist nation.*
>
> *They include some of the military's most strategically important bases: Fort Liberty (formerly Fort Bragg) in Fayetteville, North*

> *Carolina; Fort Cavazos (formerly Fort Hood) in Killeen, Texas; Marine Corps Base Camp Pendleton in San Diego, California, and MacDill Air Force Base in Tampa, Florida.*
>
> *Robert S. Spalding III, a retired United States Air Force brigadier general whose work focuses US-China relations told The Post: "It is concerning due to the proximity to strategic locations.*[97]

There is no rational explanation why our government would allow land near our military

bases to be sold to the greatest adversary facing America. For anyone that believes this is not intentionally and purposefully orchestrated by the United States government, tell me how I am wrong. After you stumble on some liberal talking points, you can explain to me how, "A report in the Wall Street Journal from September 2023 found Chinese intruders attempted to breach military facilities over 100 times in recent years, including sneaking onto a missile range in New Mexico and scuba divers spotted near a government rocket-launch site in Florida." Again, please articulate how the U.S. government is not the enemy.

The book written by two PLA Colonels, *Unrestricted Warfare*, is a guide to attacking the United States from every angle. Does it not seem that unrestricted warfare from China is in high gear now in America? The border is completely wide open and hundreds of thousands of illegal Chinese aliens are storming our border and that is only who we know has crossed. How many more Chinese nationals to include PLA soldiers and other Chinese law enforcement personnel, military assets, and intelligence spies are in the 15-18 million illegal aliens that absconded undetected through the unmanned southern and northern borders? Unfortunately, the answer to that question is that the number of 200,000 arrested illegal aliens from China can be doubled, tripled, or even quadrupled.

What are the 200,000 Chinese illegal aliens doing once they get into America? Are they assimilating and trying to become Americans? Or are they going straight to the marijuana grows, into prostitution, or to their small military cells? Chang doesn't mince words as he lays it all out:

> *There's Chinese migrants who have been in the U.S. for less than three weeks who came across the border with no identification, no money, and what are they doing? They're taking target practice — pistol shooting, rifle shooting, and we got to be extremely concerned that these are soldiers of the People's Liberation Army and that China is actually building the infrastructure in the United States to attack us.*
>
> *Remember that secret Chinese biological weapons lab at Reedley, California, that was discovered about a year ago? Well, it had almost 1,000 mice that have been genetically engineered to spread disease, as well as 20 pathogens, including the one for Ebola.*
>
> *So, we've got to be concerned that some of these saboteurs are going to take mice from labs like that and spread them around the U.S. So, we're going to have another disease, this one created by China's soldiers.*
>
> *Across our southern border, we're seeing packs of Chinese males between five and 15 — of military age — traveling without family members, pretending not to speak English. About 80% to 90% of those migrants who do cross our border from China, they fit within the category.*
>
> *The other 10%, 15% well, they could be desperate Chinese people — middle class — who've decided to give up on their society, and that's a real indication of problems inside China itself. But you know, in*

either case, we've got a great concern because we know that China has weaponized Chinese nationals in the U.S., so whether they are saboteurs, soldiers or not, we have a concern of what they are and what they plan to do.[98]

Why would our own government do this to us?

The better question needed to be asked is – Why have we allowed our government to do this to us?

CHAPTER 10

Child Sex Trafficking

The United States federal government is the world's largest child sex trafficking organization in modern history.

That was our strongly held belief after spending months filming our documentary, WHAT IS TREASON? #INVADED. My partner on this journey, Ryan Matta, and I were stunned, saddened, and angry when we reflected on the months traveling across America and then reliving it as we edited the hundreds of hours of footage. The evidence that the United States government is facilitating child sex trafficking was so overwhelming, so damning, and so in our face that we had to pause and question what we had witnessed and reanalyze the evidence before us. How could this be happening in America? How could the powerful people in Washington, D.C., not know this is happening? Or worse, how could the powerful people in Washington, D.C. know this is happening and do nothing? There were a lot of questions, and now we had answers.

We were about to expose the truth to the world.

By the end of Joe Biden's time in office, the United States Border Patrol will have arrested and released over 550,000 Unaccompanied Alien Children (UACs) and the federal government will have lost them all! Not some of them, not most of them, but ALL of them!

In a Congressional Hearing in 2023, Health and Human Services (HHS) Secretary Xavier Becerra was questioned on how his department had lost 85,000 UACs by Tennessee Senator Blackburn, "The Times reported that under the Biden Presidency the agency cannot find 85,000 children and that the agency lost contact with a third of the migrant children that are coming into the country."[99] Becerra denied this allegation stating, "I have never heard that number of 85,000, I don't know where it comes from and...so I would say it doesn't sound at all to be realistic, and what we do is we try and follow up as best we can with these kids."[99] Remember Becerra's statement for later.

In another Congressional Hearing on the same New York Times report using DHS whistleblowers (many who I have relationships with and trust) the Director of the Office of Refugee Resettlement (ORR) Monica Marcos was poorly playing defense the entire time. Ms. Marcos is unqualified, unorganized, and a liar. This is a sample of the questions and answers from this hearing:

> *Rep. Grothman: "Percentage-wise – say if we've got a group of 1,000 unaccompanied minors, what percent do you talk to one parent, what percent do you talk to two parents, and what percent do you talk to no parents?"*
>
> *Director Marcos: "I will have to get back to you on that."*
>
> *Rep. Gosar: "What is ORR's sponsor application rejection rate?"*
>
> *Director Marcos: "Congressman, I'm not sure what our rejection rate is."*
>
> *Rep. Biggs: "I think you're telling us that you don't disagree with the 85,000 number of children that we've lost contact with. I'm not saying you lost them. I'm saying you've lost contact with them. We don't know where those kids are. Is that fair to say?"*

Director Marcos: "We attempt to make a safety and wellbeing call."

Rep. Biggs continued: "When you made the call, you didn't get a response. Your letter tells me that you usually make three calls. You got no response in any of those three calls in 85,000 kids. Is that right?"

Rep Perry: "On March 31st of 2021, just a couple days later, ORR eliminated the background check requirement for immediate relatives other than a parent or legal guardian. Why would that be? How does that enhance the obligation to care?"

Ms. Marcos: "ORR's belief is that a child is best with their best or legal guardian."

Rep. Perry: "How can you be sure it's their parent? Did you look into the whistleblowers that were listed in the New York Times? Did you look into any of their cases as they were terminated after raising issues?"

Director Marcos: "Congressman, that article just came out. We have a team looking into it."[100]

This insanity went on and on and on. Both Becerra and Marcos are grossly incompetent and despite their claim that they did not know these 85,000 UACs were lost, they knew, and they lied!

Let's travel to fantasy land where the improbable is probable. In fantasy land both Becerra and Marcos knew nothing about the 85,000 lost UACs. In fact, they had nothing at all to do with this criminal neglect. Even giving both Becerra and Marcos a pass on culpability, the glaring question is why nothing was done to stop it after being alerted to obvious issues inside their respective agencies. We are not talking about misplacing a few million dollars of your budget or the loss of equipment. We are talking about losing children! I have a young son, and I never lost him, NEVER!

Fast forward to 2024 when the number of lost foreign children skyrocketed to over 320,000. In August of 2024, the Inspector General (IG) over DHS issued a scathing report detailing those agencies with oversight of these UACs. This report asserted these agencies had no contact with over 320,000 UACs, meaning they were lost. The IG is behind the curve. The real number of these children lost to sex trafficking, labor trafficking, and other horrible situations is 100%. The IG just hasn't gotten that far ahead in their findings. Before we continue, I want to take a moment to explain the process of how this all works and why I state with complete certainty that every child taken into Border Patrol custody and released is lost.

Let's follow a young five-year-old Honduran boy named Luis. Luis will have been either kidnapped, "rented," or sold by his family to human smugglers. Luis will make the journey from Honduras to the northern Mexican border. During this journey, Luis will be raped and prostituted throughout his travels. On a sick and disturbing side note – 60 to 80% of all women and children making the journey from Central America to Mexico are sexually assaulted or raped. Let me restate this because I want to make sure everyone understands that last sentence – 60 to 80 %! The smuggling cartels will bring their little product named Luis to the border fence. Before they push five-year-old Luis through, around, or over the border fence, they will staple a notecard onto Luis' shirt or place a lanyard around his neck with the name, phone number and address of Luis' sponsor. A frightened Luis now finds himself all alone on the dusty border trail. Luis has been told not to move and to wait for the Border Patrol. Luis has suffered severe sexual, emotional, and physical trauma that would shock the average American, so, out of immense fear, Luis doesn't move until the Border Patrol arrives. Border Patrol will process Luis as quickly as they can and then turn Luis over directly to HHS/ORR or if HHS/ORR are too busy, Luis is sent directly to an NGO. Luis will wait with the NGO until HHS or ORR approves the sponsor that is waiting for Luis. There is no DNA testing, house visit, or vetting of the sponsor. The coordinator at HHS or ORR simply makes the connection and then directs the NGO to make the transfer of the product, Luis. In this situation, Luis is going to Portland, Oregon. Little Luis will then be handed off to an "escort," who is employed by the NGO, and that individual, with no more than a high school diploma or GED, takes a raped and abused Luis on an airplane to his sponsor. The "escort" meets the sponsor at the Portland International Airport's baggage claim. There the "escort" takes a picture of the identification of the sponsor. In this situation, the sponsor couldn't be there to pick up Luis, so he had a friend pick him up. The "escort" is directed to release the child to this other man because this other man was able to produce a picture ID, a foreign birth certificate, or a copy of any identification of the actual sponsor. Luis and the cartel member walk into the sea of people and disappear forever. I understand if your first reaction is, "This can't be true!" Believe me, I understand because that was my first reaction as well. However, I have seen this business of governmental corruption and abuse for decades so the reality of situations like this become rationalized and accepted quickly in my law enforcement mind.

ORR is required to do a follow up welfare check on Luis. This follow up is completed by ORR or a contracted third party. Neither the ORR representative nor the third-party employee has ever seen, met, or talked to either Luis or the sponsor. What is the follow up? Is it a home visit? Is it a visit to the school Luis should be attending now? Is it an in-person visit to ensure Luis is safe? Nope! ORR or the contracted third party simply calls the sponsor. Not even a Zoom call but a simple phone call. I interviewed several DHS, HHS, ORR, and NGO whistleblowers, and they said this is how the phone call goes – "Hello is this (insert sponsor's name)?" Is Luis, ok?" The sponsor either says, "Yep, Luis is good." Or, and this is unbelievable, the sponsor says that Luis has run away, and they do not know where he is. That's it! THAT IS IT! Nothing more and HHS and ORR claim that Luis is accounted for and not lost! Understand that scenario is what HHS and ORR has classified as a positive welfare check. The other children that are classified as lost are when ORR or the contracted third party cannot connect with anyone regarding a child that was placed. Meaning the number is no good, the address doesn't actually exist, and the child is gone.

Dear God, I pray that if you, the reader, fact checks even one chapter in this book, I pray it is this chapter. Why? Because I want you to fully grasp without a shadow of a doubt that what I just wrote is the truth!

With what I just described in the forefront of your mind, let's go back to Becerra and Marcos. Both Becerra and Marcos were in congressional hearings that 85,000 children were released from their custody and were gone, lost. Both HHS and ORR have no idea where these children are, and each UAC that's been lost has been documented. Between that congressional hearing in 2023 to the August 2024 IG's report, HHS and ORR lost an additional 235,000 UACs. There are no other fantasy lands to travel to in order to explain this gross incompetence. Instead, one might believe that this egregious act could not just be gross incompetence, but intentional. How else can you explain it? Imagine if you were the Secretary of HHS or the Director of ORR and you were just told by both the House and the Senate that your agencies have lost 85,000 children. How would you react? Would you walk out of the congressional hearings and beeline it straight to your department and work nonstop to fix this heinous issue? Would you demand accountability from every position you had authority and oversight over? Would you not halt all transportation of UACs to sponsors until you had a solid and reliable process to ensure maximum safety for these children that you are ultimately responsible for?

The answers to those questions are no. HHS and ORR did not change even one aspect of their process. In fact, they doubled down and stayed with the same process that lost 85,000 UACs and increased their "success" to over 320,000 UACs lost. I use the term "success" because that is the only way to rationally explain their actions. Becerra and Marcos have facilitated the largest child sex trafficking organization in modern history.

The Biden Administration using Mayorkas' DHS, Becerra's HHS and Marcos' ORR have systematically destroyed the border that has allowed the largest mass invasion and human trafficking organization in the history of civilization. The evil that manifests from this level of treason is hard to quantify. These traitors have created a window, an access, for the narcotic and human smuggling cartels to flourish both outside and inside of America. The above-mentioned traitors know these windows and access are open and fully operational, but they all refuse to close these avenues. Instead, the windows and accesses are opened wider allowing more and more destruction to the United States of America.

How do these cartels exploit these openings created by our government?

Let me break this down to a very basic level of how smuggling a child, woman, or narcotic works in the mind of the cartels. First, stop thinking of the cartels as these stupid animals. Yes, they are savages, and they are brutally violent. However, at the end of the day they are businessmen. Think of them as no different than Amazon. The cartels deliver products. What would happen to Amazon if they didn't offer products that Americans demanded? They would go bankrupt and close. The cartels are no different. They are delivering products that Americans demand. The cartels are delivering products to the American consumer using the same distribution infrastructure as Amazon. They use the same highways, maritime lanes, and airports. They use the same style of warehouses and record profit and loss using the same financial and business models as major U.S. companies.

When you understand and view the cartels as businesses, you begin to connect the dots. A straight line appears between the cartels and the government of the United States of America. The dots create a picture of treason that becomes so clear, so obvious that you are amazed it took you so long to realize how corrupt and evil our own government has become. Have you ever seen a Mexican drug cartel member drop 100 pounds of cocaine over the border and walk away? Have you ever seen the Mexican drug cartel drop 500 pounds of heroin over the border and walk away? Have you ever seen a Mexican drug cartel member carry 100,000 fentanyl pills to the border wall and throw it over the border wall and walk away? I have never seen that happen and I have witnessed almost everything a person could imagine. Now, why would a narcotic smuggler never throw their products over the border wall and walk away? Because the Border Patrol would discover those very expensive products and seize them causing a significant loss to the cartels. Most importantly, the cartel member that caused their business to forfeit such a financial loss, would pay a heavy price for his failure in terms of his life.

Knowing that the above scenario has never happened, consider why the same cartels that would never toss their narcotic products over the border wall and walk away would toss their child product over the wall AND walk away? The answer is because the United States federal government has removed the cost, the potential product loss, and the transportation component from the smuggling process. The cartels know that the federal policies on processing and transporting children will ensure that their product is cared for, fed, clothed, medicated, and ultimately be transported back to the cartels at the exact location the cartels tell the federal government. Aaron Stevenson, a former United States Citizenship and Immigration Services (USCIS) analyst and former military analyst was fired from his job as an analyst with USCIS. Mr. Stevenson discovered that international criminal organizations from different nations with no known criminal connections had all discovered loopholes in the USCIS sponsorship program. This enabled international criminal organizations to facilitate the smuggling of children from across the globe using the federal government as the smuggling branch of their criminal organizations.[101] I interviewed Mr. Steveson for our documentary, *WHAT IS TREASON? #TRAFFICKED*, and when I asked him what USCIS' response to his discovery was, "I was fired. But do you know what they didn't do? They didn't ask me how I found the loophole, who was using it or how to correct it." Stevenson said nothing had been changed or corrected since he made this discovery public almost two years ago.

As the evil of child sex trafficking is revealed and nothing is done to stop it, one must ask the very powerful three letter question...Why?

This is where the rubber meets the road. It is difficult to write this and maybe this will be hard for the reader to digest and even accept. As much as I want to kill the demons that work and run the Mexican cartels, they are not the problem. The problem is America. America demands cocaine, heroin, and other hard narcotics, so the cartels provide the product. America demands cheap labor, so the cartels deliver the product. America demands children to rape, abuse, and use as sacrifices so, the cartels deliver the product. We, the America public are the problem. We, the American public need to look directly into a mirror and see the evil monster we have become.

Who is the number one consumer of hard narcotics in the world? America! Who is one of the top nations on planet Earth that physically pays money to rape children? America! What nation produces and exports more pornography in the world? America! And who consumes more child pornography than any nation in the world? America!

Never in a million years would I have thought I would have unknowingly filmed and produced a documentary on child sex trafficking. Over the course of several months of filming, I began to see this evil come to life in front of me. I never sought this out. I never wanted to be a part of this sick horror show. I never wanted to interview people that are deep inside this world searching for these kids. I never wanted to write a book with this as a major chapter. I never wanted to talk about this horrific topic for hours on podcasts and in speeches. But here I am. I hate it! I hate everything about this evil. I have taken several breaks as I wrote this chapter. I remember coming home from each filming trip and having to suppress what I learned so I would not allow this evil to enter my home. Am I the perfect guy to talk about this topic? No. Am I the most knowledgeable guy on sex trafficking? No. Do I feel inadequate in this field? Yes. So why am I here? Because I am unafraid to speak directly to the face of evil. I will never bend a knee to the powerful out of fear. I will stand tall in the face of this evil. I know deep in my soul that if I don't talk about the evil of child sex trafficking and who benefits with money and power; my silence will make me complicit in this sin and I will have no excuse when I stand before God.

Will I have a profound impact? I don't know. What I do know is that I won't stop exposing the sin and the evil ones destroying God's children!

The United Staes of America has facilitated the trafficking of over 550,000 children into America. These children have been discovered working in meat packing plants on midnight shifts, in dangerous construction sites, and worse of all, these children have been sold as slaves into the lucrative business of child sex. If these children are lucky, they will find the fate that President Trump has stated numerous times, "A lot of them are already dead!"

President Trump has directed the new Border Czar Tom Homan to find these lost children. Tom Homan is the most qualified and determined man for this position. He is determined to seal the border and deport every illegal alien residing in America. I pray he finds all these children. However, when Tom Homan finds these children, many will be in shallow graves. The children rescued from the grip of evil will fight a lifetime to erase the horrific pain and suffering they endured under the flag of the United States of America.

There are many answers to that three-letter question, why? I want to end this chapter with the most enraging answer I received as to why our government does nothing to stop this evil of child sex trafficking. Several prominent individuals on the good side of this evil, both men and women, with unmatched experience and success told me, "There are politicians; Congressmen, Senators, and Presidents, both past and present, that are pedophiles. Not all politicians are pedophiles, but they all know who is a pedophile. And because the ones that know and say nothing become complicit in the crime, they become open to coercion and blackmail."[21]

Where's that mirror?

CHAPTER 11

My Congressional Testimony

I testified on November 19, 2024, in front of the United States House of Representatives Committee on Homeland Security Subcommittee on Border Security and Enforcement Subcommittee on Oversight, Investigations, and Accountability. The topic was, "Trafficked, Exploited, and Missing: Migrant Children Victims of the Biden-Harris Administration." This moment in my life confirmed every strongly held belief about our government, the politicians running it, and the absolute necessity to have the smallest government possible.

When you testify in front of Congress, you must submit a formal testimony for Congressional records. My oral testimony was limited to five minutes. Below is that testimony:

> *Chairman Higgins, Ranking Member Correa, Chairman Bishop, Ranking Member Ivey, and Members of the Subcommittees, I appreciate the opportunity to speak about the evil of child trafficking caused by the open border policies under President Joe Biden and his administration.*
>
> *I served in the United States Border Patrol for 24 years until I retired as a Deputy Patrol Agent in Charge in San Diego Sector. I worked under five presidential administrations and only one President secured the border, President Donald Trump. Border Patrol*

Agents went from working and being supported by the greatest border President in American history to the worst, President Joe Biden.

My last year in the Border Patrol was Joe Biden's first year in office. On his first day in office, I watched in disbelief as ninety-four Executive Orders cascaded down from Washington, D.C. obliterating every immigration policy that had provided the most secure border in America's history. Border Patrol Agents were forced to carry out unconstitutional orders that violated every law in the Immigration and Nationality Act.

President Biden, through Department of Homeland Security Secretary Alejandro Mayorkas, created policy out of thin air, ignored federal immigration law, and facilitated the largest mass invasion into America that the world has ever seen.

The United States of America will have spent over one trillion dollars in four years to fund the needs of the over 50,000,000 illegal aliens that populate our nation. Between one in six and one in seven residents in America is an illegal alien. America has suffered the greatest demographic shift in modern history.

After serving in the Border Patrol for 24 years, spending a year researching and writing a best-selling book entitled INVADED: The Intentional Destruction of the American Immigration System, and filming two documentaries: I state, with complete certainty, that Biden, Harris and Mayorkas intentionally, strategically, and purposely weaponized illegal immigration and used it as a tool to fundamentally transform America.

Inside this invasion, the unspoken evil of child trafficking and, more specifically, child sex trafficking, has flourished. At the end of this current administration, the number of children trafficked will have grown to over 550,000 unaccompanied alien children known as UACs. This horrific number of children will have been arrested, released into America and then lost. To put this into context: during President Trump's last year in office, Customs and Border Protection (CBP) arrested 30,557 UACs who were accounted for and not lost. Conversely, in the first year of Biden's presidency, CBP arrested 147,975 UACs, most of which are unaccounted for and lost.

In 2023 Congressional Hearings, Health and Human Services (HHS) Secretary Xavier Becerra and Director of Office of Refugee Resettlement (ORR) Robin Marcos were forced to admit that their agencies had no contact with over 85,000 UACs. They were lost.

What did the DHS, HHS, and ORR do to correct this humanitarian disaster? Nothing. In fact, all three agencies created further policies and procedures to increase the efficiency of moving UACs from the border to the interior of the United States to unknown and unvetted sponsors. Unaccompanied alien children were being handed off to total strangers. They then disappeared into the darkness of labor and sex trafficking.

In fact, a year later in August of 2024, the Inspector General with oversight of DHS issued a report stating that the number of lost UACs had grown to over 320,000!

My business partner Ryan Matta and I spent 6 months traveling across America filming a documentary titled, WHAT IS TREASON? #TRAFFICKED. The evil of child sex trafficking is difficult to digest and understand. After conducting numerous interviews with officers, agents, and whistleblowers from every alphabet agency and department, it was made clear to us that the federal government knowingly and actively facilitated these criminal acts.

After several exhaustive months filming, interviewing and then editing this documentary, I state without reservation that the United States federal government is the world's largest child sex trafficking organization in modern history.

The probability that thousands of these UACs are being raped at this very moment is 100 percent.

The call to action has three parts. All three parts happen at once.

1 - Every means necessary is to be taken to ensure all four borders of the United States of America are sealed shut.

2- There is a national law enforcement emergency to locate and rescue every single one of the 550,000 unaccompanied alien children that are lost.

3 - A full-scale investigation of every U.S. department, agency and every

Non-Governmental Organization (NGO) participating in this criminal act shall be launched. Every person involved shall be arrested.

The intentional opening of our borders is an act of treason. I encourage questions so I may further articulate this allegation.[102]

Let's back up a minute before I testified in Congress, to lay out my journey to that moment before I stood up and swore to tell the truth.

After debating if I should go and testify or not, I convinced myself that since Trump was going to be President once again, I should go. My thought process was that my testimony, backed by my 24-year career in the Border Patrol, my best-selling book, and my two just released documentaries on the border and child sex trafficking would carry some weight. I believed I could articulate the problem and the solution if given the opportunity. I also knew that everything I had hoped would happen was a long shot because I was going into a den of thieves and worse, a den of stupid. Man, did I underestimate the stupid part.

The day of the Congressional Hearing, I got up extremely early to catch a flight to Washington D.C. from Kansas City, Kansas. Flying to D.C., I reviewed my oral statement once more and tried to anticipate certain questions from the Republicans as well as from the Democrats. I tried to think of every dumb thing the Left would ask and what the sophomoric responses from Republicans would likely be. I was playing a huge game of what if, so I stopped thinking about it and assured myself that I had verbally sparred with much more intelligent people than who would be sitting before me in a few hours. Again, I underestimated the level of incompetence and outright stupidity I would soon face.

I hurried out of the airport, grabbed my Lyft, and headed to the centralized power center of the world, Washington, D.C. I have been to D.C. numerous times but this time as I drove across a bridge into D.C., the feeling of power, corruption, and elitism was palpable. Two thoughts rushed into my head, what a beautiful and powerful place it was with all the marble and granite monuments; and the other thought was this place is everything our founding fathers warned us about. The centralization of power was the greatest threat to our Republic then and it is certainly the greatest threat now. I headed towards the Nation's Capital Building and was stopped at a red light near my destination, the Cannon House Office Building. As I idled at the red light, a woman in a tight-fitting leopard print pant suit walked across the street. I shrugged at the sight, thinking not a great look, but whatever and the light turned green, and I was off.

I paid my Lyft driver and walked into the Cannon House Office Building. It is an old building but beautiful inside. I met the other two witnesses that would later testify, Ali Hooper and my friend, Tara Rodas. The other witness was a Democrat witness and quite honestly, I still don't know why she was there except to counter the three of us. Heck, I can't even remember her name. The three of us walked into the room that we would testify in, and I found my name tag and seat. I sat down and waited. I waited for the four Congressmen on the committee to arrive as well as the other Congresspeople to fill out the remaining seats on the dais. Interestingly, the dais sat several feet higher from where we were all sitting. An obvious tactic to make anyone testifying feel less than the people who were physically looking down on us. The people questioning me from both sides needed a dais of at least 1,000 feet higher than me for me to ever feel as if I was less than them. I am not the smartest guy in the room, but I'm not an idiot either!

The room was filling up and I began to feel nervous, and I wanted the testimony to begin because I knew once it started and the first metaphoric punch was thrown, I would instantly be at game speed. I always approach these situations like I did playing football. Once I was hit, the game was on. Waiting for the kickoff and out of the corner of my eye, I saw the side door to the room, which was directly to my right, open and to my amazement the same lady wearing the leopard print pant suit walked in. I thought what were the odds and that she must be a reporter or a staffer. What I would never have guessed, as she proceeded to the stairs leading up to the dais, was that she would be a Congresswoman. Dear God, she is a Congresswoman! This game had not officially started but I knew the real game had been played for a lot longer than just today.

The dais was full and they had the four witnesses stand, raise our right hands, and then swear to tell the truth. It didn't hit me until much later that night after the congressional hearing was complete that no one else in that room pledged an oath to tell the truth, especially the Congresspeople. During my testimony, and the two hours of listening to lies, I should have connected the dots why these people could never be required to swear an oath to tell the truth.

Prior to the beginning of the testimony from the witnesses, the first punch was thrown, and I was the target. After Representative Correa bloviated about nothing, the California Congressman scolded me about my use of the term of treason in my formal written testimony about Biden, Harris and Mayorkas.

> *Mr. Carrell, I want to note, that I saw your prepared remarks and they don't conform to the rules of the committee. Here in Congress, you don't accuse sitting Presidents, Vice Presidents, or members of Congress of treason, but you are invited by the Chairman and in this hearing, I am going to respect that, I want to make sure we move ahead and hear your testimony sir. We want to be productive here and move forward.*[103]

I remember that moment because that was like using smelling salt before a football game to make sure all my senses were alive. I made a career arresting this Congressman's "people" in Santa Ana and the surrounding areas that has a huge illegal alien population. So, I knew he and I would become good friends by the end of this game. The way this game works, and don't you think for a second this isn't a produced event, is you can't interrupt, refute allegations, or defend any slanderous statements made about you unless you are directly asked to answer. The entire hearing was a joke. If I could have interrupted or at least answered his remarks of me being outside of the rules of decorum, I would have simply stated, "If we can't declare treason in the halls of Congress, then where do you suggest these allegations be levied?" This moron would have had no answer for that as he was left stumped by me later in the hearing.

After a few minutes of the committee lavishing praise on a retiring Congressman, I was again attacked. This time by another Democrat Congressman from Michigan named Ivey. Mr. Ivey proceeded to state that I wanted to punch the Speaker of the House and some other comments I made in one of the hundreds of podcast interviews I have given over the last two years. Again, I could not respond, but instead I had to sit there as my words were presented out of context and I was portrayed as violent. Ivey would later mock the three Republican witnesses as he laughed at the mention of child organ harvesting. He thought child organ harvesting was a myth. I already hated this event, but I buckled down and waited for my coming testimony and any questions that would be asked. After being punched by incompetent fools, I was ready to speak and confront these people head on.

I took my same attitude and demeanor into this hearing because I strongly believe we are in this current disaster because we have remained silent or cowered into suppressing our own speech. Not me and not then. I instinctively knew that these people on the dais were not intellectually sharp. They did not possess even the rudimentary knowledge of the border, child sex trafficking, or how any of the processes of HHS and ORR worked. These Congressmen and women were grossly ignorant and arrogant. Which is a deadly combination, and it usually ends in disaster for the ignorant and arrogant. And lucky me, I was about to meet one of the most ignorant and arrogant people in the Capital, Illinois Congresswomen Ramirez.

Congresswoman Ramirez used her entire five minutes to slander and disparage me. For the record, I believe Ms. Ramirez to be ignorant, unqualified, and a racist. She is basically an activist paid to be a Congresswomen. Ms. Rameriz started her testimony stating that I am a racist and I am another "witness with no credibility on the hearing topic. Who believes in conspiracy theories and write[s] about it and promote lies ultra-right extremist ideologies to be here."[103] I laughed at her as I sat in my seat looking up onto the dais filled with clowns. As I had to transcribe her statement, it would have been difficult to understand her English syntax if I hadn't already spoken to thousands of illegal aliens. More on that in a moment. Remember when I said earlier that not one congressperson took an oath to tell the truth, not one, including Ramirez. She was free to tell lies about me without recourse, she brought out a big cardboard picture of January 6 with a noose hanging in the middle of the picture claiming that it was from my X account. Of course, it was not. But who cares, she did not swear to tell the truth. She did quote me correctly and in context, once, stating that I said, "The federal government is the enemy." For that one truth out of five minutes of lies, I want to say, thank you! When given enough time and opportunity, ignorant and arrogant people always make a mistake by revealing the truth about themselves. In a moment of emotion, when discussing women being raped on the border, Activist Ramirez unknowingly and openly admitted to being something other than a United States citizen, "My mother experienced that with me. She was pregnant with me crossing that border."[103] HOLD ON A SECOND! I looked around to see if any of the other clowns on that dais just heard what I heard but, no, they are all completely stupid! The Congresswoman from Illinois, the same woman lying about me and showing 100% loyalty to illegal aliens, is a self-admitted illegal alien from Guatemala! I am rarely stunned or shocked but there I was sitting in front of the dumbest people from our population without any understanding of immigration law and our constitution while an illegal alien from Guatemala slandered me! Dear God!

The federal government is the enemy and the people running the federal government are the enemy's foot soldiers! There is a sitting congresswoman that is an illegal alien. I will later address the abuse and the misinterpretation of the 14th Amendment that gave slaves citizenship. For now, I will explain this amendment in one sentence: United States citizenship is gained by being born in America AND being born under the jurisdiction of America. Illegal alien Ramirez was born on American soil, but she was born under the jurisdiction of Guatemala. I remember sitting there fuming not only because I was being lied about by an illegal alien, but because the stupidest people in America sat there like unqualified morons who were too afraid or too stupid to say anything about the Guatemalan illegal alien! It gets worse, The Guatemalan illegal alien is married to another illegal alien.[104] Her uncle is also an illegal alien. I looked everywhere and I didn't see any evidence that Ramirez went through the immigration process and became a naturalized citizen. The enemy is running our government!

Not to be outdone by the illegal alien from Guatemala, Congressman Correa asked me if sealing the border shut, which I stated as my solution to this child sex trafficking problem, would cause any problems. What problems was this buffoon referring to? Well, Correa asked if the border was completely sealed shut how would the tourists, goods, products, and workers cross the border? Dear God, I promise he asked me that. I looked right at this man and replied like I would to a third grader, "That's why we have ports of entry!" Correa put his head down and surprisingly asked me no more questions. A sitting United States Congressman thought closing the border meant that in order to get our produce, medicines, and tourists into America, they would have to scale the border fence and run. I sat in my witness seat wondering how the hell those morons got into positions of power and authority that allows them to have a direct impact on my life.

I testified that the probability was 100% that thousands of children were being raped as I spoke. I laid it all bare for everyone to see. And do you know what the response was, "Well, we are out of time. This hearing is adjourned." I wanted to yell, STOP! Instead, I stood up and watched everyone either leave the hearing or mill around trying to make connections. I did not testify that the monetary policy is wrong or that we needed a different energy policy. I was testifying about unaccompanied alien children under our government's supervision in the United States of America are being raped right now! Let me repeat this again to make sure everyone understands - thousands of children are being raped! Everything in America should have been stopped and all resources should have been used to locate every child to ensure their safety. Instead, I was asked if I wanted to take a picture with a congressman, as if they were special! All I wanted to do was leave and I did!

I exited the Cannon House Office Building and called my wife. I called my wife because I knew she was watching the hearing live. I needed to speak to her to make sure what I just participated in was as bad as I thought or see if I was the crazy person. My wife answered my call and was as stunned as I was. As I was speaking with my wife, my phone was blowing up from friends and family that I trust and respect. They all saw the same boondoggle that I had just witnessed in real time.

This hearing was one of many congressional hearings on child trafficking and nothing has changed. There have been no processes or policies changed, no one has been held accountable, and no one cares. We have come full circle again asking that little three letter question: Why? Just because my 24-year career in law enforcement is over, doesn't mean my abilities to find answers other people would rather ignore disappeared when I turned in my gun and my badge. Instead, that talent is even more fine-tuned now than before. What I believe is from experience, research, and listening to people that have been there and done that; and what I believe is the federal government, big media, big business, entertainment, religion, and the elites peddle in pedophilia. I have discovered that everything revolves around pedophilia. Have you ever wondered why everything that comes out of Washington, D.C., never benefits America? The fires in Hawaii. The hurricane in North Carolina. The fires in Los Angeles. The wars overseas. Taxation and money policies. Funding foreign nations. I could go on and on. Every decision is bad for America.

Are there dots that need to be connected from Epstein and Diddy? Strangely, not one name of a child rapist on Epstein's Island was identified. Ghislaine Maxwell trafficked children to ghosts! Diddy parties with politicians, entertainment celebrities, and other elites raping children and not one name. Here is a great suggestion, why don't we all slow down and ask the hard questions and demand the tough answers about what the hell is happening in the United States of America! Then have the moral courage to exact punishment on these heinous criminals even if they are your favorite politician!

I got on a plane home the next morning and I knew for complete certainty three things: (1) Politicians are the dumbest people in our population, (2) The United States federal government needs to be as small as we can make her, and (3) I will never again put myself in a position to be lectured by inferior people!

CHAPTER 12

Name the Traitors!

It is necessary and important to identify the criminals and the crime if you want to stop it. What is paramount to ensure it never happens again, those criminals must be punished for their crimes. When the crime is treason and you are proven guilty of undermining the safety and security of the nation you were entrusted to protect, the severity of the punishment must be the maximum allowed under the law. For the crime of treason, the maximum penalty is death. I want to make sure I am as transparent as I possibly can – I want everyone involved in the intentional and strategic plan to destroy and then fundamentally transform America by opening our borders to 30 million illegal aliens to be tried in the court of law and if found guilty, I demand the maximum penalty of death be applied to those convicted traitors.

Also, I demand this happen as quickly as possible. There must be an example of what happens if you commit treason against our nation. I am not talking about monetary policy or energy decisions to drill for oil in the ocean or not. I am talking about intentional and purposeful decisions and planning the downfall of a nation, our nation. The powerful individuals in our nation conspired with international forces to move millions of illegal aliens up to the Mexican border and then into every state in our Union. This group of people had meetings at the highest levels of government, and they made a conscious decision to use mass migration from every corner of the world to upend America's demographics which has caused death, societal collapse, and economic struggle.

I was shocked watching 94 Executive Orders cascade down to my Border Patrol station on Biden's very first day in office. These Executive Orders obliterated every immigration policy Trump had in place which gave America the most secure border in her history. Remove the politics and the hatred Americans have for the opposite party and let's look at this from a practical position. Let's use a fictitious example with Google as the "business" in place of our government. In January 2021, Google stock price was a little over $196. Imagine if the CEO of Google stepped down right after Christmas 2020 and the new CEO started in January 2021 with a high stock price of $196. Let's call this CEO, Brandon. At the beginning of Brandon's reign as CEO, every time he walked the halls of Google, the employees excited about Google's future would chant, "Let's Go Brandon! Let's Go Brandon!" Then something went wrong. Brandon took every internal policy that guided Google to new financial and business heights and immediately banned them. Brandon replaced those policies with mandates that went against everything Google stood for and what made Google the envy of the business world. Instantly, the business tanked. Google stock was declining rapidly. The Board of Directors and major stockholders were screaming for Brandon to stop and reverse course back to what was working just a few days ago. Brandon ignored the pleas for common sense and for the CEO to honor his commitment to the company. Instead, Brandon doubled down and at the same time, Brandon and his top cabinet denounced everyone that was complaining as bigots and racists. Months later, Google shuttered its buildings as the business had completely collapsed. Investors, Google employee's pensions, and the stock price were all bankrupted. A once great business fell to ruins almost overnight.

What would have happened to that CEO when a trillion-dollar business collapsed overnight? Would the Federal Trade Commission (FTC) open an investigation? Would the employees have revolted and physically gone after Brandon? Would business leaders, cable shows, and even politicians demand answers? Would one of the answers be that Brandon must have made decisions to tank the stock price and destroy the company on purpose? Would Brandon have been arrested and charged with financial fraud, securities fraud, market manipulation, or bribery? Of course he would.

If Brandon were charged with multiple crimes against Google for intentionally and strategically destroying that business, why would Biden's purposeful decisions to open the borders thus destroying America go unpunished? The answer to why Biden was allowed to continue his treasonous ways is due to the width and depth of corruption in our federal government. The corruption that has rooted itself in the foundation of America is so layered, so deep, that a rational person would feel overwhelmed by its size. The corruption in the federal government is perpetrated and funded by both parties. The last two years of Biden's term in office, the Democrats crafted the policies, and the Republicans funded all of it. Not some of it, but ALL of it!

Stop for a second and ponder what 30 million of anything looks like. Thirty million computers, 30 million pens, 30 million cars, or 30 million dogs; 30 million of anything is hard to comprehend. Now, realize the magnitude of 30 million people pouring across our borders in four years and try to rationalize on any level how this would be positive for America. How could this process have been undertaken any other way except through collusion, blackmail, coercion, and other malicious actions? When we break this treason down into small intellectual bites, it becomes easier to digest and understand. It is still hard to swallow our government is run by traitors, and that they have become the enemy of the people.

I am very aware of the words I speak and the words I write. I take no pleasure writing these words, but they are the truth. As a former law enforcement officer, I still think in very logical and linear thoughts. I am a very black and white type of guy that sees things in simple terms. If A happens and the result is B, then who or what caused A? Who gets the most out of B when it materializes? What other outcomes came from this cause and effect? If there are other outcomes, what players in this event benefited? When I remove my resentment and anger at what has transpired these last four years, I look at this ongoing event in logical and linear terms.

Not listening to the unwise words of California Congressman Correa, "Mr. Carrell, I want to note, that I saw your prepared remarks and they don't conform to the rules of the committee. Here in Congress, you don't accuse sitting Presidents, Vice Presidents, or members of Congress of treason..." Well, Congressman we are no longer in that evil cesspool called Washinton, D.C. and in that old building with old, corrupt mindsets. We are in the real world where truth trumps everything and people like you become unprotected and vulnerable. In that vein, let's name the names of traitors!

In my prior book, *INVADED*, I showed the genesis of this treason started with the Immigration and Nationality Act of 1965 and named the names of traitors from both parties. The lies and deceit have not changed but the ferocity of malicious intent is at heights never seen. If I use the Immigration and Nationality Act of 1965 as the first chapter of a manuscript, I will use the Obama era as the prelude to the end of the book. President Obama weaponized the administrative state of immigration law. Using the administrative state, Obama was able to systematically halt all deportations of illegal aliens inside the United States. Individuals preparing to jump the border fence believed that if they could make it past the Border Patrol, they would be untouchable. As unrealistic as that sounds, those future illegal aliens were correct. I was stationed as a Supervisory Border Patrol Agent in the San Clemente Border Patrol Station during Obama's reign. The San Clemente Station is an interior station so the overwhelming majority of illegal aliens we arrested were already living in the interior of America. President Obama mandated a policy called Prosecutorial Discretion. This administrative policy placed an extremely high bar of crimes committed by an illegal alien in order for that interior living illegal alien to be deported. The bar was so high that an almost 100 percent release rate was in effect on all interior arrests.

The famous George Washinton University law professor Jonathan Turley gave a congressional testimony before the House Judiciary Committee in December 2013 that perfectly articulates how Obama's Prosecutorial Discretion circumvented immigration law:

> *The federal law mandates deportation for individuals in the country illegally. While prosecutorial discretion has been cited in individual case decisions, the Administration was using it to nullify the application of federal law to hundreds of thousands, if not millions of individuals...In ordering this blanket exception, President Obama was nullifying part of a law that he simply disagreed with. There is no claim of unconstitutionality. It is a raw example of the use of a "dispensing power" over federal law. It is difficult to discern any definition of the faithful execution of the laws that would include the blanket suspension or nullification of key provisions. What the immigration order reflects is a policy disagreement with Congress. However, the time and place for such disagreements is found in the legislative process before enactment. If a president can claim sweeping discretion to suspend key federal laws, the entire legislative process becomes little more than a pretense.*[105]

What Jonathon Turley described is what the entire Border Patrol was forced to accept and enforce. The United States Border Patrol knew what we were doing went against immigration law. However, it is extremely difficult to fight the machine when the Republican cowards in Washington, D.C. not only play along but walk side by side down this illegal path with the Democrats. Even as a young, inexperienced, and naive Agent; I knew policy cannot trump law. Policy is created through administrative mechanisms within the confines of the law. The Democrats are masters of creating policy that lives outside of the law allowing those policies to grow and flourish.

Obama was the beginning of this last push to fundamentally transform America through immigration. I believe the Democrats had a long-range plan that included placing Hillary Clinton into the position of President to seal this fundamental change. We all know Trump stymied this plan but if we are being completely honest, Trump was just a speed bump in their traitorous plan. I strongly believe this speed bump was a wakeup call to these traitors that time was not on their side and that when they held the presidency again, they would go all in without hesitation or fear of repercussion.

Enter the stolen election of 2020 and the walking dead Joe Biden. I want to clear when I say Biden, I mean the cabal that currently pulls his dead puppet strings! When Joe Biden was Vice President, he made this infamous quote about immigration:

> *It is the ultimate source of our strength, it is the ultimate source of who we are, what we become, it started all the way back in the late 1700s. There has been a constant, unrelenting stream of immigration, not in little trickles but in large numbers." Biden mumbled some incoherent nonsense about a metaphorical "buried black box" and continued with,*

> *There is a second thing in that black box: an unrelenting stream of immigration, nonstop, nonstop. Folks like me who are Caucasian, of European descent, for the first time in 2017 we'll be in an absolute minority in the United States of America, absolute minority. Fewer than 50% of*

the people in America from then and on will be white European stock. That's not a bad thing, that's a source of our strength. [24]

Biden was coherent then, albeit still an arrogant blowhard, and he pushed for the unrelenting stream of immigrants. What he did masterfully was Biden never made the distinction between legal and illegal immigration. Why does the Left and the RINOs always fail to make that distinction? They do that to convolute the two very different categories of immigration and to also make any movement to stop illegal immigration as anti-immigrant. Did this man always feel this way about unrelenting streams of immigration? Of course not! In 2006 while speaking at a rotary club in South Carolina Biden pontificated this:

Folks, I voted for a fence, I voted, unlike most Democrats – and some of you won't like it – I voted for 700 miles of fence. But, let me tell you, we can build a fence 40 stories high – unless you change the dynamic in Mexico and – and you will not like this, and – punish American employers who knowingly violate the law when, in fact, they hire illegals. Unless you do those two things, all the rest is window dressing. Now, I know I'm not supposed to say it that bluntly, but they're the facts, they're the facts. And so everything else we do is in between here. Everything else we do is at the margins. And the reason why I add that parenthetically, why I believe the fence is needed does not have anything to do with immigration as much as drugs. And let me tell you something folks, people are driving across that border with tons, tons, hear me, tons of everything from byproducts for methamphetamine to cocaine to heroin and it's all coming up through corrupt Mexico. [106]

Does it surprise anyone what this man has and will say? President Biden is a world class liar and always has been. In a debate in 2007 on the campus of Dartmouth College in New Hampshire, Biden was asked a yes or no question if he would allow sanctuary cities ignore federal law and his answer was, "No."[106] CNN Politics also cited Biden at another event in 2007 stating:

> *We've got to get tougher with employers. In fact the person we should send to jail is not the illegals, we send to jail the employers. If you knowingly hire an illegal alien, then you should be held accountable. Because let me tell you, the next person I hear tell me that my labor guys aren't willing to work hard, that's why you have illegals putting up sheetrock, then I want to tell you, you don't know my guys.*[106]

This man has been a walking contradiction on immigration, quite frankly on everything in his life, for his entire 40-plus year career. Biden is a walking contradiction and sounds like MAGA:

> *Way back in the 1980s, I was the guy who convinced a lot of my colleagues in the military that the military should get involved in this process, and so in the drug strategy thing. Whether or not we should consider someone other than those Federal agencies that traditionally have the responsibility for protecting our borders short of a literal declaration of war or an invasion in the literal sense, whether or not we should bring anybody else into this battle.*[107]

What Joe Biden has done to America is unconscionable. The total destruction of the immigration system to fundamentally transform America has reached levels of treason that would make Obama envious. Biden, in every attempt to bypass Congress, has told America up front what he wants to do without apology. At an event in 2019, Biden stated, "We could afford to take in a heartbeat another two million [immigrants]. The idea that a country of 330 million people cannot absorb people who are in desperate need and who are justifiably fleeing oppression is absolutely bizarre."[108] Biden continued to make his plan heard and the future would prove him successful, "I would in fact make sure that there is – we immediately surge to the border all those people are seeking asylum. They deserve to be heard. That's who we are."[108] No one asked him then or now, "Explain how that is who we are?" America doesn't invite the world to "surge" our borders, causing chaos and violence. What the President openly advocated for was foreign nationals to storm our borders and force America to take them in? We allowed a known racist, a known liar, a known morally deficient man, and someone known to be in severe mental decline to destroy our nation.

How did this man go from the current MAGA stance to completely opening the borders of America to 30 million illegal aliens in four years? Biden is a shell of his former self. Biden is a puppet directed by evil traitorous people. My claim that Biden is mentally unfit should not be used as an excuse for his decisions and the path of fundamental transformation and ultimate death of America. Biden, on some level, understands exactly what he is doing because he made a conscious decision to accept this path for America back in 2020 leading into the Presidential Election. Even though Biden has been a serial liar, bombastic, and grossly arrogant; he is a political genius. Sure, he is not, at all, considered an intellectual but to ignore his successful career in politics would be intellectually disingenuous. By acknowledging Biden's political prowess, I condemn him for his traitorous decisions. Biden is barely functioning on a cocktail of narcotics that allows him to muddle through one or two quick speeches then he is hidden for the rest of the day. Looking at the entirety of his career, his actions over 40 years, and his ability to weave in and out of contradictory policy and law decisions, all to his and his family's benefit, I make a definitive allegation that Joe Biden is a traitor!

I don't even want to use any space to discuss Kamala Harris because she is such an imbecile and such a pawn on this chess board of treason. However, Harris did play an important role in this betrayal of America. What was her role? She played the role of the dunce. She pushed the narrative that everything that was occurring on the border was normal and that there was nothing to worry about. Harris was the Border Czar. I don't care what lies were told by the mainstream media during the 2024 Presidential Election that Harris was not connected to the border issue at all. The media acted as if Harris was some outside entity in the Biden Administration. Just to put the media's lying into context, here is the first sentence of a Forbes article, "Vice President Kamala Harris will make her first visit to the U.S.-Mexico border since she became the Democratic nominee on Friday, speaking on immigration as Republicans have scrutinized her views on the issue and claimed she served as the Biden administration's "border czar," which misinterprets the narrow task Harris actually had."[109] The media and the Democrats tried in vain to split hairs about Harris' role as a "Border Czar." All of that is semantics because Harris, even as unqualified as she was to be Vice President much less a Border Czar, was in charge of the border issue under President Biden. The problem of being the Border Czar is one must go to the border. Kamala never did until she was forced. We are all familiar with the NBC's Lester Holt interview where Harris lies about going to the border in this extremely uncomfortable exchange:

> *Holt: "The question that has come up and you heard it here and you'll hear it again I'm sure, is, 'Why not visit the border? Why not see what Americans are seeing in this crisis.'"*
>
> *Harris: "We have to deal with what's happening at the border, there's no question about that. That's not a debatable point. But we have to understand that there's a reason people are arriving at our*

border and ask what is that reason and then identify the problem so we can fix it."[110]

Holt pressed her about visiting the border:

Harris: "At some point, you know, we are going to the border. We've been to the border. So this whole thing about the border, we've been to the border. We've been to the border."

Holt: "You haven't been to the border."

Harris: "And I haven't been to Europe. And I mean, I don't understand the point that you're making. I'm not discounting the importance of the border."[110]

Lester Holt just reinforced what we all knew and that is Harris is both unqualified and incompetent. Harris' claim to fame on the border is discovering "the root causes" of why millions of illegal aliens are invading America. Now that would be just fine if all those millions were stopped at the border and denied entry. Then we could try and understand the cause of this invasion. But that is not what the sophomoric moron was talking about because she knew what the causation of this flood of humanity was. This invasion was the result of President Biden welcoming and encouraging millions of foreign nationals to illegally enter America. Again, let me point out that I believe Harris is a moron in every sense of the word. She is an extreme Diversity, Equity, and Inclusion hire. President Biden selected her solely because Harris is a "woman of color," period. Despite her low level of intellect and her extremely limited ability to use the English language correctly, Harris participated and facilitated this treasonous plan to demographically change America. Harris' fingerprints are all over this treason as she dictated a propaganda letter from the White House in her position as Vice President:

> *Our immigration system has been broken for decades. That is why President Biden and I have spent the last three years putting forward solutions to fix it and address the root causes of migration.*
>
> *On the first day of our Administration, we sent a comprehensive immigration reform bill to Congress that included an increase in funding for border security and a pathway to citizenship for immigrants, such as Dreamers who have been here for years.*
>
> *We have partnered with countries in the Western Hemisphere to address global pressures that are forcing people from their homes, and worked with the private sector to promote investment in Central America. Last October, as part of our national security supplemental request, we asked for $14 billion for border security, which would increase personnel and technology to secure the border and provide assistance to cities to manage the influx of migrants.*
>
> *At each step, we have been clear: Congress must act. Unfortunately, we have too often been met with those who sought to play political games instead of participating in solutions.*[111]

I just can't subject the reader to this dribble, so I cut to the end of this letter to America in February 2024 because this last paragraph is so inspiring: "Let us remember: we are a nation of immigrants. Immigrants have always helped strengthen our country, grow our economy, and drive innovation. We know that in America, diversity is our strength. So rather than politicize this issue, let us all address it with the urgency and seriousness it requires."[111]

Understand that when Harris posted this letter from the Office of the Vice President, tens of millions of illegal aliens had already poured into America. At the writing of this book, over 12 million illegal aliens have been arrested and released. DHS claims another three million illegal aliens have crossed the border undetected and absconded. CBP had illegally flown in millions of illegal aliens off the books. And we are supposed to believe Harris was an innocent bystander and the fault lies with Congress. Vice President Kamala Harris is a traitor!

This brings us to my all-time favorite villain, DHS Secretary "Ali" Mayorkas. The man in charge of the most powerful law enforcement agency in the United States government is a man that became a naturalized citizen from the communist country of Cuba. If "Ali" was a pro-American, seal the border, and a protect America's sovereignty at all costs naturalized citizen from communist Cuba, I would be his biggest supporter. But he is not that guy! Instead, because he comes from a communist nation and he was on the board of HIAS, the international NGO that is playing a significant role in trafficking illegal aliens into America, coupled with "Ali's" anti-American policies and malicious actions, I question his allegiance to America. Going all the way back to 2008 when Obama descended from heaven to be President unto present day, Mayorkas has created from whole cloth every negative immigration policy and action destroying America's sovereignty today. Not some policies or most policies, but every single policy!

Mayorkas took the most secure border in America's history and blew the doors wide open. Mayorkas violated immigration law and at the same time invented policy and implemented these unlawful and unconstitutional orders in real time. Mayorkas used the old propaganda line in an interview with Fox News Neil Cavuto, "We're dealing with a terrifically broken asylum system and [this] would deliver for us resources at a level that we desperately need, that we do not have."[112] The system was not broken prior to you coming into power. The system was working so well that the border was within six to nine months of being completely secure under Trump's administration! Not a little bit or 50% sealed but all of it. How do I know this to be true outside of statistical data, I was there on the border! I was a senior leader in the United States Border Patrol during Trump's presidency and I was there for the first year of Biden and Mayorkas' betrayal. The unspoken secret about immigration law is that we do not need any more laws! The laws on the books work. Does the INA need to be cleaned and tightened up? Absolutely in terms of enforcement, but not in widening the loopholes to create more "legal pathways" into America.

The Democrats have many character flaws but the most damaging characteristic they all share is arrogance. They all feel the need to tell us exactly what they are doing as a power play. They use this power play to prove to us that they are both in charge, and you, the unwashed, can do nothing about it. In the same interview with Cavuto, Mayorkas arrogantly states that he committed absolute treason, "You know, we built, capabilities, in foreign countries, in, Guatemala, in Costa Rica, in Mexico as well. And sometimes they don't develop overnight. They take time to mature. And we continue to take action within the confines of our authorities."[112] What this traitor just stated was that he has built physical buildings and implemented processes in foreign nations to facilitate the efficient flow of millions of illegal aliens into America. This was not the only time Mayorkas arrogantly and in complete defiance of the law stated his treason. In an interview with ABC Sunday Show *This Week* he stated, "We have increased the number of refugees that we will accept from the western hemisphere. We have built Safe Mobility Offices in Columbia, Ecuador, Guatemala, and Costa Rica to reach people where they are so they don't have to take the perilous journey."[113]

I dedicated an entire chapter to Mayorkas in my book, *INVADED*, because he is the apparatus from which all this evil is funneled through. Mayorkas created and facilitated every catastrophic immigration policy we are living through today. As I stated as clearly as I could in, *INVADED*, Mayorkas is a traitor!

I would be remiss if I didn't enumerate the Republican traitors as well. How many Republican traitors are there? Well, enough fill up page after page. Unfortunately, I don't have limitless pages so I will focus on just three. I will start with two of them together because they worked in tandem to undercut President Trump during his first term in office and that would be the uber RINO House Speaker Paul Ryan and Senate Majority Leader Mitch McConnell.

When I am writing about these two, my initial reaction is to use profane language because I get emotional. Why? Because the Republicans had both houses of congress and the presidency. With this power, they could have strengthened border policies and law. They could have solidified the INA thus blocking all future attempts to open the borders as Biden would do years later. Instead, both men lead the RINOs in an upfront attack on Trump. They shot down any attempt to secure the border with more infrastructure, AKA, The Trump Wall. I am passionate about my disdain for both Ryan and McConnell because I witnessed firsthand the danger of working the border without a wall and without proper infrastructure. Because Ryan and McConnell blocked funding for Trump's wall, Agents died and were seriously injured. Border Patrol Agents were left unprotected and were assaulted constantly. If I took that sharp tongued weasel Ryan or that old, withered McConnell to the border with no security, or armed personnel they would lay down in the fetal position right there on the dirty border road crying for "momma." I despise those two and every other Republican that sided with them. Ask yourself a simple question – why did these two men vote for trillions of dollars to fight wars in the Middle East and trillions of dollars to fund physical border walls in foreign nations and deny all funding for our American border? I need an answer to that question! If you can't rationally or logically answer that question, maybe listen to my answer - TREASON!

Paul Ryan hoodwinked Trump into signing an omnibus bill with the promise from Ryan that the wall would be funded. Ryan lied! What was Trump's response to Paul Ryan and his deliberate lie on the funding of the wall,

> *Paul told me in the strongest of terms that, 'Please sign this and if you sign this we will get you that wall.' Which is desperately needed by our country. Humanitarian crisis, trafficking, drugs, you know, everything – people, criminals, gangs, so, you know, we need the wall. And then he went lame duck. And once he went lame duck, it was just really an exercise in waving to people, and the power was gone so I was very disappointed. I was very disappointed in Paul because the wall was so desperately needed. And I'll get the wall.*[114]

Mitch McConnell was on the Senate floor actively blocking the emergency funding request from Trump to build the border wall. Trump made his case very clear in a Twitter post, "Republican Senators are overthinking tomorrow's vote on National Emergency. It is very simply Border Security/No Crime - Should not be thought of any other way. We have a MAJOR NATIONAL EMERGENCY at our Border and the People of our Country know it very well!"[115] Then the old bastard blocked the border wall funding because of some parliamentary "standards," old Mitch held dear while my Agents were being killed and maimed! The standards that Mitch loved were the same standards the Democrats abused at will to destroy America through open borders. The Republicans are a bunch of gutless cowards. If I am completely honest, I respect the Democrats. I do! They believe what they believe and they do what is necessary to achieve what they believe. I don't care if it is legal or not, I have respect for them because they are determined and have a huge set of brass balls. They are everything our Republican Party is not. You may detest Trump, but tell me what the Republican Party would be like without him? In fact, I believe that if there wasn't a Trump, we would already have a third party created out of the distrust and hatred of the Republican Party by its own members.

The last Republican traitor is the current beta male, House Speaker Johnson. What does this coward do at the first sign of trouble and a Continuing Resolution (CR), he bends a knee to the mental patients and traitors running the Democrat Party. What did he concede to that he said he never would do? He funded the entire NGO machine knowing that the NGOs are responsible for unbelievable levels of child sex trafficking and human smuggling. Speaker Johnson funded this machine to the tune of $7.9 billion for several weeks of "service." We should all have seen this coming once Johnson was caught walking in the halls of congress with Paul Ryan. Johnson was then taken to the secure Skiff, to be debriefed, and then emerged from that undisclosed location a completely changed man. What happened to Johnson? What was Johnson told? Was Johnson coerced or blackmailed? I don't have the answers to these questions except commonsense tells me something happened down in that blackhole and on the long walk with Ryan that made Johnson turn his back on everything he promised he would not do.

Speaker Johnson is an obvious pawn in this high-stake politician machine in D.C. Johnson is a physically and intellectually weak man. Trump tolerates him. Do not be surprised that when Trump sees an opening to dispose of this weak and impotent man, he will discard Johnson like he was a contestant on *The Apprentice*. We need strong leaders in every position in the government to combat and defeat the evil that permeates every institution in our government.

Treason is not just at the top of our government. Unfortunately, traitors are scattered throughout the organizational charts across the entire government. The number and layers of these traitors are frightening when you look at the size of this problem coupled with how well-hidden they are. The administrative state of our government is the body of treason.

They receive their marching orders from the head, the politicians, who hate America. Like in a heavy weight fight, the body must fall so the other fighter can win. The same applies to the massive administrative state that runs the government.

CHAPTER 13

The Lieutenants

For change to happen, there must be a vision and true leadership at the top; and the ground level workers must be given clear instructions on how to achieve success. As important as the top and the bottom of an organization are, the most significant section of the operation is located at the managerial level or as I like to label them, the Lieutenants. The Lieutenants of the DHS and the White House are powerful administrators within this cabal to weaponize immigration tools to change America.

Who are these people and are they really that bad? Buckle up!

As I detail just a few of the many Lieutenants placed in influential positions within the hierarchy of DHS and the White House, remember these are the professionals that should be supplying the necessary tools and funding to complete the only mission of the DHS and that of an American President which is securing and protecting the sovereignty of the United States of America. These Lieutenants were not hired to promote and drive the mission of the DHS, instead, they were hired to destroy the DHS and ultimately our nation from within. You will be shocked to learn who the power players are within the departments of DHS and their overt hatred of what they, on paper, were hired to do.

Here is a great individual to begin this journey of discovery, United States Citizenship and Immigration Services (USCIS) Policy Analyst, Office of Policy and Strategy, Humanitarian Affairs Division Kursten Phelps.

Sounds like a fantastic position to help ensure the border is secure and that the illegal aliens that are arrested are deported quickly. Not really. Ms. Phelps began her government career in USCIS in July 2021 and currently holds this position in USCIS. Ms. Phelps worked for the Tahirih Justice Center from 2013 to 2020. It is important to describe the Tahirih Justice Center mission because it says a lot about an individual that would leave that position and enter the world of federal immigration. Ms. Phelps worked for years with an organization that proudly boasts:

How do we protect survivors of violence?

> *Tahirih works to dismantle the laws, practices, and attitudes that leave immigrant survivors vulnerable to abuse. We provide each survivor with the resources they need to secure personal protection and support their agency in their healing journey. By working at both the systemic and individual levels, we seek to have a truly transformative impact on our justice system. We take an interdisciplinary approach to secure justice for survivors. Through free legal and social services, policy advocacy, and community outreach and training, we protect and expand legal rights for immigrant survivors of gender-based violence seeking safety in the U.S.*[116]

I don't know if employing an individual into USCIS, whose sole mission is to ensure the

legal immigrants that come into America are immigrants that benefit America, from a nonprofit that "works to dismantle laws, practices and attitudes..."[116] seems like a smart choice. Ms. Phelps seems to be an odd addition to USCIS. But wait there is more. In a video on "The Role of Social Workers in Immigration Legal Services Organizations," Ms. Phelps tells the viewers bluntly, "To gain legal status...requires interaction with systems of oppression...they have to be of value to a system of oppression. Systems that can oppress or cause harm directly to their own communities, such as we see with law enforcement harming black and brown communities."[117] And my two favorites, "It ultimately places survivors at the intersection of this white supremacy rubric...There is a pipeline from criminalization and racially motivated and racist white supremacist law enforcement practices directly to a deportation pipeline."[117] Thank God, Ms. Phelps is on our side!

Let's look at one of my favorite groups inside the boondoggle of federal immigration law, the Immigration Judges (IJ). Judge Andrea Saenz is a perfect starting point.[118] Ms. Saenz was a proud member of Brooklyn Public Defenders Services. What is the Brooklyn Public Defenders Services most proud of?

> *Brooklyn Defenders' Immigration Practice protects the rights of immigrant New Yorkers by defending against ICE detention and deportation, minimizing the negative immigration consequences of criminal and family charges for non-citizens and representing immigrants in applications for immigration benefits.*
>
> *Our immigration practice represents people who are applying for immigration relief, including asylum, before U.S. Citizenship and Immigration Services ("USCIS"), and in removal proceedings in New York's immigration courts. We are one of three New York Immigrant Family Unity Project (NYIFUP) providers, which specializes in representing people who are detained while they await their deportation hearing.*
>
> *Our specialized team of attorneys also provides assessments and advice to defense attorneys across Brooklyn Defenders and all our clients about the specific impact of their legal case on their immigration status.*[119]

So here we have an Immigration Judge adjudicating immigration cases that spent six years working for an organization that fought against the very same DHS that now employs her. What type of immigrants did Saenz provide legal services to prior to being appointed an IJ? Try this one on for size - Braulio Duran Acevedo, a native of Mexico and lawful permanent resident who has lived in the U.S. since 1969, was convicted in 2015 of attempted oral or anal sexual conduct with a person under age 15 in violation of N.Y. Penal Law § 130.45(1).[120] Duran Acevedo was found guilty and ordered deported after his appeals, but at least he had representation.

Welcome to this chapter, Mr. Daniel Delgado, Acting Deputy Assistant Secretary for Immigration Policy, DHS. Per the DHS Bureaucrat Watch List website, Mr. Deputy Assistant Secretary for Immigration Policy is responsible for:

> *At a time when Cuba, Haiti, Nicaragua, and Ukraine raise geopolitical concerns the Biden administration has failed to assuage, Daniel Delgado has helped pave the way for "mass parole" into the United States from each of these nations. Daniel Delgado was listed as the point of contact on press releases from DHS announcing the following policy changes to country-specific parole implementation – indicating a senior involvement on Delgado's part in creating these policies.*[121]

Not that it matters but where did Mr. Delgado work prior to his career in DHS? He worked as an intern at the Coalition of African, Arab, Asian, European, and Latino Immigrants of Illinois (CAAAELII) and at the Voter Participation Center as a Research Fellow that focused on voting registration for, "...young people, people of color and unmarried women." Maybe I am not portraying a senior level leader in DHS in the correct light. Let's look at a social media post from his LinkedIn account to make sure that I am being fair:

> *Twelve years ago today, DACA was created to provide young people who were brought to the United States as children to live and work in the only country they've called home. Since DACA's inception, more than 800,000 Dreamers have been able to pursue an education, contribute to the economy, and strengthen our communities. #DHS continues to fortify #DACA and protect #Dremaers to the fullest extent possible.*[121]

Yep, I got this guy down perfectly!

Staying in the senior leadership ranks, let's take a hard look at Senior Executive Deputy Director – USCIS Jennifer Higgins. Ms. Higgins is a huge fan of Diversity, Equity, and Inclusion, which explains a lot of what has happened to USCIS. This quote will give you direct insight into the type of person who is making vital decisions in the upper ranks of USCIS:

> *You might have diversity in your entry level positions, but there are tremendous barriers that abound in our leadership positions. And, so, I think it's really, really important for us to dig into the reasons why that's the case. And I think, in a lot of ways, it's taking a look and recognizing at the barriers that people faced before they even joined our department. You know, whether it was, growing up in a particular community, whether it was, um, you know, challenges that they had, um, in school, um, you know, microaggressions that they had to deal with on a regular basis. All of that led people to have a particular experience even before they enter the DHS workforce. And so for us, it's really critical to recognize that and to take those things into consideration when we're making hiring choices and hiring decisions. And, so, a big part of what the department is doing is actually trying to do more "barrier analyses" to be able to really assess, okay maybe on the surface we have a diverse workforce, but if*

> *we just dig a little bit deeper we will realize that we actually have a lot of work we need to do.*[122]

Ms. Higgins does not believe the greatest threat to America is the 30 million illegal aliens that have crossed into America under Biden or the total of 50 million illegal aliens living in America at this moment. No, the greatest threat is homegrown extremism and, wait for it, is misinformation, malinformation, and disinformation:

> *It's not going to come as any surprise to the group that's listening today that, you know, homegrown extremism, lone wolf actors, cyber threats, transnational criminal organizations, [and] terrorist fighters who are exploiting conflicts that are happening right now around the world, um, ideological, ethnic driven terrorism threats, the threats abound in our landscape right now. One of the things, though, that I think is interesting given the work that I do in the immigration space is probably a threat that people don't immediately think of when they think of Homeland Security. And that is, I find an emerging area, to be particularly interesting, in the area of misinformation, malinformation, and disinformation. Um, you know, the use of those tools to be able to undermine institutions.*[122]

By this point in the chapter, it should be evident that the leaders in *DHS are anti-Americans that hate our immigration system. With great frustration, I must state without reservation that these traitors are successful, and they are winning this war to change America. It is undeniable. And the list goes on.*

The next person is an individual that is moving the ball down the field, Wilson Osorio Associate Counsel, USCIS. Mr. Osorio loves TikTok and uses other social media platforms like YouTube and Instagram. Using these large social media platforms, Osorio pushes his pro-illegal alien propaganda and ideology. For example, on his TikTok, "Undocumented immigrants play an important role in US infrastructure. I was also told that despite not having papers, they pay their taxes to Uncle Sam."[123] On Instagram, "The American Dream is alive and well. This is the story of a Honduran immigrant who entered the United States illegally [around] 20 years ago. With hard work and dedication, he is now the owner of an expanding restaurant which brings in over $1 million in sales."[123]

The founder of The American Accountability Foundation, Thomas Jones, started a website that documents these DHS employees. Mr. Jones stated with determination, "We created DHSWatchlist.com to shine a light on the swamp's darkest corners. No longer will these radicals be able to hide in anonymity."[123] And then Mr. Jones declared exactly what I believe must happen immediately or at least the first day Trump takes office, "Even as he collects his taxpayer-funded salary, Osorio pushes his radical open borders agenda that is endangering the safety, stability and livelihoods of millions of Americans. It is an utter betrayal of the American people. He must be fired immediately."[123]

Let's go to the top of the organizational chart with Katie Tobin, Biden's top migration advisor in the National Security Council as a Deputy Assistant and Senior Director for Transborder Security to the President. Wow, that is a wordy title. Ms. Tobin played a large role in the dismantling of Title 42, and she spearheaded the Los Angeles Declaration on Migration and Protection. Interestingly, she did not spearhead the Closing off the Southern and Northern Border Initiative! What was the Los Angeles Declaration and Migration Protection? Well, as you can imagine it was a lot of talk about the challenges of tackling the global migration invasion. Basically, everyone signs a document stating that they will do nothing and the invasion into America will continue. You know Ms. Tobin is not on our side when National Security Advisor Jake Sullivan confirms our worst nightmare, "Katie is departing after three years of tenacious and dedicated efforts on the migration file."[124]

Where did Ms. Tobin obtain her experience to rise to the ranks of Presidential advisor? She worked diligently for a decade at the UN Refugee Agency (UNHCR) where she advised the U.S. and governments across Latin America on refugee and migration response.[125] It only gets better. Ms. Tobin, according to her bio on the Carnegie Endowment for International Peace website, served as a refugee officer for DHS, she clerked for the greatest immigration traitor in U.S. history, Senator Ted Kennedy, and Senator "I have never seen an illegal alien I didn't love" Dick Durbin. The topping on the proverbial cake is, Ms. Tobin started her career with Annunciation House, an organization that ran migrant shelters in Mexico. Why doesn't Biden have an advisor on immigration whose prior experience was working as a frontline Border Patrol Agent or a Supervisory ICE Officer? Because those highly qualified individuals would never sell America out for another promotion or a highly paid private job.

Ms. Tobin left her role as a Presidential advisor, but her influence ensured Biden's treasonous immigration policies succeeded. The common theme so far is if you hate deportation, immigration law, and any form of law enforcement, you were hired.

If you still have any questions that the DHS and White House advisors are antithetical to America's best interest, look no further than the Director of USCIS, Ur Jaddou. Yep, her first name is Ur! And here we go with a line of questioning from Congressman Tom Tiffany from Wisconsin, "Do you have any regrets over what's happened in the last four years with the open borders policies and all its different ways here in America?"[126] Ms. Jaddou answered proudly, "I am proud of the efforts that this administration has made with regards to its efforts at the southwest border."[126] And then Representative Tiffany responded with a mic drop, "You have been part of the largest human trafficking operation since slavery in the United States of America. It is...the people of the United States voted for change on November 5 and we can only pray that it happens soon."[126] Was Congressman Tiffany being too harsh with his words? Not really! Ur Jaddou is the problem. She embodies everything that is wrong with this immigration scam costing the U.S. billions of dollars. In remarks Ur Jaddou made at the 2021 National Immigrant Integration Conference, she stated, "As we reset, USCIS is focused on ensuring that: We are processing requests in a timely manner; Making tools and resources available to people who are navigating the immigration process; and Meeting communities where they are to talk, listen, and engage in diverse and creative ways – as we are notably doing today!"[127] She continued with:

> *As we march towards fulfilling these goals, as well as new and evolving priorities, we realize that it is equally important to work towards restoring trust and confidence in USCIS and the naturalization process. At the heart of this effort is a whole of government approach to do just that: Break down barriers to the naturalization process through policy changes and operational means; and Promote naturalization and the importance of U.S. citizenship through outreach and promotion, understanding that our goal is to strengthen integration for new Americans.*[127]

Why does USCIS, under DHS with the policy guidance of the White House, need to promote citizenship? Why is USCIS providing benefits to legal residents which is against the INA and makes that individual immediately deportable? And finally, why does the United States government have to meet communities of foreign nationals "where they are?" I thought everyone came to America because they wanted to be Americans or is this another lie, we have been sold. Everything this government does is against the betterment of America and its citizens. Have you ever wondered what would have happen if millions of Americans illegally or legally resided in say Iran, Ecuador, Mexico, Uzbekistan, or Germany? Then demanded that those governments meet us in our communities, that they provide us with free everything, and speak to us in our native English language. When this insanity is written out in plain sight and not whispered in the offices of D.C. think tanks, it makes no sense at all. It is completely off the rails from reality. No other nation on Earth would placate foreigners and give away our limited resources to immigrants over our own citizens.

I want to finish with Esther Olavarria, White House's Domestic Policy Council and Deputy Director for Immigration. Ms. Olavarria previously served as Counsel and

Deputy Assistant Secretary for Policy at DHS. Now this is where you realize that this whole immigration business is completely incestuous. Ms. Olavarria worked from 1998 to 2007 on Senator Edward Kennedy's immigration counsel on the Senate Judiciary Committee. She has been involved in the immigration world for decades. The "Lion of the Senate" and known as the man that killed Mary Jo Kopechne, sponsored or cosponsored every immigration bill from 1965 to his death. Senator Kennedy changed the fabric of immigration by stopping the flow of immigrants from Europe and opening the floodgates of immigrants from third world nations from Latin American and Africa. Ms. Olavarria was in the thick of it all. The inbreeding of these immigration frauds is astounding once you line them all up and see where their common career paths crossed and from where they all embarked to. Ms. Olavarria served as a senior fellow at the Center for American Progress and a senior advisor for the UNHCR, the UN Refugee Agency. My favorite connector among the majority of them is that they all began as immigration attorneys. Oh yeah, one more connector, she was born in Cuba!

In an interview with UVA Miller Center, Ms. Olavarrio discussed her early career:

> *I practiced immigration law in Miami for about nine years working at, actually, three different non-profit organizations. I started out at the Haitian Refugee Center, representing Haitian asylum-seekers. From there I went to a legal-services-organization program to run their immigration unit. And then in '95, when Congress changed the laws and said LSC [Legal Services Corporation] organizations couldn't represent immigrants, even with private funding, we formed a new organization that didn't take any government money and continued to represent people. Nine years of doing that is a long time, and the demand for services is incredible. You can't even begin to meet it, and I just wanted to do more policy work.*[128]

Esther Olavarria has retired from federal service but she, like many other open border zealots, had a profound impact on the treason we are living through today. I despise these people because they have created an entire system to undercut immigration law and have actively, some for decades, worked to change the demographics of America. None of these people were elected. Instead, they a part of this huge administrative class of traitors that collect massive government salaries with incredible benefits as they corrupt the system they were charged to protect and serve in the best interests of the United States of America. They have all failed us, but they have been successful within the confines of their collective desire and determined ambition to demographically alter the population of America.

This small list of traitors inside our government is just a tiny representation of the numerous career bureaucrats and political appointees running the administrative state. The administrative or deep state is layered, and it is deep. From the lowest interns to attorneys to senior leaders in the White House, they are aligned in their hatred of what America is and they want to change her. These open border, limitless immigration, zealots hate you and want to replace you. That statement is not hyperbolic or written to fearmonger. Instead, it is a simple fact. Every word they utter and every action they take, proves that statement correct. If you choose to ignore it or minimize it, that is on you. Your willful ignorance will not protect you. There is an obvious line drawn in the sand and you better think long and hard on what side you choose to stand on. Be warned that the side I have chosen to stand on and the American patriots have chosen to stand on will give no quarter to the other side. Choose wisely.

In his next term, President Trump must work his way through the organizational charts of every agency and department in the federal government, but he must focus directly on the immigration agencies. President Trump must eradicate every career bureaucrat and immigration activist infesting our federal agencies. There can be no quarter given to these people. I want Trump to destroy the organizational charts of all these departments using an ax not a scalpel. I want Trump and his senior executives to error on the side of America and if there are some positions and individuals you are not completely sold on, fire them as well. America cannot sustain any level of deceit or treason. America is extremely close to failing and a purge of the administrative state must happen.

The moment Trump removes his hand from the Bible and becomes the 47th President of the United States of America, Americans demand these traitors be removed immediately. These people have proven they hate America as she is, and they want to demographically and racially change the population of America. Did anyone vote for this? Was anyone even asked about this modern-day demographic upheaval? Then why did this happen? Why did we allow this to happen? And the biggest answer yet to be revealed to the question is: What are we going to do about the criminal act of treason committed against the body of America?

CHAPTER 14

America Must Fall!

When you pull back from our narrow view of looking at America and take a bigger view of the global mass migration into the western nations, you can see the Global Reset is in its final stage. Europe has been colonized by third world immigration through an intentional invasion allowed by the global leaders of the European Union. The last piece to the Global Reset's puzzle is the United States of America. Does anyone care or more importantly, does the economic structure of the world change if Sweden, Denmark, or even a nation like France falls? The answer is that nations of that economic caliber failing could not cause a change to the structure of power in the world. However, if America falls, the world changes instantly and a mad scramble to fill that power void would restructure the entire world.

The globalists needing America to fall are why we have been living in this frenzied open border chaos. The globalists and our compromised political elites have positioned America to fall, and they have accelerated the invasion of the world into America. There has been an expedited component to this invasion. From the beginning, there has been a consensus among our corrupt politicians and outside forces that the proverbial clock is ticking. The leaders of America have felt the time to ensure transformational change was not in the future but in the immediate future. Each day that expired under Joe Biden was a day closer to the elites losing power to the reelection of Donald Trump. With the mindset that Donald Trump would again be a wrecking ball to their treason, their actions to secure the change needed to globally reset was pushed into overdrive.

When I look back at the political situation in America on Biden's first day, the anti-Americans outlook for success was looking great. America's birth rates had fallen below the replacement level, Americans were getting older by the day, COVID injuries and deaths were increasing, the borders were opened, almost two million illegal aliens were arrested and released in Biden's first year in office, and the economy began to fall apart. The mood in America was divided, full of distrust, resentment, and anger between neighbors, and worst of all a powerful cloud of hopelessness blanketed our nation. America was in a situation that was ripe for fundamental change.

In four long years, the demographics of America was artificially changed and Americans stood around not fully understanding what had happened to their nation. Americans were struggling to meet their financial needs as third world invaders from across the globe were given free housing, meals, same day laundry service, cell phones with free monthly service, and to add insult to injury, illegal aliens by the millions were receiving preloaded cash debit cards in the thousands of dollars. Anger rose and the resentment of what our own government was doing to our nation exploded into a runaway presidential landslide for Donald Trump.

The replacement of native populations with third world single adult military aged males is occurring across the globe. Let's take Sweden as a prime example. Sweden's population consists of 20% being foreign nationals. TWENTY PERCENT![129] Where did the foreigners come from? Well, countries that you wouldn't think would assimilate into a white majority nation: Syria, Iraq, Iran, Somalia, and Afghanistan. Sweden was once an all-white nation with 99% of the population in the 1980s was native born Swedes. I found an interesting article from the Boston Review, not a conservative voice, while researching Sweden. The article was from 2022, and I found it interesting because everything the author was stating was about the evils of preserving one's ethnic makeup, "The intention behind racist and xenophobic rhetoric is less about total control of the government and more about making the country as inhospitable as possible for non-whites."[130] What struck me the most was how the writer depicted Sweden as the only nation on Earth that wants to protect their racial, ethnic, cultural, and societal makeup. This is the propaganda used throughout the European Union and the western world, that you are evil for wanting to maintain a certain way of life. I wonder if this writer ventured into the same nations that now call Sweden home and asked those nations if the whites from Sweden could inhabit and change their demographic makeup. Do you think Somalia, Iraq, Iran, or Afghanistan would allow that? We all know the answer to that, but why is it ok for Middle Eastern nations to maintain their cultural and ethnic makeup and they are considered righteous? The hypocrisy is abundant on the Left. Worse that the Left's hypocrisy is their blatant racism towards white people!

What is happening in Sweden now that they are not all white and now 20% of their population is not Swedish? A lot of raping by immigrants![131] Who can explain why this is happening? As reported in the BBC, another not so conservative outlet, from an interview with a former police officer in Afghanistan that, "some young Afghans who had come to Sweden in recent years had views that differed significantly from Sweden's idea of sexual equality."[132] I say, what are a few rapes of the native women of Sweden compared to diversity, equity and inclusion? I just have to wonder if Iran would allow all those beautiful blonde Swedish women to walk around in their western clothes demanding women's rights.

I am sure this issue of third world men from the middle east is just an isolated problem in little Sweden. Nope! Another once proud European country populated with a majority white population, Germany. Under

Chancellor Angela Merkel, Germany was the epicenter of taking in millions of middle eastern men. Like Sweden, Germany has a major problem with rapes, and sadly gang rapes, of their native population at the hands of immigrant savages.[133] Google gang rapes in Germany and be ready to see the manifestation of extreme Leftist policies. Friedrich Merx, a rising star in the German centre-Right Christian Democrats made a statement that even shocked me, "On average there are two gang rapes per day, far more than half of which are carried out by migrants."[134] And then he followed up with, "This country needs to be able to live in freedom and security once again...we will find a majority to ensure that this nightmare is ended."[134]

I could go down the list of the EU nations and show either massive crime increases, terrorism, rape epidemics, and other lawlessness that dominates their once safe nations. What they all have in common is a massive invasion of third world men into their communities. What is encouraging is that western Europe is waking up to the multi-cultural global reset and they are vomiting that poison out of their nation's body. For years now, I have been saying that America is about three to five years behind Europe in this global conspiracy to demographically change the western world. Europe is in the purge phase of this cabal. America is still in the intake phase and trying to come to grips with the devastation that has been strategically and purposefully placed on America.

When you look at Europe and you see the cultural and societal chaos that has engulfed their nations, coupled with the media and political elites' suppression of the atrocities, you can see great cultures that are dying. Interestingly, the only nations that have not had terror attacks or migrant gang rapes are two nations that denied the mass invasion into their respective nations. Both Poland and Hungary have stood their ground and would not bend a knee to the globalists and destroyers of western Europe. Hungarian Prime Minister, Victor Orban, a staunch believer in national sovereignty declared his belief of the European Union's mass migration efforts, "If you look back from 2014 period until now, this period is a disintegration process period of European Union."[135] Orban is correct that since the establishment of the EU, the disintegration process of national sovereignty has been systemically destroying every nation in the EU. Orban is the evil isolationist bogeyman; the Leftist in the media and in Brussels hate him. Why do they despise him so badly? Because he will not bend a knee to their global reset by allowing an invasion of military aged men from third world countries. Orban stated clearly and with precision, "If Brussels wants illegal migrants, Brussels can have them."[135] Orban is cut from the same cloth as Donald Trump. Both men are determined, unafraid, and patriotic. Trump praised Orban, "Let me just say about world leaders, Viktor Orbán, one of the most respected men, they call him a strong man. He's a tough person. Smart prime minister of Hungary."[136] This friendship is important for many reasons, but the best reason is that they can stand shoulder to shoulder and declare that national sovereignty is of paramount importance. Not only can they declare this to be true, but they can also point to the suffering nations that have submitted to the global reset and mass illegal immigration. In fact, Trump can point directly at his own country!

Poland Prime Minister, Donald Tusk, who has control over the government, believes in Poland's sacred sovereignty just as much as Orban and Trump. Tusk is fighting the EU and has made it crystal clear that Poland will defend her borders, "Tomorrow and the day after tomorrow in Brussels we will defend the Polish border, and we will use all legal instruments. Poland cannot be and will not be helpless."[137] Poland's President Andrzej Duda, who has control over the state, is in line with his Prime Minister on the EU's push for mass migration into Poland, "The European elites are trying to impose their position and ideological approach to the issue of migration on European nations. We will defend our position and defend our borders." [137] Prime Minister Tusk stated the obvious to patriotic citizens of Poland, "We are at a turning point that will determine how Polish borders, and Polish sovereignty will be treated in the future."[137]

Take anything Trump, Orban, Tusk or Duda has stated and convince any patriot in those three nations that national sovereignty does not matter. I challenge you to take any word, phrase or sentence these men have stated about protecting their homeland, their culture, and their societal norms that is incorrect or out of step with rational thought.The irrational thought of open borders, mass migration, blending cultures, diversity of languages, and customs defies logic. The mental disease of liberalism causes delusion and condemns God's natural order and human behavior.

Because of the mental deficiencies of the Left, their argument will be that diversity is a strength, and that multiple languages and culture have made America great. That is pure nonsense. The entire European Union now understands that it is a fairy tale. American history proves that America's greatness was unification of languages into one language, English. American history has proven one culture is supreme and thrives in our Christian nation and that is the American culture. American history has proven that only one set of societal norms, expectations, and the sanctity of our God given rights matter and should be cherished and that is the American way of life. When did the citizens of the United States of America begin to believe we were great because of other cultures? When did Americans shortchange our greatness and strangely give praise to foreigners instead of the men and women that built our nation? When did Americans believe we were equal to other cultures and societies? The truth is we were once a great nation because of the culture norms and societal customs. America was once great because we were united in our devotion to America. A rational and intellectually honest American can answer all the prior questions with the fact that America lost her greatness when we turned from our Christian values and beliefs, when we turned to greed by erasing the middle-class jobs in favor of cheap foreign labor domestically and abroad. We can turn this ship toward greatness, but it will take a herculean effort. It will be worth it. The only question left is do we still want it?

The EU and their global mission to erase national sovereignty is crumbling like a house of cards. America is right behind the EU. Because of the acceleration of abuses to our border and the actual numbers of illegal aliens entering the United States, I believe that same sense of urgency and acceleration the Left felt and used will be the same feeling MAGA patriots will use to move illegal aliens out of the country.

We must stop the invasion into America. We are importing third world individuals to replace the native population. The Left can hurl racist and xenophobic insults and allegations at me but, after the Left catches their breath from yelling and screaming, I will ask one question: What have I said that is factually incorrect? I will tell you the response to that question because I have asked Leftists this question several times. Their response is complete silence for several seconds. There is a moment when we look right at each other, and they have a look of shock and horror because they have no response. Then there is a barrage of verbal insults and profanity thrusted at me because their policies and beliefs are superficial and based on feelings. As I have stated numerous times on my podcast and in speeches, "I do not care about your feelings, all I care about is the truth!"

Americans are demanding a sovereign nation. A nation without strong and secure borders is just a piece of land that people trample, abuse, and rape. That is exactly what is happening in America today. The number of assaults, rapes, and murders at the hands of illegal aliens is frightening. The ecological disaster caused by 30 million illegal aliens crossing and then trampling on America's body is beyond comprehension. The idea that

America can sustain her greatness by opening the southern and northern borders wide open is gross incompetence and willful stupidity. Europe is awakening to a dismal future of mass deportations, violence, and degradation. They are left with no other action but to attack because if they do not, Europe is dead.

Americans are facing the same chaotic future of violence, mass deportations, and civil unrest. America's only option in this situation is to fight or die. One great thing about the situation in America is that the sides are so clearly defined that no one can sit in the middle because there is no middle ground to be found.

A war for the soul of America has been raging for years. The end is near. Which side will you choose to fight on? Your very life may depend on your decision, so decide wisely.

CHAPTER 15

New Sheriffs Are in Town!

By the time this book goes to publishing, there will be new Sheriffs in charge. That means traitors like Mayorkas will have been removed and I am praying he will be in jail. Border Czar and the Queen of Word Salads, Kamala Harris, will be on some obscure cable news show babbling about nothing important. White House advisors that hate America and work diligently behind the scenes to ensure fundamental change is occurring as quickly as possible are now working in some unimportant think tank in D.C. The entire atmosphere and environment in Washington, D.C. are changing.

This transition from a weak, impotent, and self-loathing administration to a super charged patriotic administration is unprecedented. Trump's first term began with a thunderous clap then into a whimper as the deep state and RINOs dominated every policy and national security issue. Trump was dumbfounded at the level of stupidity, coercion, and corruption in the federal government. Think back to those times. They were filled with extreme disappointment as we watched Paul Ryan and Mitch McConnell sabotage Trump's initiatives. We watched insane impeachment hearings and suffered through Russia Collusion allegations. It wasn't until Trump's last two years or even his last 18 months that his administration began to make significant changes.

This time feels completely different. Trump has a thorough understanding of what D.C., and the federal government is capable of, and Trump is ready to fight. Trump has had four years to train and be ready to throw massive amounts of blows to the enemy. There is a palpable feeling in the air that something huge is about to happen. The Democrats are frightened, and the impotent and soft Republicans know their time has passed them by. There will be no whimper to start this administration off. Instead, Executive Orders are ready to be signed, and the personnel will be in place on day one to enforce the changes demanded. America is ready for a new life. We have been, if we are honest, in a hopeless depression for four solid years. We were led down into a dark, wet, and hopeless basement with the expectation that we would never escape. Those days are gone. There is an excitement of possibility. Even more than that, there is a belief that significant change is upon us and the lives of Americans are going to be infinitely better.

The individuals that have been selected to serve in Trump's administration with a focus on sealing the border, locating, and deporting every illegal alien, and removing the administrative state in DHS has been a presentation on playing chess when your opponent is trying to locate the checkerboard. Trump made strong appointments to become his Lieutenants who will carry out policies that will deliver Trump's and America's desired outcomes. Trump cannot carry this weight for America alone. The burden is too heavy, too broad, and too consuming. By placing determined and patriotic Americans in specific positions to ensure America's interests are carried out, Trump has become the overseer instead of being in the weeds. Trump needs the freedom to move from one disaster to another left behind by Biden and his flunkies. The reconstruction of America can't be handled by one man. Trump must lean on and depend on these men and women to deliver powerful knockout punches daily.

Trump has selected several exceptional individuals that are ready to go full throttle on day one.

One of Trump's best and most unheralded moves was selecting South Dakota Governor, Kristi Noem, to be the next Department of Homeland Security Secretary. Many people thought this would fall to Tom Homan. Trump made a chess master move because if Trump placed Homan in such a huge bureaucratic organization, Homan would have been pulled every which way from Sunday. Anchored down by the size and scope of DHS, Homan would have never been able to enforce the arrests and deportations of tens of millions of illegal aliens. Kristi Noem was the perfect fit for this position.

Governor Noem has proven to be an excellent executive, overseeing an entire state and all that entails. Noem was not just an average do-nothing Governor, but rather her state of South Dakota excelled. Noem is ferocious and will not bend a knee to the insane Left. Noem has been through the proverbial fire and has come out clean. She has proven loyal to Trump and that carries a lot of weight with the President. The Department of Homeland Security is a mess right now. Kristi Noem is going to have to turn this gigantic ship around with little to no time to spare. She can't go into DHS and waste even a second because time is ticking away quickly. She is going to have to use her executive skills and locate the cancerous employees and surgically remove them from the department. This is not a job for the faint of heart and Mrs. Noem possesses the strength, determination, and resiliency of a woman from the state of South Dakota.

I met Governor Noem several times when I lived in South Dakota, and I have spoken to her staff on immigration issues. When I lived in South Dakota, there was an instance where a religious NGO tried to set up delivery of illegal aliens, but it was halted. One of those times I spoke with the Governor, I asked her, "Was it you that stopped that illegal alien drop off?" She smiled and said it was. The Governor told me that Biden's strategic dumping of illegal aliens wasn't going to happen in South Dakota. I believed her and I don't believe many people! That was in 2021, and Governor Noem tweeted about this situation on X, "South Dakota won't be taking any illegal immigrants that the Biden Administration wants to relocate. My message to illegal immigrants...Call me when you're an American."[138] That is the type of bold declarations needed in this war against America. Unapologetic, patriotic, and determined language, backed up with strong and decisive actions is what we need now more than ever before in our Republic.

Noem is not a novice, but a seasoned politician rooted in common sense. The kind of common sense you would find on a farm or cattle ranch in South Dakota. Noem is the perfect pick because she is not of the D.C. ruling class and no matter how hard she would try; she would never be allowed into the east coast elite crowd. Kristi Noem will always be a rube and a member of the class of deplorables to those insufferable elites. Noem will have no ties to the administrative state, no unpaid "paybacks" to the invisible power players on K Street, and her only loyalty will be to the man that tapped her for this position and to America. One of the elites that will be questioning her on her nomination to be Secretary of DHS will be Connecticut Senator Richard Blumenthal. You remember ol' Dick? Dick liked to tell the lie that he served in the theater of war in Vietnam but that was a complete lie. These elites are immune to shame so he is standing by with his skeleton frame pontificating about his private meeting with Noem when he discussed, "the kind of Family Separation Policy that 'horrified' Republicans during the first Trump Administration."[139] I don't remember being horrified and I was there on the border doing the arresting of these family units. With all of his combat experience in the dark recesses of Connecticut, he followed up with the tough guy stance, "Governor Noem declined to be fully specific on a number of issues and I certainly hope to hear more during her upcoming confirmation hearing..."[139] Men like Dick Blumenthal are little, weak, beta males and these betas desire, no they long for, the attention of beautiful women like Kristi Noem. Too bad Dick, you are a weak, pathetic, lying sack of crap from the gutless beta class of east coast elites.

I don't worry about Noem because this is the same woman that refused to close South Dakota during the fraud and abuse of COVID. South Dakota stayed open when the entire nation closed and surrendered their state's sovereignty to the abusive federal government. Kristi Noem was vilified as a denier of science and a rube. Time reveals the truth. Sometimes it takes a little longer than we like but the truth always finds the light. Time revealed that Kristi Noem was correct and everyone else was either cowards or frauds. Handling the mental patients on her nomination process will be a circus but she will come out clean because she is smarter, and she has more commonsense in the tip of her pinky than the entire Democrat Party combined.

I have so many favorite Trump picks, but the selection of Stephen Miller is great because of two factors: Miller is incredibly intelligent, and his best superpower is he can make liberals' heads explode. Miller will be Trump's White House Deputy Chief of Staff for Policy which will place him in a powerful position to provide Trump with the truth of what is happening and strategic plans to correct the treasonous invasion. Miller is not a newcomer to the illegal alien war that has been ongoing for decades. Miller's activism can be traced all the way back to his high school days. Did Miller attend some high school in the middle of Nebraska or some other red state? Nope! He attended Santa Monica High School in deep blue California. Miller's patriotism and belief in America's sovereignty was so pronounced in high school that if you Google that period in his life, article after article will appear. He had such an impact in his teenage years, Univision, a radical Hispanic television channel, has done numerous articles and in one such article Univision was offended that in Miller's yearbook he was quoted repeating the famous President Teddy Roosevelt line of, "There can be no fifty-fifty Americanism in this country."[140] Univision loathes Miller so much that they did an investigation all the way back to his high school days and interviewed his former classmates.[141]

You know you are on the right side of history when the Southern Poverty Law Center (SPLC) provides a lot of space for you on their website and space in their minds.[142] Miller is labeled "anti-immigrant" in the extremist files. SPLC credits Miller with, "...shaping the racist and draconian immigration policies of President Trump, which include the zero-tolerance policy, also known as family separation, the Muslim ban, and ending the Deferred Action for Childhood Arrivals (DACA) program."[142] What is so ironic about this SPLC's description of Miller is that they portray him as a staunch America first, protector of national sovereignty, and an extreme patriot. What is wrong with any of that? Well, a lot of it is wrong if you are a member of the racist SPLC. The SPLC offers this gem to their members trying to paint Miller as a zealot of enforcing immigration laws, "It was a simple decision by the administration to have a zero-tolerance policy for illegal entry, period. The message is that no one is exempt from immigration law."[142] Quotes like that from Miller make him even more awesome!

Miller is a tough as nails political figure. He will never bend a knee, and he has a unique way of mocking the Left. His ability to articulate the Left's insanity has become so perfect that it is considered an art form. Miller is a lightning rod of criticism that brings the tired slanderous terms of racist, xenophobe, extremist, and most of all white nationalist. I'll always find the term white nationalist applied to Jewish men telling because when the world thinks of white nationalism, we think of the Nazis. The Left are void of original thoughts. All the Left have available are words and even the nastiest words they use have become tired and boring. Think about what the Left has accomplished, they took the word Nazi and watered that word down to mean anything, even Jewish men! Well, the Jewish man they call a white nationalist owns them and they know it.

Trump tapped Rodney Scott to be the next Commissioner of Customs and Border Protection (CBP). Rodney Scott was the Border Patrol Chief under Trump, and he lost that position when Biden took power, as Scott would not conform to Mayorkas' wokeness. Chief Scott was my sector Chief in San Diego. I know Chief Scott well as he promoted me into management in San Diego Sector. We have spoken several times during the depressing times under Biden.

Let me tell you the type of man Chief Scott is to assure you he is the right man for the job. When Mayorkas took control of DHS, he sent out a policy directive stating that the term "illegal alien" would not be used in any internal documentation, conversations, or criminal documents. That racist term would be replaced with "undocumented immigrant." The problem with that policy directive, besides being asinine, was that the term illegal alien is a lawful term used in the court of law. Chief Scott immediately followed that policy directive with his own policy directive to ignore the stupidity of Mayorkas. Well, that didn't go over well and Chief Scott was forced out. When he retired, he explained:

> *The U.S. Border Patrol (USBP) is and must remain an apolitical federal law enforcement agency...Despite every attempt by USBP leadership to ensure that all official messaging remained consistent with law, fact, and evidence, there is no doubt that the reputation of the USBP has suffered because of the many outside voices. Mandating the use of terms which are inconsistent with law has the potential to further erode public trust in our government institutions.*[143]

Chief Scott could have towed the party line and remained in a powerful position but his integrity, and most importantly, the integrity of the Border Patrol would not allow him to comply with stupidity. Chief Scott garnered the respect of the Agents well before accepting his fate by standing on his honor but that decision to defy that little rat bastard Mayorkas solidified the respect and admiration of the thousands of Border Patrol Agents serving under him.

Chief Scott has a mild-mannered way about him. His demeanor is 180 degrees from Tom Homan, and he is not a lightning rod like Miller. However, he is as hard lined and determined to secure our nation's borders and to eradicate every illegal alien from our communities as those two men. I trust Chief Scott and would bet a year's salary he will be successful. Not just that he will have a little success, but that his impact on illegal immigration will be profound and have a lasting effect. Chief Scott has dealt with the D.C. politicians and elites, he belongs among them as much as Kristi Noem does. Chief Scott has been in front of Congress numerous times and understands that it is all theater. In the middle of the circus, he remains focused on what must be done because time is not our friend in this war.

The last Trump pick that I want to write about is Tom Homan because he is the most vocal and the poster child for the "world's largest deportation force" ever. I could go on for days about why I love Homan. His greatest strength is his ability to speak truth right at evil and stupidity. He is unflinching and a firm believer in his role in this war for the soul of America. One of my favorite Tom Homan interactions with Congress was when Congresswoman Pramila Jayapal got verbally smacked by Homan when he was giving his congressional testimony.

Homan was in front of the House Judiciary Committee's Immigration and Citizenship Subcommittee as the Acting Director of ICE to discuss "The Expansion and Troubling Use of ICE Detention."

The interaction started off exactly how I would figure it would and that was with Homan coming out hot. "I understand this hearing is important, but where are hearings on the Southern border, on sanctuary cities? It seems like they have a quick hearing when those who violate our laws may find [themselves in] a difficult position, [and] they say they're not being treated fairly."[144] Then it went downhill for Jayapal from there as Homan continued as Jayapal banged her gavel for Homan to stop talking, but Homan ignored the ignorant congresswoman,

> *You want to know why there's 50,000 people in detention? You want to know why we have 1 million illegal entries in the United States? You want to know why we're having these issues? Because you have failed to secure the border. You have failed to work with this president to close the three loopholes we've asked for two years to close!*[144]

Jayapal banging her gavel declared, "Mr. Homan, please respect the chair and the authority of the chair. The time of the gentleman has expired."[144] Having none of this theater Homan fired back, "I have asked you politely to go beyond my time and you let other people go beyond their time. But not to Tom Homan. He don't [sic] get to go beyond his time. This is a circus!"[144] Jayapal was furious and made the fatal decision to challenge Homan directly. Homan's response has become legendary, "You work for me! I'm a taxpayer. I'm a taxpayer, you work for me."[144]

The other "Best of Tom Homan" was his congressional testimony exchange with one of the dumbest congresswomen in the House, AOC. Ms. AOC was trying to educate Mr. Homan on immigration law pertaining to the family separation policy. Ms. AOC somehow forgot who Homan is and what he did for over three decades in law enforcement. It didn't go well for AOC:

AOC: Three different options presented, the third included the option for family separation. This initiative would pursue prosecution of all amendable adults including those presenting with a family unit. Mr. Homan, your name is on this, is this correct?

Homan: Yes, I signed that memo.

AOC: So, you are the author of the Family Separation Policy?

Homan: I am not the author of this memo.

AOC: You are not the author, but you signed the memo.

Homan: Yes. A zero-tolerance memo.

AOC: So, you provided the official recommendation to Secretary Neilson so the United States could pursue family separation?

Homan: I gave Secretary Neilson numerous recommendations on how to secure the border and save lives.

AOC: But it says here that you gave her numerous options, but the recommendation was option three family separation.

Homan: What I am saying is [this is] not the only paper where we have given the Secretary numerous options to secure the borders and save lives.

AOC: So, the recommendation of the many that you recommended, you recommended family separation.

Homan: I recommended zero-tolerance.

AOC: Which includes family separation.

Homan: The same as it is with every U.S. citizen parent gets arrested when with a child.

AOC: Zero-tolerance was interpreted as the policy that separates children from their parents.

Homan: If I get arrested for DUI and I have a young child in the car, I will be separated. When I was a police officer in New York and I arrested a father for domestic violence, I separated that father from his family.

AOC: Mr. Homan with all due respect, legal asylees are not charged with any crime.

Homan: When you are in the country illegally it is violation 8 United States Code 1325.

AOC: Seeking asylum is legal.

Homan: If you want to seek asylum, go through the port of entry and do it the legal way. The Attorney General of the United States has made that clear.

AOC: Ok...[145]

What Tom Homan did in that exchange is what every politician and political appointee must do when faced with ignorance and malintent, attack them with facts and never backdown. AOC is an intellectual lightweight compared to Homan. That little bartender was trying to school a former Border Patrol and ICE Officer, who was then the Acting Director of ICE, on immigration law. AOC's interpretation of immigration law is based solely on her feelings. The Left's beliefs and their understanding of those beliefs are built on a foundation of sand. Take no quarter when telling them the truth, in fact, use the Homan tactic when he seems tired and perturbed having to talk to someone with such a low IQ.

There is no greater Homan moment than the 60 Minutes piece with Cecilia Vega when Vega tried to corner Homan, "Is there a way to carry out mass deportation without separating families?" Homan leveled the hammer, and the mic dropped, "Of course there is. Families can be deported together."[146]

Tom Homan is the perfect selection to be the Border Czar. This position will not be for the faint of heart and it will take a man of devotion and determination to be successful. This job can only be successfully completed if the man in charge knows the immigration laws inside and out, is unafraid to enforce those laws, and will steamroll anyone that foolishly tries to impede him. Tom Homan is that man.

All four of these people that have been strategically selected by Trump are precision moves on the chest board. Trump has his Lieutenants in place who will not only support the desired goals of the President, but they will all take the direct heat off Trump allowing him to move freely and correct the insurmountable challenges left by the worst president in modern times, maybe ever.

CHAPTER 16

TRUMP and WASHINGTON

A hundred years from now, historians are going to write volumes and volumes of books describing this period in history. Truly great historians have a unique way of peeling away the emotions, political fervor, and the biases of that specific time in order to write historical documents that are factually correct. Historians will look back on the early 2000s and scoff at the level of insanity. They will be appalled at what the average citizen accepted as truth even when the "truth" was proven to be lies. Historians will be shocked at the level of propaganda, lies, and deceit that our own government forced onto their citizens. Historians will also rightly portray the brave individuals that fought, in the face of adversity and evil, for the sovereignty and protection of the United States of America as patriots.

Historians will write about one specific man that saved America and guided her to a future of prosperity in the face of extreme adversity: Donald J. Trump.

I have a book on George Washington sitting on my desk titled, *The Real George Washington* by Jay A. Parry and it is at least three inches thick. It is also one of my all-time favorite books. George Washington is a historical hero of mine, and I firmly believe that Washington earned and deserves the title of The Indispensable Man. Without George Washington, there is no United States of America. Could the colonies have eventually formed the United States, maybe, but with complete certainty, I ascertain it would not resemble the United States of America forged under the leadership of George Washington. As I read about the founding of our nation and the trials and insurmountable challenges it faced, I am always intrigued by how a single leader would emerge from uncertainty and turmoil to lead the charge of change. It is easy to sit in my office and type away about the greatness of Washington, but it would be another completely different experience to have walked in his boots for just one day. What a giant in American history.

One hundred years from now, there will be another man like me writing about another point in American history that threatened to destroy the Republic. That man will look back into history and he will use Donald Trump as the example of strength, determination, unshakable optimism, and patriotism, as I have used George Washington. At first glance, the side-by-side comparison of these two men would make them seem incredibly different with no apparent similarities. However, strip away the clothes and stop the comparison of modern times to the founding of our nation over two hundred years ago and you realize they are more similar than not. They are cut from the same cloth and share the same qualities of determination and strength that singularly focused leaders possess. The most profound similarity is they both have a belief that they were called by God. Both men proclaim God is divine and that He is all powerful. I am not suggesting that Trump is as articulate about God as Washington was, but I am making the claim that both men feel touched by God. That belief that God had dominion over them is a powerful driving force in their lives that almost forces them forward.

George Washington wrote a letter to Reverend John Rodgers in June of 1783 proclaiming, "Glorious indeed has been our Contest: glorious, if we consider the Prize for which we have contended, and glorious in its Issue; but in the midst of our Joys, I hope we shall not forget that, to divine

Providence is to be ascribed the Glory and the Praise."[147] Washington's faith in God is undeniable. His belief that God's hand was guiding the colonies to ensure the creation of the United States of America was firmly imprinted in Washington's writings and speeches. Trump, though less eloquent, feels the same about God and the nation He created. Many individuals on the Left mock any talk about a higher power, Divine Providence, or just the whisper of his name – God. They now mock Trump as they believe Trump is using God as a sort of political tool. Christians believe Trump to be sincere because no man could have walked through the valley of darkness and emerge from that darkness unchanged. If a man survived that type of intense fire, and ascended from the ashes, he could easily be changed into a man of resentment, anger, and violence. Or that same white-hot fire, could change a man's life for the better and be yoked to God in a deeper relationship. I believe the latter happened to Trump. Trump's life, in all matters, changed toward the direction of God and I believe Trump began to understand that his life is not his own but belongs to the will of God. Many Christians look at Trump as a living example of the figures written about in the Bible. God used flawed and sinful men to lead His people and speak His words. I believe Trump's belief in God was solidified when he walked away from the attempt on his life in July 2024. In a speech, to the 11th Hour Faith Leaders in Concord, North Carolina, Trump stated,

> *But as I look back at my life's journey and events, I now recognize that it's been the hand of God leading me to where I am today. And my faith took on new meaning on July 13th in Butler, Pennsylvania, where I was knocked to the ground, essentially, by what seemed like a supernatural hand...I would like to think that God saved me for a purpose. And that's to make our country greater than ever before.*[148]

Believing God has placed you in the exact location you need to be, is powerful. When a man accepts his position in life and, more importantly, understands why God placed him in his position in the world, the manifestations of greatness and grand events become common. There is a form of greatness that happens when a man accepts and understands his responsibilities of being a father to his children and a provider to his wife. There is power when a man accepts and understands his purpose in life. There is power in accepting and understanding God's plan for a man causing him to turn over his life to the Creator. Trump now understands and accepts God's plan, as did George Washington. There is overwhelming evidence that God's hand has created and protected America from her inception to now. How else can you explain America defeating the world's most powerful army without the proper training, weapons, or manpower? How else can you explain the emergence of America to superpower status within a short time compared to civilizations that have been in existence for thousands of years and have never achieved a fraction of the success America has? The only answer is that we have been blessed by Divine Providence.

The characteristics of strength and determination, that both men share, are the two most important leader attributes of their time in history. Washington's determination and his shear strength led the colonies to victory against the greatest military power up to that moment in history. Trump's determination and resiliency to fight through slander, threats of imprisonment, assassination attempts, fraudulent elections, and having his family be forced, by outside evil actors, into unsafe and dangerous positions have strengthened his resolve as a leader. Trump could have walked away from the cesspool of D.C. and the corruption of the 2020 elections, but he didn't because he knew his life had a bigger purpose.

Trump has a large ego as did Washington. Men do not achieve greatness by being meek and gentle. Instead, men that become great are driven, bold, and yes, they believe that they were created for greatness.

That ego that persists in the minds of great men, drive them to the outer edges of risk because they believe that is where the greatest rewards lie. To assume the great men of the past were soft and mild mannered would be a ridiculous idea. Life was a grueling adventure in Washington's time. There were no safe places or men running around in dresses. Instead, Washington lived in a world that was harsh and was brutal. A world where the weak were devoured and the strong barely got by. Washington could have stayed on his Mount Vernon estate and lived one of the best lives in modern times, but he made a conscience decision to join the fight. I am sure he believed, on some level, that the war for the sovereignty of the colonies and the creation of the United States of America needed him. That being said, he still had to make a choice of leaving the safety and security of his home to enter into a war with almost certain death and then dive in the political world that would force him away from his family. Washington famously said about leaving his home at Mount Vernon and facing the political world, "the 10,000 embarrassments, perplexities and trouble to which I must again be exposed in the evening of a life, already consumed in public cares."[149] In a letter to his friend and future Secretary of War, Henry Knox, Washington lamented, "My movements to the chair of government will be accompanied by feelings not unlike those of a culprit, who is going to the place of his execution; so unwilling am I, in the evening of a life nearly consumed in public cares, to quit a peaceful abode for an ocean of difficulties."[150] Washington could have chosen his life in Mount Vernon, but he chose to fulfill God's plan for him. His acceptance of this responsibility was an act of obedience.

I can only imagine how Trump has felt in the beginning of his political life and what his inner most thoughts were in the quiet of his limited private life. He had to be exhausted, angry, and resentful. Despite those humanly and righteous feelings, Trump was optimistic and forward thinking even in his farewell address in 2021, "To serve as your President has been an honor beyond description. Thank you for this extraordinary privilege. And that's what it is—a great privilege and a great honor."[151] Trump made a poignant statement about him entering the arena, "So I left behind my former life and stepped into a very difficult arena, but an arena nevertheless, with all sorts of potential if properly done. America had given me so much, and I wanted to give something back."[151] Like Washington, with the choice to retire back into his normal life, Trump chose to enter the arena again.

Both George Washington and Donald Trump share the same unwavering optimism and patriotic fervor that has physically, spiritually, and emotionally defined our nation. Their belief that the American flag represents a great nation with great citizens and that the future is waiting for Americans to harness and shape it for the betterment of our country is unwavering. In one of Trump's patriotic promotional videos released in January 2024, right before his inauguration, Trump proclaimed, "What will we do in this moment? How will we be remembered? Look at the opportunities before us!"[152] This is the spirit of optimism that both men share. It is the belief that America's future will be her best days. That America's future challenges are not just an obstacle to overcome but an opportunity to join the fight and become great. That is the essence of America. Our nation was once great because of what our founding fathers, our grandparents, and even some of our parents fought for and overcame. God didn't just hand us a great nation. Instead, God gave us an opportunity to have a great nation. There is a huge difference in the obtainment of something given to you compared to obtaining something earned. In George Washington's farewell address, he stated the importance of what the citizens had achieved through the creation of the United States of America and the importance of national unity:

For this you have every inducement of sympathy and interest. Citizens, by birth or choice, of a common country, that country has a right to concentrate your affections. The name of American, which belongs to you in your national capacity, must always exalt the just pride of patriotism more than any appellation derived from local discriminations. With slight shades of difference, you have the same religion, manners, habits, and political principles. You have in a common cause fought and triumphed together; the independence and liberty you possess are the work of joint counsels, and joint efforts of common dangers, sufferings, and successes.[153]

Washington was imploring Americans to understand that the differences between Americans are small, almost insignificant, compared to the commonalities. Americans have not changed despite the constant attempts to divide us and make each other the enemy. We share the same commonalities forged through wars, economic depressions, and through daily life all under the protection and unification of the flag of the United States of America. Washington's words are as correct today as they were two hundred years ago. Our slight shades of difference pale to the shared love of our country and the collective desire, as citizens, to return to greatness together.

One of the defining characteristics of both men is their unwavering patriotism and unapologetic pursuit of freedom. George Washington may not be one of your favorite presidents, as he is mine, and many people despise Donald Trump. However, no one that is intellectually honest can deny the feverish love of country that they both exude. On July 4th of 2020 Trump gave a speech on the exceptionalism of America:

On this wonderful day, we celebrate our history, our heroes, our heritage, our great American flag, and our freedom. Happy Fourth of July to everyone. I want to thank the U.S. Army Golden Knights for that truly awe-inspiring display. Tremendous talent. The Golden

> *Knights, and every member of the Armed Forces here this evening, we just want to say that you have earned the eternal gratitude of our entire nation.*
>
> *Two hundred and forty-four years ago in Philadelphia, the 56 signers of our Declaration of Independence pledged their lives, their fortunes, and their sacred honor to boldly proclaim this eternal truth: that we are all made equal by God. Thanks to the courage of those patriots of July 4th, 1776, the American Republic stands today as the greatest, most exceptional, and most virtuous nation in the history of the world.*[154]

The truest example of Washington's leadership and his steadfast belief of freedom was evident in his plea to his men to re-enlist in the Army:

> *My brave fellows, you have done all I asked you to do, and more than can be reasonably expected; but your country is at stake, your wives, your houses and all that you hold dear. You have worn yourselves out with fatigues and hardships, but we know not how to spare you. If you will consent to stay one month longer, you will render that service to the cause of liberty, and to your country, which you probably can never do under any other circumstances.*[155]

Both Presidents, Washington and Trump, are forces of nature demanding America continues toward greatness. Would Trump's over the top brashness rub Washington wrong or would Washington's rigid manner make Trump bristle? Probably so, but that's not the point in the comparison of these two men. Yes, these men lived in different times of American history and yes, they have different personalities, but their tenacious determination to ensure America is strong, and her future bright cannot be argued against. One incredible feat both men can claim is no wars took place in the eight years of Washington's Presidency and no wars started under Trump's first term in office. Their ability to project strength protected America from war under their leadership. Both men were alpha males never playing second fiddle to anyone. God created them for the exact moment in American history. Presidential American history has proven over hundreds of years that Americans demand an alpha male to lead us. Melissa Heldman, who has long studied masculinity in presidential politics, said masculinity is the "central requirement" for winning the presidency.[156] I don't know what Heldman's political views are or not, but she is spot on, "The idea of the president as the hypermasculine father protector figure has been with us since the start."[156] Yes, it has! America demands that our nation resume its place as the most powerful, the most dominant, and the most resourceful nation ever. That will only happen through power and strength.

Both men sacrificed a great deal to be the President of the United States of America. They also both gained a great deal. History has been kind and generous to Washington and history has portrayed him as the great and powerful leader he was on both the battlefield and in the political world. Trump's portrayal in history is still undetermined. However, time will remove the lesser figures in modern times and Trump will stand, like Washington, as a giant in America history.

President Washington faced an enemy that stood between the colonies and the future of the United States of America as freedom was at stake. That same type of leader is needed as America stands in the crosshairs of another enemy. An enemy that is more terrifying than the British Army. An enemy that another great president, President Lincoln, stated was the only enemy that could destroy America and that was the enemy within – traitors. History will be watching Trump closely to see if he should be placed on the same pedestal that Washington now sits alone. If Trump can continue to present the strength, determination, and courage of George

Washington, I believe Trump will be able to return America to greatness. If Trump can Make America Great Again, Washington will need to make a little room on that pedestal.

Future authors of history are waiting.

CHAPTER 17

Make America Great Again!

How?

Every time I give a speech, or I am interviewed about the treason America has suffered through, I am asked, "What can we do to Make America Great Again?" Americans have been in a fog of depression for four years because we have been witnessing the slow death of America from cultural destruction, societal chaos, crime, economic struggles, endless wars, inflation, and the real time demographic shift caused by open borders. My response to that question is, "The question is not 'What can we do?' but 'How do we do it?'"

How do we change the course of history that America is hurtling into? How do we regain America's power, strength, and optimism? How do we fight the internal enemies that have brought us to the doorstep of failure? How do we recapture America's sovereignty? And ultimately, how does America gain control of her future? All those questions must be answered and the answers to those questions will dictate the path America takes to the future. However, all those questions lead to the last question, which is the most important of them all.

Think about America in terms of your personal life, your personal future. If you have no control of your life and you are living in chaos and uncertainty, you feel helpless and hopeless. There will come a time in your life when you will either surrender to your hopelessness or you will hit rock bottom and change the course of your life. Either decision will require suffering and pain. However, one decision delivers constant pain and suffering until you die, while the other option will be painful and you will suffer but, and this is a huge but, you will come out of that darkness, a stronger, more determined, and more appreciative person that will do everything in your power to never fall back into that despair. That is where we are as a nation and as citizens.

America has been staring into darkness, but we can see light. That light is getting brighter but there is a nagging fear that this time we might not overcome the darkness. The enemy has been inside our walls for a long time, and they have destroyed so much and have caused so much damage that we all feel a sense of hopelessness and despair. We look around and see strangers inside our homes, helping themselves to all our food, our woman, and our children. When we go to work, the strangers stay in our homes and relax and play as we toil for wages to support them. When we try to revolt, the masters of our neighborhood shout us down and call us vile names. They suppress our rights and force us to work harder and longer as the strangers ruin our homes to the point, we eventually throw our hands up and succumb to the life we never wanted. When we surrender to the powerful, we submit to the horror; we wallow in fear, and then we die. However, it does not have to be this way. As horrible as the last four years have been, we have been presented a gift from God. That gift is time. Time to make the necessary life changes to become a nation under God, restore God's natural order, and become the great nation we were once.

This battle for the soul of America is different from any war we have faced in the past because the enemy is our own government. The enemy is our own people. The idea that once Trump is in office, everything will be "a ok" is ridiculous. That lie is as believable as men can have babies! The government has layers upon layers of American hating bureaucrats that have already openly discussed sabotaging the Trump Administration. The war we now find ourselves in has been raging for decades. What has changed is the enemy that was once hidden has been drawn out into the light for all to see. There is no more wondering who is on what side. The division of America's citizens is clearly defined, and the battle lines are real.

The old days of trying to be civil and have polite discussions died long ago. For every weak kneed, impotent, and cowardly Republican that makes the claim that we need healing and unity, I say, "Go pound sand!" Are we supposed to forget the COVID Nazis, as Americans are still dying and suffering severe medical aliments, because you lied to us about the origins of the virus and how to treat it? You lied to us and forced most Americans to take a drug that was not thoroughly tested and found to not work. If people like me and my family refused to take the shot, we were demonized, called vile names, cancelled by society, and many of us were forced to quit our jobs.

For the sake of unity, we are required to ignore the endless wars we have been lied to about. Wars that caused tens of thousands of U.S. soldiers to die. Wars that have caused untold numbers of soldiers to suffer severe injuries, both mental and physical. For the sake of healing, we must ignore the destruction of the American dollar because they print and spend money to the complete detriment of America and her future. For the sake of unity, we must ignore the pain and suffering of our neighbors and family when young girls and women are raped and murdered by illegal aliens allowed into America caused by the intentional open borders. Are we supposed to accept the insanity and perversion of the gender issue that allow our young children to be confused and mutilated for the sexually perverse in our society? Unity and healing will only happen if those that sinned against America and caused severe damage to Americans come before us all and apologize and ask for forgiveness. Otherwise, take your sorry asses to your side of the battlefield and prepare for war.

It does not matter to me if the traitors do or do not apologize for their treasonous actions against the body of America. I do not expect them to apologize because they completely believe what was done to America was a righteous action. These traitors intentionally created the policies and acted on those policies to fundamentally transform America. The borders were open on purpose. The wars across the globe were intentionally started and managed by the United States government. Losing 550,000 UACs was purposely allowed to happen. The murders and rapes of our citizens were ignored by our government to further their treason. Our government purposely and strategically used tens of millions illegal aliens to create demographic upheaval. All the individuals that are identified as traitors must be dealt with the harshest punishments allowable by our laws.

Before I continue to enumerate the actions needed to be taken to Make America Great Again, I want to take a few more words to complete my argument against accepting a false unity and healing. The people that have committed the crime of treason want forgiveness as quickly as they can get it. However, those traitors have no true understanding of what forgiveness stands for. Their understanding of forgiveness is rooted in secular beliefs thus forgiveness to them just means no punishment for their actions. America's belief of forgiveness is anchored in Christian doctrine and faith. To achieve forgiveness, one must confess their sins, be contrite and remorseful, and try in earnest to never commit that sin again. Then you will be forgiven, but God never commanded us to forget what was done to us.

Even if those traitors begged for forgiveness from the ones they harmed, I will never forget what they did to us! Never forget that we were called vile names, and they mocked us. Never forget that they claimed we were liars about open borders and about criminals running free causing destruction across our nation. Never forget that we were cancelled, and they removed our ability to voice our God given rights of free speech.

Never forget that many of our loved ones were injured and killed by a man-made virus created by our own government. Never forget that they covered it up causing more suffering and death. Never forget that they tried to fundamentally transform the United States of America from a nation of citizens to a nation of non-citizens. Never forget that the federal government, the government of the people, was weaponized and then used against the American people. Never forget that they made the federal government the enemy of the people!

The enemy is strong, they have been diligent in preparing for war, and the pieces of their army are in place. Every institution in America is run by the Left. The enemy controls every federal government department and agency: the national education system, healthcare, economic and banking sectors, intel agencies, media and entertainment, professional sports leagues, large corporate companies, and our religious denominations. Try to name any institution that has an impact on your life that you thoroughly trust. That's what I thought. If you can't name just one entity that you trust, then you are at war because you are being attacked from every angle.

I want unity and I want healing because I want peace and prosperity. However, the Left and the traitors that created the situation we find ourselves in today will never stop fighting. They will never relent in their pursuit of changing America. They hate what this country is because they believe with the strongest convictions, that America was built on slavery, oppression, and colonialism. To them America was founded on evil, and they must bring America to her knees so that she can be fundamentally changed.

How do we Make America Great Again? How do we secure the future we want for America? We move with urgency and power.

1. Place Loyal Lieutenants in Positions of Power

President Trump has completed the first step in this war for the soul of America and that is placing the most competent, patriotic, aggressive, fearless, and loyal people in the highest positions of authority. Trump obviously created a war board in Mar-a Lago well before the presidential election because the moment he was elected, he began announcing his picks. He was playing chess when the Democrats couldn't even find their board pieces. Trump has placed individuals into positions over the same departments and agencies that attacked and harmed those individuals. I would pay a month's salary to see that first meeting when the new Director of National Intelligence (DNI) Tulsi Gabbard requests to see her file and the people who initiated it. The file where she was placed on the Transportation Security Administration's (TSA) list requiring additional screening. Gabbard was irate when she was placed on this list, "The TSA placed me on the Quiet Skies domestic terror watchlist in what I can only describe as the ultimate betrayal. The Harris-Biden regime has now labeled me a domestic terror threat. Why? They see me as a threat to their power."[157]

I would pay another month's salary to be present at RFK Jr.'s first meeting as Secretary of Health and Human Services. Oh boy, that's going to be a special event, "FDA's war on public health is about to end. If you work for the FDA and are part of this corrupt system, I have two messages for you: 1. Preserve your records, and 2. Pack your bags."[158]

And I would pay another year's salary to be standing right next to Tom Homan when he steamrolls the beta male blue city sanctuary mayors! Homan is the stereotypical alpha male that enjoys confrontation, "But look, me and the Denver mayor, we agree on one thing -- he's willing to go to jail, I'm willing to put him in jail because there there's a statute. It's Title 8 United States Code 1324 (iii). And what it says is it's a felony if you knowingly harbor and conceal an illegal alien from immigration authorities. It's also a felony to impede a federal law enforcement officer."[159]

These Lieutenants are placed, now turn them loose to fundamentally transform America back to her founding and to her greatness.

2. Arrest All the Traitors

Trump made a fatal mistake on day one of his presidency in 2016, he did not arrest Hillary Clinton. I understand his thinking and what he wanted to accomplish, but he was wrong. The power-hungry immoral cretins, to include Hillary, saw that gesture of kindness in an attempt for unity, as a sign of weakness and like sharks, they attacked. The most ironic thing in this entire criminal atmosphere is that the Democrats have left Trump no other recourse except to arrest and imprison these traitors. If he doesn't, they will smell blood in the water and these morally bankrupt traitors will attack him and his family.

Current historians will shred Trump to pieces for arresting these people that tried to destroy America. They will use the phrase "imprisoning his political opponents" over and over. This will be difficult to withstand but Trump is left with no other option but to arrest, present his case in trail, and if convicted, punish the criminals. The nation can't be attacked from the inside by individuals that intentionally and strategically injure our nation, and no one is punished. That would perpetuate future treason furthering the vulnerability of our sovereign nation. If Trump can buckle down and do what needs to be done, future historians will applaud and hold him up as the greatest example of strength, courage, and patriotism. Historians will be able, from the distance of time, to articulate to future Americans that in the face of extreme duress he did what few men could have done to save America.

3. Seal All the Borders

The moment Trump removes his hand from the Bible, and he instantly becomes the 47th President of the United States of America, every military branch descends on the southern, northern, western, and eastern borders and seals them shut. No one crosses outside of the port of entries. Every Biden Executive Order is rescinded and every unlawful policy in DHS is cancelled. At the very same time, Homan begins to hunt down every illegal alien that is living in the country. No quarter given and a new policy will be instituted and turned into a law: anyone found illegally present in the United States after a seven, ten, or 30-day grace period will be given a 20-year ban from entering America. Period and no exceptions!

The new Commissioner of Customs and Border Protection, Rodney Scott will ensure every border, port of entry, and every inch of America is secure and not one illegal alien enters and escapes. The Commissioner will remove all bad policy from the Biden Administration and institute legal and lawful policy back into the daily assignments and mission of CBP. Removal of all illegal aliens will be facilitated by contracting with private prisons, erecting supersized tents along the border, and having air flights around the clock deporting illegal aliens back to their home countries. Nations that will not take their nationals back will lose all federal foreign aid. If that does not incentivize that nation, America will use military force to repatriate the nationals back to their third world hellholes.

4. Remove All Incentives for Illegal Aliens and Punish Governments, Businesses, and People that Facilitate the Movement and Care of Illegal Aliens

The Real ID will be mandatory in May of 2025. The Real ID has all your biographical data to include your social security number. The possession of this Real ID will validate that the individual is a United States citizen. Non-U.S. citizens are forbidden from receiving any federal, state, or local social services to include welfare. Illegal aliens cannot rent a residence, obtain employment, get any type of medical attention outside of emergency care that will be strictly enumerated, illegal alien children cannot attend school, and illegal aliens will be forbidden to receive any other service or amenity offered to United States citizens. Any violation of this law by sanctuary states, municipalities or businesses will result in criminal prosecution. Sanctuary cities that will not work with or help federal immigration law enforcement will first have all federal monies stopped and the officials will be arrested for harboring and assisting illegal aliens.

The laws are already in the Immigration and Nationality Act. The quickest way to deport tens of millions of illegal aliens is to make life so difficult for them to even function in our society that they will voluntarily depart from our nation.

5. End Birthright/Anchor Baby Citizenship

Birthright/Anchor Baby citizenship is a lie. The 14th Amendment was instituted to provide citizenship to black slaves and their children. The 14th Amendment in the Constitution of the United States of America has a two-prong system to determine citizenship. In Section 1 it states, and I quote, "All persons born or naturalized in the United States, and subject to the jurisdiction thereof, are citizens of the United States and of the State wherein they reside." In both lawful and practical terms those important words mean that an individual must be born on United States soil AND be under the jurisdiction of the United States to be a citizen of America. Let me give you two examples where the baby born on America soil is not a United States citizen. A German husband and wife come to America to see the Grand Canyon and the woman is in the third trimester. The young pregnant woman has been walking all day and her water breaks, and she has the baby right there overlooking the Grand Canyon. The baby is healthy, and this new German family has an incredible story. However, that baby is not an American citizen! Why? Because the baby is under the jurisdiction of Germany thus making that baby a German citizen. Example number two. A pregnant Guatemalan woman is crossing the border and gives birth to a little baby girl named Delia Rameriz. Little Delia is a citizen of Guatemala. Yes, she was birthed on American soil, but she was and is under the jurisdiction of Guatemala.

The morons in our government have been pedaling this lie that if you are born in America, you are a citizen. Has this always been the law? Well, no because the United States Constitution is the law. So where did this magically appear? I will let the conservative writer Ann Coulter explain:

> *The late Supreme Court Justice William Brennan invented the anchor-baby policy out of whole cloth and snuck it into a footnote of an opinion written in 1982. Yes, this ancient bedrock principle, this essence of "Who We Are," dates all the way back to the Reagan administration.*
>
> *The Brennan footnote was not part of the decision. It does not have the force of law. Yet, today, we act as if Brennan's absurd dicta is the law of the land for no reason other than: a) sheer ignorance and b) a fear of being called "racist."*
>
> *No U.S. Congress or Supreme Court ever debated and then approved the idea that children born to mothers illegally present in the country should automatically become citizens. Consequently, any president or Congress could simply state that children born to illegal aliens are not citizens. If only we had a president or Congress that would do so.*[160]

This lie must be put to death immediately. The citizenship of the United States of America has cost our citizens a great deal so the cost applied to foreigners must be a lot higher than just crossing into America illegally.

I think that is fair.

6. Defund Every NGO in America

Instantly stop all federal funding to every NGO operating in America. The network of NGOs is the engine that drives the illegal alien invasion, and they are a direct adversary to America. When you remove the engine, the machine can't move! Once all NGOs are defunded, the federal government will slowly and carefully reinstate any NGO that has not participated in the treason against America.

7. Never Apologize for Removing Illegal Aliens from America and Do Not Stop Until Every Illegal Alien Is Removed from the United States of America!

Securing the borders of America is not rocket science, hell it's not even fifth grade science. Simple common sense is what is needed to secure the borders of America thus providing America with a safe and sovereign nation. The problem seems insurmountable because the level of treason was so great, and their crime has been so well planned and executed. However, understand that this entire strategy of fundamentally transforming America had to be done with lies, propaganda, and deceit. The entire foundation of this plan was built on sand. It is all falling on top of itself. The leaders of this treason are being forced out and new patriotic individuals that are determined and have actual skin in the game are ready to fight for America. They are ready to bring America's foundational cornerstones of law and order back as anchors to provide freedom and opportunity.

We have been lied to, mocked, ridiculed, and called vile names as we were socially marginalized. Never forget that. Never forget what they did to us. Do not give an inch as any kindness is seen as a character weakness to exploit. Remain civil until you can't. Be ready to defend yourself, your family, and your country. Throw away the religious lies we have all been programmed to accept as the truth. God despises men and women that are weak, undecided, and cowardly when faced with evil. Instead, we are all called to stand strong in our beliefs of God and country. Never apologize for the greatness of America and the greatness of our brothers and sisters. Be prepared to fight to the death as our founding fathers did when they swore an oath to each other to and to the future of America.

This time in history is no different from the time of our founding. The line in the sand has been drawn and the sides are being selected. Choose wisely. There will be a heavy price to pay for aligning on the wrong side of this war for the soul of America. Our ancestors deserve better than what we have given America. It is now time to reclaim our nation's prosperity and have the courage to love, appreciate, and desire America to be great again.

I can think of no worse sin against your fellow citizen than treason, except for allowing treason to go unpunished.

America's future depends on how we handle the traitors of our nation. History is waiting to judge us!

CHAPTER 18

Twenty-Four Hours Changed the Course of America

In the first 24 hours from when Donald J. Trump pledged his oath to become the 47th President of the United States of America, the entire nation changed. It was and continues to be the most fascinating and amazing experience I have ever witnessed. One man changed the course of America's future because he has the experience, determination, love of country, and most of all; President Trump possesses the courage to do what is right and what is needed.

One's thoughts, feelings, or understanding of Trump do not matter because if you love him or hate him; it was abundantly obvious when he walked into the inauguration, he was The Alpha. Not the alpha in the room, not the alpha in America, but The Alpha in the world. Everyone felt it, everyone witnessed it, and everyone knew it. America changed in 24 hours.

I wrote this final chapter of this book as it was going to print because it is important to document what one man has done to the course of American history. As I write, Trump is strategically attacking and unraveling the effects and conditions of Biden's treason. One man has literally picked up the entire nation of America and turned her around facing a completely different path. America was once traveling at breakneck speed into a dark abyss and now she is heading towards prosperity and greatness. The entire cabal of treason is being eradicated piece by piece and all at once. Every part of the last four years of Biden's reign is being destroyed. From economic policies to energy decisions, to the endless and useless wars, to the gender insanity, to the DEI policies, and to every decision made these past four years that has paralyzed our nation and made American citizens question their own sanity.

The greatest attack on Biden's treason has been the full assault on the traitorous open border policies that allowed 30 million illegal aliens to cross into America.

Trump wasted no time as he signed over 200 Executive Orders with the emphasis on the open borders. Trump declared a national emergency on the border. He immediately removed the CBP One App, it no longer exists! Trump sent 1,500 soldiers to the border with more to follow. Trump immediately closed all "legal pathways" that Mayorkas unconstitutionally created. Trump fired the top brass throughout DHS' organizational chart. Trump ended catch and release and mandated that every person arrested was returned to their nation of origin. Trump threatened and then instructed law enforcement agents and officers to arrest anyone that interferes with their lawful duties to include politicians. Trump then instructed his Department of Justice to prepare to prosecute those felony violations in the court of law. Trump ended birthright citizenship that has violated the 14th Amendment of the U.S. Constitution for decades. The alpha lion roared and every living animal in his kingdom heard him. I cannot over state what President Trump has done in the immigration world. As I am writing these words, thousands of illegal aliens are being stopped at the border, thousands are being arrested in the interior of America, and thousands are being deported right at this moment. The greatest part of Trump's decisive actions is it will continue until every illegal alien is removed from the United States of America!

When you hear, "we must close the border," understand that the enemy has opened the border in many ways. Trump is aware of all these illegal avenues that were created during the past four years. Trump is attacking the system all at once and on all fronts. First, he is physically closing the border. On day one, I received calls and texts from front line Border Patrol Agents telling me that everything had changed instantly. The orders were clear and direct. No one is to be released, and everyone will be deported back to their country of origin. New vehicle pursuit policies and use of force policies were being developed and implemented as soon as possible. The border wall is being built, and the demeanor, attitude, and morale of the Agents are off the chart.

Trump did not hesitate as he fired four of the top executives in the Executive Office of Immigration Review (EOIR). This is the agency inside the immigration beast that issues final orders of deportation, stays of deportation, asylum and pending immigration cases, oversight of the Immigration Judges, and immigration courthouses. EOIR has enormous control of the flow and or the lack of flow in immigration proceedings and the EOIR is a disaster. How bad is the EOIR? There are over 3.5 million cases pending. There are over 4.5 million immigration asylum cases backlogged. There are less than 1,000 asylum officers to adjudicate almost five million cases. There are only 642 immigration courthouses across America. As any eight-year-old child can see, the immigration system has been completely sabotaged. This was the plan of Biden, Mayorkas, and the Lieutenants in order to get to the final stage of this treasonous plan and that was amnesty. Amnesty has always been the final objective, and they almost crossed that proverbial goal line! Trump is using the EOIR as the starting point of taking a meat clever to the DHS' organizational hierarchy.

Trump issued the Executive Order "Realigning the United States Refugee Admissions Program" directing the State Department to stop all partnerships with refugee resettlement organizations. Every refugee NGO must halt all appointment reservations to the United States Refugee Admissions Program (USRAP). Trump's order stated, "Over the last 4 years, the United States has been inundated with record levels of migration, including through the U.S. Refugee Admissions Program (USRAP)."[161] Trump's EO followed up brilliantly dictating when this order will be lifted, "...until such time as the further entry into the United States of refugees aligns with the interests of the United States."[161] What a novel idea that the people we allow to enter and live among us must be the type of individual that we want to be here and an individual that will benefit America!

In typical Trump fashion, he listed the path forward on immigration enforcement on the White House website, titled "Donald J. Trump Protects the States and the American People by Closing the Border to Illegals via Proclamation." The first bullet point on the site was, "In joining the Union, the States agreed to surrender much of their sovereignty in exchange for the federal government's promise in Article IV, Section 4 of the U.S. Constitution, to "protect each of [the States] against Invasion."[162] Trump has started his presidency with firing cannons not bullets. He has looked directly at the enemy, without blinking or stuttering, telling them everything he is going to do, when he is going to do it, and then proclaiming they can do nothing to stop him!

The attacks and lawsuits from all the anti-American haters are already beginning. However, we have a strong leader that simply does not care. I agree with Trump, file lawsuits all you want, and we will slow roll them through the court system. If sanctuary cities and politicians want to play dangerous games with dangerous outcomes, then ok here we go. Trump must and is meeting every afront to his Executive Orders with power and strength. Just like our founding fathers inherently understood, there is no longer any middle ground on which we can meet and discuss issues. The battleground has only enough room for the winner. Our founding fathers took that limited space on the battlefield by force, and they never apologized for winning. Trump must do the same as our founders.

Do not fool yourself that because Trump is in office and he is winning out of the gate, the enemy will retreat. Instead, the enemy is still fighting because they are at war with you, me, and the United States of America. Trump is just one man. Yes, he is the alpha, he is unique, and he is rare, but this nation needs all of us. We must support Trump, and we must meet him on the battlefield to defeat the enemy of America. The enemy has completely revealed itself to us and us to them. The sides in this war are clearly defined. The future of America hangs in the balance and the soul of America is the prize.

The war is raging.

The only question now remains: What side wants to win the most?

Treason is a game played for keeps!

There can only be one winner...

ENDNOTES

1 "Nationwide Encounters," US Customs and Border Protection, date accessed December 13, 2024, https://www.cbp.gov/newsroom/stats/nationwide-encounters

2 U.S. Congress. *United States Code: Immigration and Nationality,* retrieved from the U.S. Citizenship and Immigration Services, date accessed December 13, 2024, https://www.uscis.gov/laws-and-policy/legislation/immigration-and-nationality-act

3 Salgado, Catherine, "A Shocking Number of Illegal Aliens Flagged as National Security Risks," PJ Media, September 7, 2023, https://pjmedia.com/catherinesalgado/2023/09/07/a-shocking-number-of-illegal-aliens-flagged-as-national-security-risks-n1725073

4 "Former CPB head expresses belief that US more vulnerable today than it was on 9/11," The National News Desk, November 5, 2024, https://cbsaustin.com/news/nation-world/former-cpb-head-expresses-belief-that-us-more-vulnerable-today-than-it-was-on-911-mark-morgan-customs-and-border-patrol-immigration-ice-chicago-racism-hate-crime-terrorism

5 Blankley, Bethany, "Northern border sector encounters break records again in fiscal 2024," The Center Square, November 4, 2024, https://www.thecentersquare.com/national/article_d586f7f6-9ad3-11ef-82e5-a3f297c024e7.html

6 https://cbpone.cbp.dhs.gov/ [This link was removed by President Trump on January 20, 2025]

7 Montoya-Galvez, Camilo, "Migrants in Mexico have used CBP One app 64 million times to request entry into U.S.," February 12, 2024, https://www.cbsnews.com/news/immigration-cbp-one-app-migrants-mexico-64-million/

8 Green, Mark, "Chairman Green Statement of Reports Cartels Are Abusing the CBP One App," Homeland Security, August 5, 2023,

https://homeland.house.gov/2023/08/05/chairman-green-statement-on-reports-cartels-are-abusing-the-cbp-one-app/

9 https://homeland.house.gov/2023/10/23/mew-documents-obtained-by-homeland-majority-detail-shocking-abuse-of-the-cbp-one-app/ [This link was removed by President Trump on January 20, 2025]

10 Bensman, Todd, "New Records: Biden DHS Has Approved Hundreds of Thousands of Migrants for Secretive Foreign Flights Directly into U.S. Airports," September 21, 2023, Center for Immigration Studies, https://cis.org/Bensman/New-Records-Biden-DHS-Has-Approved-Hundreds-Thousands-Migrants-Secretive-Foreign-Flights

11 "Millions of Illegals being FLOWN into our Country! SITREP 12.21.23," December 21, 2023, Monkey Werx US, YouTube, https://www.youtube.com/watch?v=1z8mWwVwZpg&t=957s

12 White, Nic, "Christmas chaos in Eagle Pass as THOUSANDS more migrants cross US border into Texas after wading across the Rio Grande and wait to be processed," December 25, 2023, Daily Mail, https://www.dailymail.co.uk/news/article-12899949/Christmas-crisis-Eagle-Pass-Texas-border-migrants.html

13 Bensman, Todd, "Biden Admin. Sends Millions to Religious Nonprofits Facilitating Mass Illegal Migration," January 30, 2024, Center for Immigration Studies, https://www.congress.gov/118/meeting/house/117010/documents/HHRG-118-GO06-20240321-SD004.pdf

14 "HIAS Congratulates Board Member Alejandro Mayorkas on DHS Nomination," November 23, 2020, HIAS, https://hias.org/statements/hias-congratulates-board-member-alejandro-mayorkas-dhs-nomination/

15 "HIAS Welcomes Five New Members to National Board." June 30, 2020, HIAS, https://hias.org/statements/hias-welcomes-five-new-members-national-board/

16 "Civil Society and NGOs," date accessed December 20. 2024, IOM UN Migration, https://www.iom.int/civil-society-and-ngos

17 "Civil society and NGOs with observer status," date accessed December 20, 2024, IOM UN Migration, https://www.iom.int/civil-society-and-ngos-observer-status

18 https://hias.org/news/cross-border-programs-provide-vital-support-gbv-survivors-and-lgbtq-people-darien-gap/ [Link No Longer Available]

19 "MAYORKAS: "We have built safe mobility offices in Columbia, Ecuador, Guatemala, Costa Rica to reach people where they are so they don't have to take the perilous journey," Townhall.com X, https://x.com/townhallcom/status/1800185756427899386?lang=en

20 https://www.state.gov/about-us-bureau-of-population-refugees-and-migration/ [This link was removed by President Trump on January 20, 2025]

21 "This is Treason," Film Website, accessed January 14, 2025, www.ThisIsTreason.com

22 Montero, Carlos, "DHS Awards Millions to NGOs Facilitating Illegal Immigration," FAIR: Federal for American Immigration Reform, May 14, 2024, https://www.fairus.org/blog/2024/05/14/dhs-awards-millions-ngos-facilitating-illegal-immigration

23 118th Congress, "H.R. 6363 – Further Continuing Appropriations and Other Extensions Act, 2024," November 17, 2023, https://www.congress.gov/bill/118th-congress/house-bill/6363

24 Shaw, Adam, "Flashback: Biden praised 'constant,' 'unrelenting' stream of immigration into US," Fox News, December 12, 2020, https://www.foxnews.com/politics/flashback-joe-biden-constant-unrelenting-immigration

25 "Birth Rate by Country 2024," World Population Review, accessed January 15, 2025, https://worldpopulationreview.com/country-rankings/birth-rate-by-country

26 "BODYCAM: Ohio woman arrested for eating a cat," September 11, 2024, WKYC Channel 3, You Tube, https://www.youtube.com/watch?v=jNh9clZUU3Y

27 Binder, John, "Mass Immigration Pushes Middle America to the Brink: 'Not Sustainable,'" September 6, 2024, Breitbart, https://www.breitbart.com/politics/2024/09/06/mass-immigration-raises-housing-costs-strains-healthcare-services-in-middle-america-this-is-not-sustainable/amp/

28 DeMio, Terry, “Mauiritanians in Lockland wait for work as village struggles to cope. What to Know,” October 30, 2024, Cincinnati Enquirer, https://www.cincinnati.com/story/news/2024/10/30/immigrants-lockland-ohio-wait-work-village-loses-tax-revenue/75937082007/

29 Camarota, Steven & Zeigler, Karen, “Foreign-Born Population Grew by 5.1 million in the Last Two Years,” May 13, 2024, Center for Immigration Studies, https://cis.org/Report/ForeignBorn-Population-Grew-51-Million-Last-Two-Years

30 Zarandi, Mohammad Fazel, Feinstein, Jonathan, & Kaplan, Edward. “Yale Study Finds Twice as Many Undocumented Immigrants as Previous Estimates,” September 21, 2018, Yale Insights, https://insights.som.yale.edu/insights/yale-study-finds-twice-as-many-undocumented-immigrants-as-previous-estimates.

31 Batalova, Jeanne, “Frequently Requested Statistics on Immigrants and Immigration in the United States,” March 13, 2024, MPI: Migration Policy Institute, https://www.migrationpolicy.org/article/frequently-requested-statistics-immigrants-and-immigration-united-states-2024

32 “Mayor Eric Adams in 2021: Illegal Migrants Keep NYC Running,” June 16, 2021, Grabien, https://grabien.com/story?id=438525

33 Allen, Virginia, “NYC on Track to Spend $10 Billion on Illegal Aliens Over 3 Years,” August 15, 2024, The Daily Signal, https://www.dailysignal.com/2024/08/15/nyc-on-track-to-spend-10-billion-on-illegal-aliens-over-3-years/

34 Gonen, Yoav, “Mayor Adams on Trump Border Czar: ‘We Have the Same Desire,’” December 12, 2024, The City, https://www.thecity.nyc/2024/12/12/eric-adams-tom-homan-immigration-border/

35 “Transcript: Mayor Adams Delivers Address on Asylum Seeker Humanitarian Crisis and Takes Q&A,” August 9, 2023, NYC, https://www.nyc.gov/office-of-the-mayor/news/585-23/transcript-mayor-adams-delivers-address-asylum-seeker-humanitarian-crisis-takes-q-a#/0

36 “NYC Mayor Eric Adams Welcomes Asylum Seekers Bused from Texas,” NBC News You Tube, September 7, 2023, https://www.youtube.com/watch?v=WWX_ThcpIsQ

37 Taer, Jennie, Marino, Joe, & Fitz-Gibbon, Jorge, "Fiend accused of burning woman to death on NYC subway is illegal migrant from Guatemala who sneaked into US after he was deported," December 23, 2024, New York Post, https://nypost.com/2024/12/23/us-news/nyc-subway-burn-suspect-is-illegal-migrant-from-guatemala-who-sneaked-into-us-after-being-deported/

38 Hogan, Gwynne, "Hundreds Pack Clinton Town Hall About 'Frustrating, Disastrous' Migrant Mega Shelter," May 7, 2024, The City, https://www.thecity.nyc/2024/05/07/hall-street-migrant-shelter-crystal-hudson/

39 "Growing Costs of Illegal Immigrants on Illinois Taxpayers," April 11, 2024, Rep C Miller, https://repcmiller.com/2024/04/11/growing-costs-of-illegal-immigrants-on-illinois-taxpayers/

40 "Davidsmeyer Blasts Pritzker for Spending $638 Million on Chicago's Migrant Crisis; Reiterates Call to End Sanctuary State," November 16, 2023, C.D. Davidsmeyer, https://cddavidsmeyer.org/2023/11/16/davidsmeyer-blasts-pritzker-for-spending-638-million-on-chicagos-migrant-crisis-reiterates-call-to-end-sanctuary-state/

41 Coggina, Madeline, "Chicago resident slams mayor, calls out city's illegal immigration 'Ponzi scheme': 'Gotten out of hand,'" December 14, 2024, Fox Business, https://www.foxbusiness.com/media/chicago-resident-slams-mayor-calls-out-citys-illegal-immigration-ponzi-scheme-gotten-out-hand

42 Cherone, Heather, "City Council Votes 30-18 to Spend $70M More to Care for Migrants in Chicago," April 19, 2024, WTTW News, https://news.wttw.com/2024/04/19/city-council-votes-30-18-spend-70m-more-care-migrants-chicago

43 Joseph, Jamie, "Chicago mayor urges Biden to grant work permits to half million illegal immigrants," April 4, 2024, Fox News, https://www.foxnews.com/politics/chicago-mayor-urges-biden-grant-work-permits-half-million-illegal-immigrants

44 Kelty, Bennlto, "House More Homeless, Serve Fewer Migrants Among Mayor Johnston's 2024 Goals," February 26, 2024, Westword, https://www.westword.com/news/denver-mayors-2024-goals-center-largely-on-migrants-and-homeless-19607042

45 Lewis, Ray, "Democratic Denver mayor warns migrant crisis has city 'very close' to breaking point," January 31, 2024, The National Desk, https://abc3340.com/news/nation-world/democratic-denver-mayor-warns-migrant-crisis-has-city-very-close-to-breaking-point-colorado-mike-johnston-west-coast-illegal-immigrants-immigration-asylum-seekers

46 Del Puerto, Luige, "With Denver at a breaking point from illegal immigration, mayor heads to DC to plead for action," January 16, 2024, Colorado Politics, https://www.coloradopolitics.com/denver/denver-city-council-immigration-help/article_48177344-5d38-5c7d-9833-c442863ccec9.html

47 Zalubowski, David, "Denver councilmembers tie rise in 'hot spots' crime to illegal immigration surge," July 10, 2024, The Denver Gazette, https://denvergazette.com/news/denver-city-council-crime-illegal-immigrants/article_ef07c79e-3f0e-11ef-a6ab-a7f0b21fce50.html

48 Arenas, Jasmine, "Denver Health on brink of breaking point due to uncompensated medical care costs," January 12, 2024, CBS Colorado, https://www.cbsnews.com/colorado/news/denver-health-brink-breaking-point-due-uncompensated-medical-care-costs/

49 Parks, Kristine, "Dever city official caught on camera begging migrants to leave, head to Chicago, NYC: 'Going to suffer,'" April 1, 2024, Fox News, https://www.foxnews.com/media/denver-city-official-caught-camera-begging-migrants-leave-head-chicago-nyc-going-suffer

50 Sallinger, Marc, "Denver Mayor Mike Johnston backtracks comments about sending Denver Police officers to block Trump deportation efforts," November 22, 2024, 9News, https://www.9news.com/article/news/politics/denver-mayor-mike-johnston-police-officers-block-trump-deportation/73-99dcea89-e9ad-4e11-ad1e-d3facd6e5519

51 Garcia, Armando, "Trump border czar Tom Homan says he's willing to jail Denver mayor over mass deportation protest," November 26, 2024, ABC News, https://abcnews.go.com/US/trump-border-czar-tom-homan-jail-denver-mayor/story?id=116235385

52 Sallinger, Marc, "Denver Mayor Mike Johnston backtracks comments about sending Denver Police officers to block Trump deportation

efforts," November 22, 2024, 9News, https://www.9news.com/article/news/politics/denver-mayor-mike-johnston-police-officers-block-trump-deportation/73-99dcea89-e9ad-4e11-ad1e-d3facd6e5519

53 Taer, Jennie, "Indian AG investigating 'coordinated effort' that flooded small town with thousands of Haitian migrants,'" November 4, 2024, New York Post, https://nypost.com/2024/11/04/us-news/indiana-ag-opens-investigation-into-haitian-migrant-influx-to-small-town-caused-by-border-czar-kamala-harris/

54 Shaw, Adam, Tenney, Garrett, & McGovern, Patrick, "Haitian migrants overwhelming small Indiana town: 'It's just overrun,'" October 24, 2024, Fox News, https://www.foxnews.com/politics/haitian-migrants-overwhelming-small-indiana-town-its-just-overrun

55 "Yet Another Small Town Struggling with Migrant Surges," October 23, 2024, FAIR: Federation for American Immigration Reform, https://www.fairus.org/blog/2024/10/23/yet-another-small-town-struggling-migrant-surges

56 Downard, Whitney, "Migrants in Indiana: an opportunity for some, a strain for others," November 18, 2024, Inside Indiana Business, https://www.insideindianabusiness.com/articles/migrants-in-indiana-an-opportunity-for-some-a-strain-for-others

57 Szypula, Paul, "PA Residents Divided on Impact of Haitian Migrant Influx," September 20, 2024, X, "https://x.com/Bubblebathgirl/status/1837151528227852318

58 Rufo, Christopher & Buttons, Christina, "How 2,000 Haitian migrants changed Rust Belt town of Charleroi, Pennsylvania," October 10, 2024, New York Post, https://nypost.com/2024/10/10/opinion/how-2000-haitian-migrants-changed-rust-belt-town-of-charleroi-pennsylvania/

59 Needham, Michael, "A Constructed Crisis in Charleroi," September 26, 2024, Understanding America, https://americancompass.org/a-constructed-crisis-in-charleroi/

60 "Gov. DeWine calls out GOP lies on Springfield," September 24, 2024, Cleveland.com, https://www.cleveland.com/letters/2024/09/gov-dewine-calls-out-gop-lies-on-springfield.html

61 Casey, Evan, "Whitewater adjusts to changing population amid increase of immigrants," January 25, 2024, Wisconsin Public Radio, https://www.wpr.org/social-issues/immigration/whitewater-adjusts-to-changing-population-amid-influx-of-immigrants

62 Salina, Juan & Salhotra, Pooja, "What you need to know about the Venezuelan gang that Texas is targeting," September 18, 2024, The Texas Tribune, https://www.texastribune.org/2024/09/18/texas-venezuelan-gang-tren-de-aragua-abbott-crackdown/

63 "Mayor, Council Member Address Gang Concerns," September 11, 2024, Aurora Colorado, https://www.auroragov.org/news/whats_new/mayor__council_member_address_gang_concerns

64 Haaf, Landon & Lopez, Kristian, "'I thought I was going to die': Victims recount violent kidnapping by alleged TdA members in Aurora," December 18, 2024, Denver 7, https://www.denver7.com/news/front-range/aurora/i-thought-i-was-going-to-die-victims-recount-violent-kidnapping-by-alleged-tda-members-in-aurora

65 Pinedo, Peter & Rumpf-Whitten, Sarah, "Aurora, Colorado, police say home invasion 'without question' Tren de Aragua gang activity," December 20, 2024, Fox News, https://www.foxnews.com/politics/aurora-colorado-police-say-home-invasion-without-question-tren-de-aragua-gang-activity

66 Taer, Jennie, "Colorado Gov. Jared Polis dismisses migrant gang takeover of apartments as 'imagination'—despite video, mayor confirming truth," August 29, 2024, New York Post, https://nypost.com/2024/08/29/us-news/colorado-gov-jared-polis-dismisses-migrant-gang-takeover-of-aurora-apartments-as-imagination/

67 Bordelon, Colette, "Aurora Mayor Mike Coffman addresses claims of Venezuelan gang activity in one-on-one interview," September 3, 2024, Denver 7, https://www.denver7.com/news/front-range/aurora/aurora-mayor-mike-coffman-addresses-claims-of-venezuelan-gang-activity-in-one-on-one-interview

68 Michels, Ashley, "City, state leaders weigh in on what to do about Aurora crime, gang problems," December 17, 2024, Fox 31,

https://kdvr.com/news/local/city-state-leaders-weigh-in-on-what-to-do-about-aurora-crime-gang-problems/

69 Sanchez, Sandra, “Explainer: How immigrants end up on ICE’s non-detained docket,” October 1, 2024, Border Report, https://www.borderreport.com/immigration/explainer-how-immigrants-end-up-on-ices-non-detained-docket/

70 Geraghty, Jim, “ICE Drops a Bombshell,” September 30, 2024, National Review, https://www.nationalreview.com/the-morning-jolt/ice-drops-a-bombshell/

71 Taer, Jennie, “Exclusive: Feds Flagged Nearly 75,000 Illegal Migrants as Potential National Security Risks,” September 1, 2023, Daily Caller, https://dailycaller.com/2023/09/01/illegal-migrants-national-security-risk/

72 Bier, David & Nowrasteh, Alex, “45,000 “Special Interest Aliens” Caught Since 2007, But No U.S. Terrorist Attacks from Illegal Border Crossers,” December 17, 2018, CATO at Liberty, https://www.cato.org/blog/45000-special-interest-aliens-caught-2007-no-us-terrorist-attacks-illegal-border-crossers

73 Lillis, Katie Bo, Alvarez, Priscilla, & Bertrand, Natasha, “Exclusive: Smuggler with ties to ISIS helped migrants enter US from Mexico, raising alarm bells across government,” August 30, 2023, CNN Politics, https://www.cnn.com/2023/08/29/politics/migrants-us-southern-border-smuggler-isis-ties/index.html

74 Shaw, Adam, “ICE sounds alarm on what migrants are failing to bring to border as fears mount after ISIS arrests,” June 14, 2024, Fox News, https://www.foxnews.com/politics/ice-sounds-alarm-migrants-failing-bring-border-fears-mount-isis-arrests

75 “ICYMI In The New York Post: ‘House Committee Demands Answer of Eight Tajik Border Crossers Arrested for Terror Plot,’” June 18, 2024, Homeland Security, https://homeland.house.gov/2024/06/18/icymi-in-the-new-york-post-house-committee-demands-answer-on-eight-tajik-border-crossers-arrested-for-terror-plot/

76 Doba, Hena, “Southern border sees increase in crossings by Tajikistan immigrants,” June 21, 2024, News Nation,

https://www.newsnationnow.com/us-news/immigration/southern-border-increase-crossings-tajikistan-immigrants/

77 Bensman, Todd, "Thousands of 'Special Interest Aliens' Posting Potential National Security Risks Entering via CBP One App," October 24, 2023, Center for Immigration Studies, https://cis.org/Report/Thousands-Special-Interest-Aliens-Posing-Potential-National-Security-Risks-Entering-CBP-One?gad_source=1&gclid=Cj0KCQiA7NO7BhDsARIsADg_hIbobis2-JL-ClAqOOcJDVTOkIMYgNM8euKdiUcwOAh8EV_QK9TJQRIaAmSPEALw_wcB

78 "Sarah Adams – Is the Pentagon Ignoring the Most Dangerous Threat of All," December 12, 2024, Shawn Ryan Show, You Tube, https://www.youtube.com/watch?v=T50pRCNaQCA

79 "Shawn Ryan," January 1, 2025, Shawn Ryan, Twitter, https://x.com/ShawnRyan762/status/1874518346332295493

80 Green, Mark, "Fact Sheet: How Secretary Mayorkas' Open Borders Helped Unleash a National Crime Wave," accessed December 28, 2024, Homeland Security Committee, https://homeland.house.gov/wp-content/uploads/2024/02/Fact-Sheet-Secretary-Mayorkas-Open-Borders-Crime-Wave.pdf

81 "Harris County DA seeks death penalty for men accused in 12-year-old Joceyln Nungaray's murder," December 13, 2024, Eyewitness News 13, https://abc13.com/post/joceyln-nungaray-murder-harris-county-da-seeks-death-penalty-men-accused-houston-girls/15652915/

82 Mejia, Jonathan, "Mother of Jocelyn Nungaray seeks justice for daughter's murder as case ties to Venezuelan gang surface," October 3, 2024, Fox 26 Houston, https://www.fox26houston.com/news/mother-seeks-justice-daughters-murder-case-ties-venezuelan-gang-surface

83 Thompson, Adam, "Mother of murdered Maryland mom Rachel Morin testifies on Capitol Hill on immigration policies," September 10, 2024, CBS Baltimore, https://www.cbsnews.com/baltimore/news/mother-of-murdered-maryland-mom-rachel-morin-to-testify-on-capitol-hill-on-immigration-policies/

84 "Criminal? Come on in! DHS Monitoring 617K Illegal Migrants Released into U.S. With Criminal Records," April 16, 2024, The Drill Down, https://thedrilldown.com/newsroom/criminal-come-on-in-dhs-monitoring-617k-illegal-migrants-released-into-u-s-with-criminal-records/?utm_source=googlegrant&utm_medium=cpc&gad_source=1&gclid=Cj0KCQiAj9m7BhD1ARIsANsIIvDC-bpI9EV0pYYk65i0vHOLRlCiant9-Bcm4v8yQW_JzdWDOJSbOOUaAogHEALw_wcB

85 Deliso, Meredith, "Timeline: Laken Riley's last moments retraced during trial on Georgia nursing student's murder," November 20, 2024, ABC News, https://abcnews.go.com/US/laken-riley-case-murder-trial-texts/story?id=116009547

86 "Bodycam Footage Reveals Moment Laken Riley's Family Found Out About Her Death," November 20, 2024, Law & Crime Trials, You Tube, https://www.youtube.com/watch?v=MueAPX7bY4I

87 "Senate Democrats Ask FBI to Release File on Gaetz Investigation; Jose Ibarra Awaiting Sentencing for Murder of Laken Riley in Court," November 20, 2024, Transcripts, https://transcripts.cnn.com/show/ip/date/2024-11-20/segment/02

88 Lindstrom, Rebecca, Bri'd Fisbie, Ciara, & Nunez, Gabriella, "Did Laken Riley's accused killed fall through the cracks of US immigration enforcement? Here's what we know," February 27, 2024, 11 Alive, https://www.11alive.com/article/news/crime/jose-ibarra-accused-killer-laken-riley-georgia-immigration-system/85-0294133e-f5e1-4e2f-a2df-ab017b498508

89 Malanga, Steven, "No, You're Not Imagining a Migrant Crime Spree," Autumn 2024, City Journal, https://www.city-journal.org/article/no-youre-not-imagining-a-migrant-crime-spree

90 "Governor Gianforte Announces Fentanyl Trafficking Penalties After Surveying Southern Border," May 15, 2023, State of Montana Newsroom, https://news.mt.gov/Governors-Office/Governor_Gianforte_Announces_Fentanyl_Trafficking_Penalties_After_Surveying_Southern_Border

91 "Examples of Serious Crimes by Illegal Aliens," accessed January 11, 2025, FAIR: Federation for American Immigration Reform, https://www.fairus.org/issue/examples-serious-crimes-illegal-aliens

92 "Hordes of Military-Aged Chinese Men with the Same Clothing, Haircuts, and Tattoos Swarming Our Southern Border," September 9, 2023, AR15.com, https://www.ar15.com/forums/General/Hordes-of-Military-Aged-Chinese-Men-With-the-Same-Clothing-Haircuts-and-Tattoos/5-2675988/

93 Chang, Gordon, "Gordon Chang: Chinese Agents Are Slipping Across Biden's Broken Southern Border," July 1, 2023, Daily Caller, https://dailycaller.com/2023/07/01/opinion-chinese-agents-are-slipping-across-bidens-broken-southern-border-gordon-chang/

94 Taer, Jennie, "Exclusive: Illegal Chinese Pot Grows Are Taking Over Rural Blue State and Law Enforcement Isn't Stopping Them," November 22, 2023, Daily Caller, https://dailycaller.com/2023/11/22/china-marijuana-grows-immigrants-maine/

95 Yalch, Garrett & Adcock, Clifton, "How Chinese organized crime is dominating Oklahoma's illegal medical marijuana market," March 14, 2024, The Norman Transcript, https://www.normantranscript.com/news/how-chinese-organized-crime-is-dominating-oklahoma-s-illegal-medical-marijuana-market/article_9cd874d4-e214-11ee-b19a-4f569b0be4b3.html

96 "China Expert, Author: 'Why Are We Allowing Chinese Nationals onto Our Farm and Ranch Lands,'" September 6, 2024, Federal Newswire, https://thefederalnewswire.com/stories/664084612-china-expert-author-why-are-we-allowing-chinese-nationals-onto-our-farm-and-ranch-lands

97 Jacob, Mary, "Map shows Chinese-owned farmland next to 19 US military bases in 'alarming' threat to national security: experts," June 20, 2024, New York Post, https://nypost.com/2024/06/20/us-news/chinese-owned-farmland-next-to-19-us-military-bases/

98 Weatherholtz, Nicole, "Gordon Chang to Newsmax: Chinese Entering US Could Be PLA Soldiers," February 21, 2024, Newsmax, https://www.newsmax.com/newsmax-tv/gordon-chang-china-migrants/2024/02/21/id/1154477/

99 Shaw, Adam, "HHS chief 'unfamiliar' with reports that agency can't contact 85,000 unaccompanied migrant kids," March 22, 2023, Fox

News, https://www.foxnews.com/politics/hhs-chief-unfamiliar-reports-agency-cant-contact-85000-unaccompanied-migrant-kids

100 "Hearing Wrap Up: ORR Director Fails to Answer Questions About 85,000 Lost Unaccompanied Alien Childre, Flawed Vetting of Sponsors, and More," April 18, 2023, Committee on Oversight and Government Reform, https://oversight.house.gov/release/hearing-wrap-up-orr-director-fails-to-answer-questions-about-85000-lost-unaccompanied-alien-children-flawed-vetting-of-sponsors-and-more%EF%BF%BC/

101 "DHS Insider Who Exposed 'Reasonable Fear' Migrant Asylum Loophole goes Public," October 18, 2021, Project Veritas, https://www.projectveritas.com/news/dhs-insider-who-exposed-reasonable-fear-migrant-asylum-loophole-goes-public

102 Carrell, JJ, "Trafficked, Exploited, and Missing: Migrant Children Victims of the Biden-Harris Administration," November 19, 2024, US House of Representatives Subcommittee on Border Security and Enforcement Subcommittee on Overnight, Investigations, and Accountability, https://homeland.house.gov/wp-content/uploads/2024/11/2024-11-19-BSEOIA-HRG.pdf

103 "House Hearing on Migrant Children Victims," November 19, 2024, The Union Herald, You Tube, https://www.youtube.com/watch?v=LmYmeuzHag4&t=855s

104 Dickinson, Tim, "Married to A 'Dreamer;' Dreading Trump's Nightmare," September 16, 2024, Rolling Stone, https://www.rollingstone.com/politics/politics-features/delia-ramirez-married-to-dreamer-trump-evil-1235102112/

105 Arthur, Andrew, "Joe Biden's Immigration Plan," January 3, 2020, Center for Immigration Studies, https://cis.org/Arthur/Joe-Bidens-Immigration-Plan

106 Kaczynski, Andrew, "Joe Biden once said a fence was needed to stop 'tons' of drugs from Mexico," May 10, 2019, CNN Politics, https://www.cnn.com/2019/05/10/politics/kfile-biden-drugs-fence-2006/index.html

107 Marcetic, Branko, "Joe Biden, Anti-Immigrant Enabler, April 4, 2019, Jacobin, Jacobin, https://jacobin.com/2019/04/joe-biden-anti-immigrant-deportation-policies

108 Kaczynski, Andrew & Steck, Em, "Joe Biden promised to 'absorb' 2 million asylum seekers 'in a heartbeat' in 2019 – he now faces an immigration crisis", March 7, 2024, CNN, https://www.cnn.com/2024/03/07/politics/kfile-biden-2-million-migrants-asylum-seekers-immigration-crisis/index.html

109 Durkee, Alison, "What to Know About Kamala Harris's Immigration Record Before Border Visit Today," September 27, 2024, Forbes, https://www.forbes.com/sites/alisondurkee/2024/09/27/what-to-know-about-kamala-harriss-immigration-record-before-border-visit-today/

110 Joyella, Mark, "Kamala Harris Tells NBC's Lester Holt 'We've Been to The Border.' He Responds: 'You Haven't,'" June 8, 2021, Forbes, https://www.forbes.com/sites/markjoyella/2021/06/08/kamala-harris-tells-nbcs-lester-holt-weve-been-to-the-border-he-responds-you-havent/

111 https://www.whitehouse.gov/briefing-room/statements-releases/2024/02/04/statement-from-vice-president-kamala-harris-on-the-bipartisan-senate-national-security-agreement/ [This site was removed by President Trump on January 20, 2025]

112 Carnahan, Ashley, "Mayorkas urges passage of border security bill, say Biden admin has enforced the law since 'day one,'" May 21, 2024, Fox News, https://www.foxnews.com/media/mayorkas-urges-passage-border-security-bill-says-biden-admin-enforced-law-since-day-one

113 "'We stand by the legality of what we have done': Mayorkas on new Biden border rule," June 9, 2024, AVC News, https://abcnews.go.com/ThisWeek/video/stand-legality-mayorkas-new-biden-border-rule-110965163

114 Klein, Betsy, "Trump blames former Speaker Paul Ryan for not getting border wall funding," January 31, 2019, CNN, https://www.cnn.com/2019/01/30/politics/trump-paul-ryan-border-wall/index.html

115 Clark, Lesley, "Senate might fail Trump on wall, but McConnell still has the support of his GOP," March 13, 2019, Lexington Herald Leader, https://www.kentucky.com/news/politics-government/article227506654.html

116 "What We Do," accessed January 4, 2025, Tahirih Justice Center, https://www.tahirih.org/what-we-do/

117 "Phelps – Kursten – The Role of Social Workers in Immigration Legal Services Organizations," October 21, 2024, American Accountability Foundation, You Tube, https://www.youtube.com/watch?v=I_ReyYlYsPY

118 "Andrea Saenz," accessed January 5, 2025, DHS Bureaucrat Watch List Targets, https://www.dhswatchlist.com/targets/andrea-saenz

119 "Immigration," accessed January 5, 2025, Brooklyn Defenders, https://bds.org/our-work/immigration

120 "97 No. 1 Interpreter Releases Art. 27," June 6, 2020, Federal Case Summaries, https://cdn.prod.website-files.com/6653ec7bf72b6002b2326036/670c5d2cc9db159de3d1abaf_SAENZ-ANDREA-Federal%20Case%20Summaries%20%5BSexual%20Contact%20minor%20under%2015%5D-07302024.pdf

121 "Daniel Delgado," accessed January 5, 2025, BHS Bureaucrat Watch List Targets, https://www.dhswatchlist.com/targets/daniel-delgado

122 "Higgins – Jennifer – "Fireside Chat," October 10, 2024, American Accountability Foundation, You Tube, https://www.youtube.com/watch?v=Jbv3Tf4KVkc

123 King, Ryan, "Conservative watchdog unveils list of 'radical leftist' officials it wants Trump to fire if elected," October 23, 2024, New York Post, https://nypost.com/2024/10/23/us-news/american-accountability-foundation-unveils-list-of-radical-leftist-officials-it-wants-trump-to-fire-if-elected/

124 Alba, Monica, "Top migration adviser to depart White House after three years," January 26, 2024, NBC News, https://www.nbcnews.com/politics/white-house/top-migration-adviser-biden-depart-immigration-talks-senate-rcna135856

125 "Katie Tobin," accessed January 7, 2025, Carnegie Endowment for International Peace, https://carnegieendowment.org/people/katie-tobin?lang=en

126 Binder, John, "Rep. Tom Tiffany Torches Biden Official 'Proud' of Border Policies: 'You Have Been Part of Largest Human Trafficking

Operation Since Slavery,'" December 5, 2024, Breitbart, https://www.breitbart.com/politics/2024/12/05/tom-tiffany-torches-biden-official-proud-border-policies-you-have-been-part-largest-human-trafficking-operation-since-slavery/

127 "Remarks delivered by Director Ur M. Jaddou at the 2021 National Immigrant Integration Conference," October 4, 2021, U.S. Citizenship and Immigration Services, https://www.uscis.gov/newsroom/speeches-statements-testimony/remarks-delivered-by-director-ur-m-jaddou-at-the-2021-national-immigrant-integration-conference

128 "Esther Olavarria Oral History," accessed January 7, 2025, UVA Miller Center, https://millercenter.org/the-presidency/presidential-oral-histories/esther-olavarria-oral-history

129 "Immigration to Sweden from 2010 to 2023," accessed January 7, 2025, Statista, https://www.statista.com/statistics/523293/immigration-to-sweden/

130 Hubinette, Tobias, "Race and Sweden's Fascist Turn," October 19, 2022, Boston Review, https://www.bostonreview.net/articles/race-and-swedens-fascist-turn/

131 Khoshnood, Ardavan, Ohlsson, Henrik, Sundquist, Jan, & Sundquist, Kristina, "Swedish rape offenders – a latent class analysis," February 22, 2021, Forensic Sci Re, https://pmc.ncbi.nlm.nih.gov/articles/PMC8330751/

132 "Sweden rape: Most convicted attackers foreign-born, says TV," August 22, 2018, BBC, https://www.bbc.com/news/world-europe-45269764

133 "Ten men convicted over gang rape in Germany," July 23, 2020, BBC, https://www.bbc.com/news/world-europe-53517022

134 Luyken, Jorg, "Migrants behind gang rapes and knife crime, says German opposition leader," September 7, 2024, The Telegraph, https://www.telegraph.co.uk/world-news/2024/09/07/migrants-behind-gang-rapes-knife-crime-german-opposition/

135 Skujins, Angela, "'We never let them in': Hungary's PM Viktor Orban demands new laws tacking migration," June 9, 2024, Euro News, https://www.euronews.com/my-europe/2024/09/06/we-never-let-

them-in-hungarys-pm-viktor-orban-demands-new-laws-tackling-migration

136 Ordonez, Franco, "Trump points to Hungary's Viktor Orban as example of his support from foreign leaders," September 10, 2024, NPR, https://www.npr.org/2024/09/10/nx-s1-5107967/viktor-orban-hungary-donald-trump-presidential-debate

137 Charlish, Alan & Florkiewicz, Pawel, "Poland's Tusk vow to defend EU border amid asylum row," October 16, 2024, Reuters, https://www.reuters.com/world/europe/polands-tusk-says-future-liberal-democracy-hinges-migration-policy-2024-10-16/

138 Rahman, Billal, "Kristi Noem: 5 Things the New Homeland Security Secretary Has Said About Immigration," November 12, 2024, Newsweek, https://www.newsweek.com/kristi-noem-new-homeland-security-secretary-1984221

139 Meyer, Josh, "Kristi Noem, key to Trump's immigration agenda, faces senators in confirmation hearing," January 14, 2025, USA Today, https://www.usatoday.com/story/news/politics/2025/01/14/kristi-noem-trump-homeland-security-hearing/77677959007/

140 Peinado, Fernando, "How White House advisor Stephen Miller went from pestering Hispanic students to designing Trump's immigration policy," February 8, 2017, Univision News, https://www.univision.com/univision-news/politics/how-white-house-advisor-stephen-miller-went-from-pestering-hispanic-students-to-designing-trumps-immigration-policy

141 "Stephen Miller: From Harassing Latino High School Students to Drafting Trump's Muslim Ban," accessed January 8, 2024, PBS SoCal, https://www.pbssocal.org/shows/democracy-now/clip/stephen-miller-from-harrassing-latino-high-school-students-to-drafting-trumps-muslim-ban

142 "Stephen Miller," accessed January 8, 2024, SPLC, https://www.splcenter.org/resources/extremist-files/stephen-miller/

143 Chatham, Joe, "Former Border Patrol Chief Rodney Scott Nominated to Lead Customs and Border Protection," December 16, 2024, FAIR: Federation for American Immigration Reform, https://www.fairus.org/news/executive/former-border-patrol-chief-rodney-scott-nominated-lead-customs-and-border-protection

144 "Former ICE director shouts at lawmaker: You work for me!," September 27, 2019, CNN, You Tube, https://www.youtube.com/watch?v=28CWbymxBeA

145 Guerrero De Leon, Carola, "Heated Family Separation Exchange Between AOC and Returning 'Border Czar' Makes Viral Comeback," November 11, 2024, The Latin Times, https://www.latintimes.com/heated-family-separation-exchange-between-aoc-trumps-returning-border-czar-goes-viral-again-565437

146 "Cecilia Baga asks: "Is there a way to carry out mass deportation without separating families,'" October 27, 2024, 60 Minutes, X, https://x.com/60Minutes/status/1850689458590384212?lang=en

147 Vicari, Chelsen, "10 George Washington Quotes Pointing to God's Providence," February 20, 2017, Juicy Ecumenism, https://juicyecumenism.com/2017/02/20/10-george-washington-quotes-pointing-to-gods-providence/

148 "Speech: Donald Trump Holds a Campaign Rally in Concord, North Carolina," October 21, 2024, Factbase, https://rollcall.com/factbase/trump/transcript/donald-trump-speech-campaign-rally-concord-north-carolina-october-21-2024/

149 Henriques, Peter, "George Washington and the Challenge of Launching the New Government," May 9, 2011, George Mason University: College of Humanities and Social Sciences, https://chss.gmu.edu/articles/2924

150 Dunn, Susan, "A Sacred Union," George Washinton's Mount Vernon, https://www.mountvernon.org/george-washington/the-first-president/george-washington-s-sacred-union

151 "Farewell Address of Donald J. Trump, 45th President of the United States of America," accessed December 19, 2024, Trump White House, https://trumpwhitehouse.archives.gov/farewell-address/

152 "Wow! President Trump just posted this beautiful campaign ad featuring himself, Tulsi Gabbard, RFK Jr, Elon Musk, and more heroes," January 13, 2025, Bo Loudon, X, https://x.com/BoLoudon/status/1878992707286421868

153 "Washington's Farewell Address," 1796, accessed January 19, 2025, American Battlefield Trust,

https://www.battlefields.org/learn/primary-sources/washingtons-farewell-address

154 "Remarks by President Trump at the 2020 Salute to America," July 4, 2020, U.S. Embassy & Consulates in Italy, https://it.usembassy.gov/remarks-by-president-trump-at-the-2020-salute-to-america/

155 "Washington, Encouraging His Men to Re-Enlist in the Army," December 31, 1776, accessed January 19, 2025, George Washington's Mount Vernon, https://www.mountvernon.org/library/digitalhistory/past-projects/quotes/article/my-brave-fellows-you-have-done-all-i-asked-you-to-do-and-more-than-can-be-reasonably-expected-but-your-country-is-at-stake-your-wives-your-houses-and-all-that-you-hold-dear-you-have-worn-yourselves-out-with-fatigues-and-hardships-but-we-know-not-how-to-sp

156 Leonor Barclay, Mel, "Trump is man in a man's world. The RNC underscored that," July 18, 2024, the 19th, https://19thnews.org/2024/07/rnc-trump-masculinity/

157 Bo Lillis, Katie, Cohen, Zachary, & Lybrand, Holmes, "Trump's intel pick was placed on government watch list for overseas travel and foreign connections," November 22, 2024, CNN Politics, https://www.cnn.com/2024/11/22/politics/tulsi-gabbard-government-watch-list-travel-connections/index.html

158 Cohen, Joshua, "RFK Jr. Says He Wants to Untie Links Between Industry and FDA," December 4, 2024, Forbes, https://www.forbes.com/sites/joshuacohen/2024/12/04/rfk-jr-says-he-wants-to-untie-links-between-industry-and-fda/

159 Ventura, Juliann, "Homan says he is willing to put Denver mayor 'in jail' over deportation position," November 26, 2024, The Hill, https://thehill.com/homenews/state-watch/5009692-tom-homan-denver-mayor-marty-johnston-deportation-plans/

160 Coulter, Ann, "Ann Coulter: How we became the world's suckers on immigration," July 29, 2019, The Hill, https://thehill.com/opinion/immigration/455126-ann-coulter-how-we-became-the-worlds-suckers-on-immigration/

161 Knudsen, Hannah, "Refugee Flights Canceled Following President Trump's Executive Action," January 22, 2025, Breitbart, https://www.breitbart.com/pre-viral/2025/01/22/refugee-flights-canceled-following-president-trumps-executive-action/

162 "Fact Sheet: President Donald J. Trump Protects the States and The American People by Closing the Border to Illegals Via Proclamation," January 22, 2025, WhiteHouse.gov, https://www.whitehouse.gov/briefings-statements/2025/01/fact-sheet-president-donald-j-trump-protects-the-states-and-the-american-people-by-closing-the-border-to-illegals-via-proclamation/

ABOUT THE AUTHOR

J.J. Carrell recently retired from the United States Border Patrol after a 24-year career as a Deputy Patrol Agent in Charge in San Diego Sector. Carrell brings a different view on immigration and what is now transpiring on this forgotten and unknown place called the border.

Carrell's unique perspective is from years as a frontline Journeyman Agent to a Senior Leader in the United States Border Patrol. Carrell uses his experience to articulate who has created this disastrous situation on the border, how these policies are being enacted, and why these intentional policies are being implemented in his Amazon "Best Seller" book, *INVADED: The Intentional Destruction of the American Immigration System.*

Carrell has released two documentaries, *WHAT IS TREASON? #TRAFFICKED*, and *WHAT IS TREASON? #INVADED*. These documentaries expose the traitors that run our government, the evil of child sex trafficking, and the peril the United States of America now finds herself.

Made in the USA
Middletown, DE
20 February 2025

71580718R00146